CALLED TO LEAD

CALLED TO LEAD

Paul's Letters to Timothy
for a New Day

Anthony B. Robinson *&* Robert W. Wall

WILLIAM B. EERDMANS PUBLISHING COMPANY
GRAND RAPIDS, MICHIGAN / CAMBRIDGE, U.K.

© 2012 Anthony B. Robinson and Robert W. Wall
All rights reserved

Published 2012 by
Wm. B. Eerdmans Publishing Co.
2140 Oak Industrial Drive N.E., Grand Rapids, Michigan 49505 /
P.O. Box 163, Cambridge CB3 9PU U.K.

Printed in the United States of America

18 17 16 15 14 13 12   7 6 5 4 3 2 1

Library of Congress Cataloging-in-Publication Data

Robinson, Anthony B.
Called to lead: Paul's letters to Timothy for a new day /
Anthony B. Robinson & Robert W. Wall.
p.   cm.
ISBN 978-0-8028-6740-7 (pbk.: alk. paper)
1. Bible. N.T. Timothy — Commentaries.
I. Wall, Robert W.   II. Title.

BS2745.53.R63 2012
227'.8307 — dc23
2012007733

www.eerdmans.com

Dedicated to Reinder Van Til, editor and friend

With deepest gratitude to you, Reinder,
for your faithful ministry of the word

Contents

Contents

Foreword

This book is a surprising and generative gift because it dares to propose and develop an interface between two matters that we seldom connect. It moves back and forth between an intractable contemporary bewilderment and two books of the Bible that are rarely read. In the process it greatly illuminates both the intractable bewilderment and the New Testament books.

The intractable bewilderment concerns the destiny of the church in our society. We know about the common worry in the church concerning dollars and members and numbers and programs. We quibble about the reason for decline and play the blame game, all the way from charging that the church is too authoritarian to saying it's too liberal. Or perhaps it is just the larger scene of secularism, because people are not so much alienated from the church as they are easily indifferent to the church.

Whatever the reason for the decline that is offered, the antidotes tend to arise from marketing strategies that propose quick fixes or new slogans but do not in fact lead to much substantive change. This bewilderment, taken by itself, is unmanageable: it leads, variously, to "Eisenhower era" romanticism, to fatigue, to further anxiety and cynicism, or to despair.

The books of 1 and 2 Timothy are not much read, especially among the "main-line, progressive" churches that this book addresses. These books are regarded as later and non-Pauline; the continuing critical paradigm, moreover, reflected in popular thought, is that these books portray "early Catholicism" (not of the Roman variety) that transposed a movement into an institution. (It is clear that in more conservative circles, which do not fear authoritative institutions, these books of the Bible do get a better read.) Thus the books reflect growing institutional self-awareness with a fixed body of doctrinal formulation, a fixed canon, as in "all Scripture," and "orders and offices" of ministry that serve the beginning of a hierarchal ordering that seems remote from an earlier church that was propelled by the Spirit. As a result, we may, it has been tacitly agreed, safely disregard these Pastoral Epistles, which do not strike many readers as contemporary or imaginative.

The bewilderment, taken alone, yields a self-help propensity; the Epistles, taken alone, turn out to be an unwelcome testimony to which attention need not be paid. But this volume by Robinson and Wall brings the bewilderment and the letters to Timothy together for a fresh thought about the life of the church. When the bewilderment is brought into the presence of the letters, the bewilderment is reshaped and reformulated. It turns out that the apparent failure of the church is the result of practices that lack rootage in the gospel, rootage that gives staying power among the vagaries of cultural reality. Conversely, the books of Timothy are read very differently when held up in the midst of that bewilderment. Thus the book, with this juxtaposition, invites us to a compelling task of quite practical theology in which the practices of the church reflect the gospel, empower the ministry, and summon the church to be a vigorous player in contemporary life.

This book is a manual on practical theology that is itself grounded in the old post-Pauline manual of Timothy, after the initial zeal of the spirit had waned and the church was left with the daily grind of being followers of the risen Christ, a daily grind that is very ancient and very immediate in the life of the church. A movement may do things once with excitement; an institution has to continue to re-perform those same daily tasks over and over, and lapses, compromises, and cost cutting inevitably occur. This exposition of Timothy attests to what the church must do, over and over, to order its internal life, what the church must do, over and over, to sustain disciplines that are necessary for sustained discipleship.

The interface of bewilderment and 1 and 2 Timothy suggests that steady, regular, intentional practices constitute a sine qua non for church renewal. Such church practices provide identity and the disciplines the church must have in order to counter the deep disciplines and practices that sustain our culture in its pursuit of commodity, power, and control. In the ancient text the disciplines are designed to counter the work of empire, and it is not different for us now.

It is not surprising that these authors can discern the ways of the old text for our time and place. Robinson is a longtime pastor and more recently a consultant who has been able to observe and engage many congregations in various stages of emergency. On the other hand, Wall has kept his attention on the text and has been a witness to its contemporaneity in the demanding world of undergraduate education. This work, shared by pastor and scholar, by a pastor-scholar and a scholar-pastor, invites us to think afresh about rootage and discipline, intentionality and distinct identity. The books of Timothy, read with contemporary alertness, provide a way to move through our current bewilderment with courage and freedom. This book is a recital of "the ancient paths" that we thought we could shortchange. It turns out that being church is inconvenient. But that inconvenience to which we are called most assuredly yields buoyancy and joy and emancipation from bewilderment when there is practice that matches clarity of vision.

WALTER BRUEGGEMANN
Columbia Theological Seminary

Preface

Called to Lead is the second harvest of a friendship three decades long. Ours is an enduring friendship of two people who come from different sides of the theological track, from different denominational backgrounds, and who serve the church in different professional roles.

Robert W. Wall is a biblical scholar and professor at Seattle Pacific University. As a teaching elder of the Free Methodist Church, he is sometimes labeled "evangelical," even though his preference is "Wesleyan" because his activist politics and theology are most significantly shaped by the preaching of John Wesley and the lyrics of Charles Wesley and their ideals of a sanctified discipleship. His published scholarship ranges widely, including numerous published studies and a commentary on the pastoral epistles (Eerdmans, 2012). That commentary supplies the exegetical foundation on which much of the dialogue in the present book rests.

Anthony B. Robinson is a pastor and teacher. He has been a minister and senior pastor in four congregations of the Congregational/United Church of Christ. In conventional terms he would be described as "mainline" or "liberal." Theologically he has been shaped by the Reformed tradition of Calvin and Edwards. Today he writes and teaches on congregational renewal and leadership, often drawing on our previous study of Acts *(Called to Be Church)* and now from 1 and 2 Timothy for lessons that encourage congregational change and challenge thinking and direction.

This second collaboration once again testifies to God's capacity to transcend the labels and categories of which we often make so much — entirely too much in our experience. We hope its publication serves the church as one modest public sign of what many have come to see as an urgent matter within the American church: to overcome ecclesiastical barriers and religious stereotypes in order to serve more faithfully Christ's church and its mission in today's world. Much in today's political culture gives evidence that the old liberal/conservative divide is not at all helpful and is even counterproductive to a mutually enriching conversation between people of different traditions and backgrounds. Our partnership in this non-dogmatic religious venture testifies to what John Wesley called a "catholic spirit."

Not only are the authors of this book two friends in Christ from different religious backgrounds, but we are also teachers whose common calling is embodied in different ways and settings. Rob is a scholar of Christian Scripture and teacher at a liberal arts university, while Tony is a pastor and teacher of Christian congregations and their leaders. Their complementary perspectives on Scripture, shaped by a common vocation worked out within different locations, are set out in the opening chapter: Tony raises the practical problem of a culture deeply suspicious of its leaders, to which Rob responds as a biblical scholar by pointing out that 1 and 2 Timothy often occasion similar suspicions about their authority to speak God's word to today's church. In the chapters that follow these suspicions are set aside to fashion a conversation over selected passages from two Pauline letters whose ecclesial intention from the moment of their canonization is to shape and enrich the spiritual leaders of every Christian congregation.

Rob reads each passage as sacred Scripture intended for Christian formation, while Tony adapts this reading to target a wide array of hard issues with which congregational leaders struggle today. The book thereby combines scholarly and pastoral perspectives on this canonical correspondence between apostolic leader and protégé with the aim of providing today's congregations and classrooms with intellectual and spiritual beginning points, not simple conclusions. For this reason, discussion questions are added at the end of each chapter to facilitate conversations among our readers that will move what they have read in directions that enable them to carry what they have learned back into the church or marketplace where they work and worship, or into the dorm rooms and neighborhoods where they live. Only in this sort of dialogue with Scripture can a people belonging to

God hear a new word that helps to redeem this hard moment for God's sake.

For this reason, we pray that our exploration into the contemporary meaning of these precious texts will provoke and evoke, challenge and encourage, and in the end lead us to a closer walk with Jesus Christ as pastors and scholars, students and parishioners. Thank you for joining us and enlarging our partnership!

We wish to acknowledge with thanksgiving those wonderful students at Seattle Pacific Seminary who studied 1 and 2 Timothy with us during fall quarter, 2010, at various levels of enthusiasm but with an ever-critical eye toward the production of this book: Sophia Agtarap, Sybil Besheer, Bob Do, Matt Gebhart, Nate Goldbloom, Brian Gregory, Kelsie Job, Criss Mitchell, Erin Rodenbiker, Keith Snavely, Nick Timoshuk, and Aaron Willett. Their puzzlements, probing questions, and insightful comments helped to motivate and guide this project.

We wish also to thank and acknowledge the encouragement and work of our editor at Eerdmans, Reinder Van Til. Reinder, more than anyone else, has championed our collaboration from the beginning, participating in its conception, birth, and growth to maturity. We are in his debt as authors, and more so because our work together is deeply rooted in friendship. To him we dedicate this book, not only to celebrate our friendship of many years, but to affirm his insistence that biblical scholarship target the practical needs of the body of Christ.

EPIPHANY, 2012

Abbreviations

Ant.	Josephus, *Antiquities of the Jews*
ANTC	Abingdon New Testament Commentaries
BNTC	Black's New Testament Commentaries
Cong.	Philo, *De congressu quaerendae eruditionis gratia*
HBT	Horizons in Biblical Theology
ICC	International Critical Commentary
JSNT	*Journal for the Study of the New Testament*
JSNTSup	Journal for the Study of the New Testament Supplement Series
KJV	King James Version
NASV	New American Standard Version
NICNT	New International Commentary on the New Testament
NIGTC	New International Greek Testament Commentary
NIV	New International Version
NTC	New Testament in Context
NTL	New Testament Library
SJT	*Scottish Journal of Theology*
TDNT	*Theological Dictionary of the New Testament*
THNTC	Two Horizons New Testament Commentary
WBC	Word Biblical Commentary
WUNT	Wissenschaftliche Untersuchungen zum Neuen Testament

Itching Ears

Ministry in a Time of Lost and Contested Authority

An Introduction for Congregational Leaders

The topic of my presentation that day was "Leading Change and Living to Tell the Story." My audience was a group of clergy, young and old, male and female, some new to the ministry and others seasoned practitioners. I was addressing the subject of the complexity of leadership and leadership's multidimensional nature and challenge. "One dimension of leadership," I intoned, "is the person of the pastor, the leader. Who is that person — what's going on with him or her? Is he clear about his core commitments and convictions? Is she able to hold steady in the face of anxiety and resistance?"

A hand flew up in the back of the room. "Isn't that the problem right there?" said a pastor, a woman perhaps in her forties. "I mean," she continued, "you're assuming that the pastor is the leader in a congregation. In my experience, congregations don't always share that assumption. 'Who's on first?' so to speak, is an open question. Authority is contested. Just because you're the pastor doesn't mean you have any real authority. In churches, all sorts of people seem to think they are in charge." She had clearly found such a situation difficult, frustrating, and probably painful.

She is certainly correct. We live in a time and society where authority is contested, up for grabs, or altogether lost. We seek to serve and provide leadership in a church where both leadership and authority are frequently misunderstood and often contested. (Note: leadership and authority, while related, are not identical; more on that below.) Moreover, such contesting and testing is neither difficult to understand nor is it necessarily or always a bad thing. On one hand, there has been a sea change in our culture in North America with respect to authority — and particularly the authority of religious institutions and organized belief. Diana Butler Bass, a historian of religion in America, links this loss of authority to "a third disestablishment of religion."

> [S]ince the 1960's, a third disestablishment of religion has been underway. In this phase, all organized belief — especially traditional Western religion — has been dislodged even as a custodian of national morality and ethics — replaced instead by the authority of the autonomous individual.[1]

Increasingly, authority has been located in the individual, and subsequent developments, such as the growing plurality of religious and spiritual choices in North American culture, a prevailing ethos of consumerism, as well as technological changes like the Internet have only added to these trends. But these trends should not be simply characterized as either negative or positive; it is more complex than that. Nor are these trends the only contributors to the loss or contesting of almost all authority. The sad truth is that many established authorities — and those charged with leadership responsibilities — have violated the sacred trust placed in them. Stories of clergy sexual abuse and cover-up are legion. Problems with fraudulent résumés, phony degrees, plagiarism of sermons, and financial malfeasance are also all too common. Such violations of trust and the attendant suspicion of authority are not, of course, limited to clergy or the church. Educators, politicians, university coaches, doctors, and police all have their stories of failure and challenge. All such traditional authorities are met with scrutiny and suspicion. These violations of trust are not the only factor contributing to a climate of distrust and suspicion, but they are a part of it.

These days trust in leaders is hardly ever simply granted by virtue of office or title. And perhaps that is a good thing. When trust in leaders exists, it is because it has been earned. It has been earned slowly,

---

1. Diana Butler Bass, *The Practicing Congregation* (Herndon, VA: Alban, 2004), p. 24.

painstakingly, and deliberately. But here's the thing: while earning and gaining trust takes time, losing trust happens very quickly. Trust is lost — or jeopardized — easily and seemingly in an instant. A mistake, a misstep, an allegation, even a rumor can undo years' worth of work at trust-building.

Authority is contested, leadership is challenged — and not without reason. We can understand it. This has become part of the air we breathe, seemingly in the water we drink. Leadership and authority, while they may overlap, are not identical, and the loss or contesting of authority doesn't rule out leadership or the need for it. In many ways, these changes heighten the need for leadership. They also make leadership more complex and dangerous.[2]

Here's one further — and final — observation about the confusing matters of authority and leadership. At this time in both church and society, we tend to be very clear about the potential for abuses when leaders have too much power or authority, or when leaders are granted wide latitude. We are not so clear or aware of the other side of the coin: we do not see clearly the dangers or abuses that lurk when those called to lead are shorn of appropriate authority or legitimate power. To put that slightly differently, we are on the alert for and ready to question, challenge, and scrutinize the ways leaders may misuse power and authority — and then to disperse power and authority. But we are not nearly so clear about the problems and abuses that arise from an absence of authority or a vacuum of leadership.

A vacuum of leadership or an absence of legitimate authority is particularly dangerous to the most vulnerable among us. When there is a vacuum of leadership in a congregation, stuff will fill that vacuum. Often unhealthy and immature people seeking to grab power enter the vacuum. Or the vacuum gets filled with chronic and disabling conflict. Moreover, congregations that do not have able leaders tend to lose sight of their mission or purpose. Without able leadership, direction

---

2. Ronald Heifetz and Marty Linsky, *Leadership on the Line* (Boston: Harvard Business School Press, 2002), p. 12. For more on both the dangers of leadership and the distinction between leadership and authority, see this and other of Heifetz's books and articles. Heifetz tends to see "authority" as granted by an organization in order to maintain stability; "leadership" may be exercised by either those who have or who do not have organizationally sanctioned authority. Moreover, leadership focuses less on stability and more on the challenges facing a group or organization — engaging and making progress on those.

becomes unclear, and "mission-drift" frequently sets in. Needy and immature people often demand attention, sometimes holding others hostage to their anxieties and neediness. While we may not find it easy these days to trust authorized leaders, reflexive distrust is no answer either. While we aren't sure what constitutes legitimate authority, a vacuum of authority is not wise.

These are some of the open questions that make pastoral leadership very tough and challenging today. They also make it critically important and exciting. And here's the point: these are some of the key questions and themes at the heart of 1 and 2 Timothy and of this book. The Pastoral Epistles have in view a situation in which authority is contested and leadership is urgent for the health and future of the church.

When my friend and colleague Rob Wall suggested that we join forces to teach a course, and subsequently write a book, on the Pastoral Epistles and pastoral leadership, I was skeptical. As Rob notes in his portion of this introduction, 1 and 2 Timothy — Paul's "Timothy Correspondence" — have long suffered from "bad press and neglect." Like others, I had drunk the Kool-aid. I had heard that these letters were not really Paul's own and therefore of dubious value. And while I loved selected verses of 1 and 2 Timothy, I was aware of other texts in them that were quite problematic, even "texts of terror." We will unpack some of the reasons for these prevailing views and offer an alternative perspective on authorship and problematic texts.

More importantly, however, here's what I have learned in the course of working on 1 and 2 Timothy and team-teaching these texts: these "letters to a young pastor" address another time of contested authority and testing of leadership. They address a leader in another time of "itching ears," a time when people "accumulate teachers to suit their desires." What precipitates 1 Timothy is the fact that the church planter and founding pastor, Paul, is gone. He has hit the road, leaving a young Timothy to pastor and lead the fledgling congregation in Ephesus. In 2 Timothy, Paul's own death is on the horizon. Whether by absence or death, the established leader and trusted authority is no longer here, and a new young leader and pastor, Timothy, is on the job. But what is that "job"? What is Timothy supposed to be doing as a pastoral leader of a congregation in the mission field of the Roman Empire? What is the nature of, and what are the sources of, Timothy's authority? How is he to lead? Is Timothy to exercise power and, if so, how? As in our own time, when authority is contested regularly, what does it mean to lead a congregation wisely and well? We address these questions in this book.

These are a pastor's letters to another pastor. They have in view a time and mindset that will sound somewhat familiar to the contemporary pastor. Listen. "For the time is coming when people will not put up with sound doctrine but, having itching ears, they will accumulate for themselves teachers to suit their own desires, and they will turn away from listening to the truth and wander away to myths" (2 Tim. 4:3-4). Sound at all familiar?

How is Timothy to deal with a host of challenging situations including, but not limited to, different teachers and alternative teachings? How is he to handle the care of the needy in the congregation, the use of money, the interpretation of Paul's own teaching and of Scripture, the governance of the congregation, the role of elders in the church, worship leadership, and pastoral care? In other words, in these letters Paul addresses himself to all the important matters that face a pastor. Here he takes up the questions of what it means to be a pastor and to lead a congregation in such a way that the congregation is sound and healthy.

Many, of course, have argued that the Pastoral Epistles (1 and 2 Timothy and Titus) are not authentically Pauline. I will leave it to my co-author, a biblical scholar, to offer a more detailed examination of these questions and our approach to them. I will note only this: when one considers the Pauline collection as a whole, the majority of the letters — and those most well known — are addressed to congregations. Whether to the congregations in ancient Rome, Corinth, Thessaloniki, Ephesus, or other cities and towns of the Greco-Roman world, the bulk of this canonical collection is addressed to congregations in ways that are helpful, brilliant, challenging, and memorable. As we study those letters, we begin to see the issues those congregations faced, and we are able to extrapolate, often by analogy, to the church and to congregations in our own time. Those letters to congregations address pastoral leaders, though mostly in implicit — rather than explicit — ways.

But where does Paul address himself explicitly to pastors and pastoral leaders? Where does he speak, not to congregations generally, but to pastors particularly? And does it not make sense that he would at some point do so? We think it does make sense that Paul would turn from congregations to pastoral leaders. Moreover, it is here, in the Pastoral Epistles, that he does so. So we who are called to pastoral leadership may turn to these letters with special interest, anticipating a particular benefit.

This is the invitation we offer to you in this study. Ours is a time when pastoral leadership is arguably both tougher and more important than ever. It was the venerable church consultant Lyle Schaller who not long ago observed that, if ministry was a high-status and low-stress profession fifty years ago, today it appears just the reverse: low status but high stress. It is not an easy time to lead a congregation. And yet, faithful and competent leadership is more urgent than ever. Moreover, as both a pastor and a congregational consultant, I can testify that I seldom if ever see a healthy congregation that does not have a healthy and effective pastoral leader. While leadership is not the only factor in congregational health and vitality, it is an absolutely crucial factor. There are healthy, vital congregations all across the country. Almost without exception, they are led by healthy and vital leaders.

In the 2011 Academy Award–winning film, *The King's Speech,* a speech coach with unorthodox credentials, Lionel Logue, takes on the stutter-afflicted Duke of York, "Bertie," as a client. In time, Bertie will become King George VI, succeeding his brother, Edward VIII, to the throne just as England is facing the growing menace of Nazi Germany. Will Bertie be able to speak clearly and with the conviction required by a nation amid crisis? In some ways, the situation and the question are parallel in the Pastoral Epistles. Will Timothy be able to speak clearly and with the necessary conviction to a church facing a succession crisis and a shifting and challenging mission field? And will we, pastors and teachers of the church in the twenty-first century, be able to speak clearly, compellingly, and with conviction to and for the church in a time of huge cultural change?

Lionel Logue, the speech coach and expatriate Australian, turns out to be something more than a speech teacher to Bertie. He is a combination mentor, therapist, teacher, life-coach, and friend to the stammering duke. Moreover, Logue focuses on more than the mechanics of Bertie's problem, and offers more than techniques for speech improvement. He goes to the deeper questions of relationships, fear, disabling parental expectations, courage, self-knowledge, and hope. He both provokes his royal client and encourages him. He believes in and befriends a man whose birth and station have left him largely isolated. In doing so Lionel helps Bertie find his voice and lead his people.

There are in this inspiring film, as I've suggested, parallels to what Paul is up to in his two letters to Timothy. Timothy, too, faces a succession crisis: he is unsure of his abilities and capacity to rise to the challenge. And in a somewhat less grand way, there are parallels in what we attempt to do in this book. Today the church also faces a crisis, as do its leaders. Current pastoral leaders often seem to be overcome by the complexities and challenges we face. Like Bertie, pastors often lead lives of public isolation and loneliness. Some respond to the challenges of these times with timidity and a lack of confidence in both themselves and their message. They struggle to find their voices. Other pastoral leaders go to the opposite extreme in asserting themselves in voices that are loud and shrill, betraying a lack of inner conviction and confidence.

If the church is to face these times and the challenges they bring, it will need leaders who hold steady, who speak calmly — and with the authority born of both conviction and compassion. It will need leaders who have found their voices as messengers of the gospel and teachers of the church. While some works on leadership offer a largely technical and atheological approach, providing a host of methods and sometimes gimmicks that are lacking in theological depth and content, we hope this book will offer an alternative to such limited approaches. Like Lionel Logue, we seek to go deeper than technique alone. We believe that 1 and 2 Timothy and this book, which has been inspired by those Letters, may in some way be a Lionel Logue for pastoral leaders in our time. We hope you will find here both encouragement and challenge. We hope that you will find colleagues who believe in you and your work, and who join you as friends in Christ in this important calling.

Reading 1 and 2 Timothy as Scripture

For nearly two centuries, the Pastoral Epistles (1 and 2 Timothy and Titus) have suffered from bad press and neglect. The academy's verdict is that their authorship (not by Paul) and social location (long after Paul's death) have rendered them useless for scholars interested in questing for the historical Paul and by implication for a clergy they train who are interested in preaching the "real" Paul — if Paul at all. Indeed, if these are letters written by nameless pseudepigraphers (spurious writers claiming to be biblical characters) in Paul's name, who only selectively remembered and reinterpreted his apostolic legacy for a later church in which a politically domesticated and patriarchal "household of God" had become the ecclesial norm, then their instruction of the Pastorals might seem irrelevant for a congregation of postmodern readers shaped by a more liberal Zeitgeist.

Moreover, despite an array of famous (and even important) one-liners found in these letters that have been the staple of catechism classes for centuries, there are also "texts of terror" that have been used or abused to push sisters and brothers to the harsh margins of a community called to instantiate God's love in the world. The text of 1 Timothy 2:11-14 is one of these, especially when received with its history of patriarchal interpretation that has denied God's call of gifted women to Christian ministry or has restricted them to domestic chores. In a similar way, the catalog of credentials for church leadership given in 1 Timothy 3, even though presented as a guideline, has been prescribed in an artless manner to exclude mature believers from using their talents to secure the congregation's spiritual and social well-being. And the sentiment that the role of slaves is to benefit their masters (1 Tim. 6:1-2), even when contextualized by the social world of ancient Roman culture, sounds a discordant note in today's world, which has been put on alert by the horrors of human trafficking. No wonder many modern Christians, who, like the author of these letters, seek to adapt the gospel to culturally acceptable patterns of behavior, find these instructions offensive.

Within more conservative communions, however, whose grammar of faith is typically ordered by Protestantism's *sola Scriptura,* the situation is far different but no less tortured. The Pastoral Epistles are approved reading, and their instructions are practiced, but not until considerable effort has been expended to protect them from modern criticism and to hold them as genuinely Pauline and thus divinely inspired. While accepted as such, their instruction is typically applied only selectively to defend a congregation's countervailing orthodoxy or social practices against liberal religion, which these conservative communions believe advances women clergy too quickly or has been too soft in the face of perceived heresy and modernity's moral relativism.

Coming at it from a different angle, we suggest that whether or not the Pastorals are paraded and practiced in a Christian congregation — mainline or conservative — is less the result of a verdict about their authorship or hip factor and more the result of a theology of the Bible. We approach these letters as sacred texts, made so by the inspiration of the Holy Spirit for use as a means of grace, not because they were written down by inspired apostles — without error — or because they need interpretation by others. We agree that a congregation's Bible practices may confidently target holy ends — deeper communion with God and loving fellowship with others — not on the condition that a text's attributed author is affirmed or its ancient history is reconstructed by the tools of modern criticism, but on the belief that God's Spirit sanctifies and uses these same texts to lead Jesus' followers into the truth about God's providential way of ordering the world.

Even if a reader's theology underwrites the importance of Bible practices, rendering the meaning of a text without paying careful attention to its variegated contexts is often the pretext for using biblical interpretation to render proof-texts of self-interest. The trigger mechanism for doing so is sin, and the result of doing so is to fracture the body of Christ. For this reason, one of the most important tasks of congregational leaders is to give responsibility to teachers who are well prepared to teach others well. Such preparation to teach 1 and 2 Timothy well, especially in matters of congregational leadership, requires that careful attention be paid to the following five questions. Bible scholars will respond differently to each question in turn; however, their various responses will expose and clarify what "rules of engagement" will guide their interpretive approach to 1 and 2 Timothy. And so it is for us.

1. Is the author of 1 and 2 Timothy human or divine? Modern criticism has made it abundantly clear that biblical texts are human productions. Each biblical book was written, edited, preserved, and canonized during an extended period of time, subject to a variety of social, political, and ecclesiastical forces. On the rare occasion that biblical writers reflected on what they were doing, they did not characterize their writing as a magical performance or a divine dictation but as an occasional and conventional literary activity that targeted real people and was read aloud to them in response to their real needs (e.g., Luke 1:1-4; Eph. 3:3-4; 1 Tim. 4:13; Rev. 1:1-4, etc.). They did not suppose they were writing an inspired text for a Bible-to-be-named-later.

How might a theology of Scripture understand the humanity of biblical texts? Drawing on Paul's own confession as an apostle, we might regard the Bible as a "treasure in an earthen vessel" (2 Cor. 4:7). All those earthy, historical complexities that shaped Paul's ministry as Christ's apostle — his language, time zone and social location, religious background and experiences, intramural conflicts, sociopolitical struggles — also shaped his correspondence. In a similar way, then, when we engage 1 and 2 Timothy as Scripture, we do so in part by treasuring the Letters in their earthy particularity, subject to the factors and forces at work that shaped and sized them when they were written. But in doing so we are not on a treasure hunt for *the* normative meaning of a text, whether because the author intended it or because God inspired it; rather, whatever attention we pay to historical circumstance and linguistic analysis has the purpose of clarifying the text's theological subject matter.

We grant priority to text-centered exegesis because of the importance the church has always granted the text itself. But in doing so, we recognize the inherent elasticity of words used over time and the multiple possible functions of their grammatical relationships. Further changes in the perception of a text's meaning may result from new evidence and different exegetical strategies, as well as from interpreters who sort out a text's natural ambiguity within diverse social and theological locations. In fact, the kind of neutrality toward biblical texts that modern criticism applauds is now viewed with deep suspicion because our ordinary experience with texts of all kinds teaches us that textual meaning cannot be considered absolute for all time, whether as the assured conclusion of the scholarly guild (which is constantly adjusting its assured claims) or as some meaning determined by — and known only to — God at the time of a text's composition. Thus, the fluid nature of exegesis resists the old dichotomy between past and present meanings, and between authorial and canonical intentions.

2. Did Paul write 1 and 2 Timothy? Our conversation about 1 and 2 Timothy in the ensuing pages will name "Paul" as the author of, and "Timothy" as the recipient of, these letters. These attributions are not secured by historical analysis, since the hard evidence necessary to do so is much too sparse and uncertain to validate such a claim with confidence.[3] Furthermore, historical constructions of authorship are

---

3. Virtually every modern commentary on the Pastorals begins with a treatment of authorship. Most are much too immodest in their claims for or against Pauline authorship of these letters. These claims are rarely benign and typically linked with other judgments about the purpose or usefulness of these letters, whether for critical or practical ends. But to approach any biblical text as sacred and Spirit-inspiring forces its current community of readers to adapt prayerfully what the text plainly says for a new day and for new concerns.

largely irrelevant considerations when we are deciding a text's religious authority. The most striking feature of modernity's preoccupation with the real authors of biblical texts is the tacit connection, which has been made since the Reformation, between the text's author and its apostolic authority.

Modernity's marginalization of 1 and 2 Timothy on historical grounds is based on what Andrew Lincoln has called an "authorial fallacy."[4] According to this fallacy, the criterion of a text's apostolicity is based on whether or not modern historical reconstructions "prove" that a real apostle had a hand in the production of the text. A critical orthodoxy based on the "assured results" of leading scholars on this point often predetermines a judgment about a text's usefulness or continuing authority. In fact, Luke Timothy Johnson implies that an *idola theatri* ("theatrical idol") is in play as the principal reason that 1 and 2 Timothy are marginalized within the academic guild, because most scholars accept the verdict of critical orthodoxy regarding their authorship without carefully examining it.[5]

We suggest a range of different practices, especially when we approach the final redaction of the Pauline corpus as Scripture and useful as an auxiliary of the Lord's Spirit for Christian formation. Not only are the epistemological, historical, and theological interests in the phenomenology of a text's canonization different from the circumstances of a text's composition; the definition of apostolicity is also different. No longer is it attached to a particular historical figure, but it is attached to a broadly defined apostolate or tradition. In this regard, the apostolicity of a sacred text is recognized by the church, not through the modern historical constructions of its author, but whether or not what is written coheres to what is remembered of what the apostle taught (see 2 Tim. 1:13-14; 2:1-2; 3:10-14) and produces a mature wisdom necessary for salvation and good works (see 2 Tim. 3:15-17). In fact, most biblical compositions are anonymous or come with attributions that are difficult to nail down on historical grounds. Judgments about the apostle Paul's authorship are mostly intuitive rather than critical, and they are based on a track record of practical use by Christians as a means of divine grace. Thus the church, in treasuring

---

4. Andrew T. Lincoln, *Ephesians* (WBC) (Waco, TX: Word, 1990), pp. lxxii-lxxiii.

5. Luke Timothy Johnson, *1-2 Timothy* (Sacra Pagina) (Collegeville, MN: Liturgical Press, 1991).

these earthen vessels, does not blindly take it as a given but predicates it on hard evidence of a practical kind.

3. Why were 1 and 2 Timothy written? Commentaries typically introduce the Timothy correspondence by plotting the unwritten (and mostly unknown) narrative of the events that occasioned its composition. Most of them tell the story of Christian teachers who oppose Paul's orthodoxy; therefore, the instructions and exhortations each letter contains are interpreted as responses to intramural conflicts within earliest Pauline Christianity. In fact, however, while Paul mentions opponents and sometimes even names them, he gives only passing reference to them; in any case, their presence in the text can hardly explain either of the Timothy epistles as a whole. The profile of Paul's opponents is too thinly drawn, and most instructions are directed at congregational or personal practices that have little to do with the presence or teaching of the opponents.

The character of these letters is better understood by their salutation, which mentions Paul's departure (cf. 1 Tim. 1:3; Titus 1:5) and thereby implies the absence of his apostolic persona and authority (cf. 1 Tim. 2:7; Titus 1:3) in pagan Ephesus, where a fledgling Christian congregation is being formed under the leadership of a newly appointed and still unproven leader, Timothy. By analogy, then, the various instructions, theological formulae, and pastoral admonitions found in both letters are appropriate to a succession of new leaders who must struggle to get their religious bearings afresh in the absence of their charismatic and experienced leader — Paul. Indeed, false teachers, immature believers, incompetent and unprepared leaders, uncertain organization, disorderly relationships with others inside and outside the congregation all pose real threats to apostolic succession after Paul is no longer the go-to person when it comes to dealing with a congregation's needs. It's up to the next in line, with only Paul's instructions as a guide.

Reading 1 and 2 Timothy may well help construct what Charles Taylor has called a "social imaginary" of how an apostolic succession challenges a variety of social and political relationships at ground level.[6] Paul's instructions to Timothy, which have since been canonized for the church catholic of every age, define a set of normative practices and beliefs, both congregational and individual, that help every new

6. Cf. C. Taylor, *A Secular Age* (Cambridge, MA: Harvard University Press, 2007).

batch of congregational leaders reimagine how they should follow Paul's apostolic lead but in an ever-changing postapostolic setting. Simply put, these letters help readers imagine what Paul might do if he were here among us today. Their force is less prescriptive than intuitive of how a sacred household should be organized, why it should be organized in this way (practically and theologically), and what anticipates the material effects of doing so. Indeed, the earliest canon list (Muratorian, ca. 200 CE) that includes the Pastorals among Paul's canonical letters claims that their significant role is to provide "ecclesiastical discipline." We suggest that this is chief among their ongoing performances as Scripture.[7]

4. How does the literary form of 1 and 2 Timothy convey a word about God? Since the genre of sacred literature carries theological freight, it is an important element of interpretation. In this regard, whatever occasions a letter also helps to determine the form of written response. Letters of succession such as 1 and 2 Timothy are written to instruct and exhort, to provide examples and models to imitate (cf. Acts 20:17-35). But, in doing so, they target a particular crisis occasioned by any succession of leadership, which is even more critical in this case because the leader is an apostle who is providentially given a word from God for this moment of salvation's history (see comment on Titus 1:1-3). This is an apostolic succession, and its sacred deposit must be safeguarded for the next generation (cf. 2 Tim. 1:13-14; 2:1-2). Significantly, this kind of letter also facilitates the role that the Pastoral Epistles perform within the Pauline canon.

It is true that letters took many forms in the ancient world. Most were written communications that bridged the distance between two parties. Oratory was an important social convention of Paul's world, and letters were the literary expression of speech. Among the various kinds of letters preserved from the ancient world, perhaps the most common is private correspondence, similar in function and form to the Pastoral Epistles. We now possess literally thousands of ancient papyrus letters, stored in museums around the world, which reflect a variety of

7. In explaining why the Pastoral Epistles were chosen as the first commentary of the *African Bible Commentary*, S. Ngewa says that the focus of the letters is the same as the series: to focus on the church leaders and pastors of a new movement (Association of Evangelicals in Africa) who need to "examine themselves in light of Scripture to lead the people of God in a way that conforms to Scripture." Ngewa, *1 and 2 Timothy and Titus*, Africa Bible Commentary Series (Grand Rapids: Zondervan, 2009), p. xix.

transactions, even though they follow a standard literary pattern: an opening greeting, the main body, and a concluding benediction.

Letters of antiquity began with formal greetings so that the recipient would know the sender immediately upon unrolling the scroll. Paul's letters generally followed this well-known script: Sender to recipient, greetings. In personal letters such as 1 and 2 Timothy, this formula was amplified to highlight the nature of the relationship between sender and recipient; this, in turn, clarified the expected response of the letter's recipient to its instructions. In the case of his Timothy correspondence, Paul's address does more than emphasize his personal relationship with Timothy; it deals with his spiritual authority as well. Especially when the New Testament reader has the Paul of Acts in mind, Paul's identification of himself as an "apostle of Christ Jesus" posits the religious importance of his mission and message for the future of the church, which Timothy has been delegated to organize in Ephesus.

The main body of a personal letter takes up the business at hand. (In this sense, it functions much as a sermon does in a worship service.) Differences of emphasis and vocabulary that the careful reader notes from letter to letter in the Pauline corpus reflect the range of controversies and crises that Paul considers and seeks to resolve. He offers advice, gives instruction, makes commands, corrects doctrine, rebukes false teachers — all according to his understanding of Scripture's roles within the faith community (see 2 Tim. 3:16b). The personal letter follows this strategy but ostensibly with a particular person rather than congregation in view. The subject matter of 1 Timothy (and Titus) primarily gives instructions that would order congregational life in pagan places, much like the early-second-century Didache and other Christian writings across the next several centuries for an expanding missionary church. The main body of 2 Timothy is quite different: it has a heightened sense of Paul's passing and the importance of Timothy's role to carry on his legacy to the next generation — a kind of literary "last will and testament" of the revered apostle.

The concluding words of Paul's letters, including these letters to Timothy, include many elements. While one can always find an invocation of divine blessing of some kind, Paul also includes miscellaneous greetings, exhortations, itineraries, summaries of concern, and other personal reminders. What this suggests about these letters is that they were not intended by Paul as "private" letters but for a wider readership beyond Timothy.

Of the various functions performed by private letters, both 1 and 2 Timothy are letters of "instruction and order," though the instructions contained in 1 Timothy are to order a congregation, while those given in 2 Timothy are more personal in that they seek to order Timothy's life after the model exemplified by Paul. The more personal tone and themes of 2 Timothy suggest a professional relationship between a mentor and apprentice that seems to require equal measures of encouragement and a firm reminder of the important mission at hand. This observation is important for understanding the particular literary genre of 2 Timothy as a private letter and underscores the astute observation of Luke Timothy Johnson that 2 Timothy is written in the manner of a personal paraenetic letter: not as a farewell brief, but as a "succession letter," as we would call it. Likewise, 1 Timothy is written in the manner of *mandata principis* ("mandates," or instructions, from the principal of the group): an official letter from a superior to an administrative associate for use at a specific location, which mixes instruction (probably read publicly) with personal exhortation (probably kept private).[8] These literary observations not only explain the occasion of the letters but their continuing role for a church that does its work in the absence of the apostle and is charged, as Timothy was, to safeguard the Pauline apostolate for the next generation.

5. Why are 1 and 2 Timothy included among Paul's canonical letters? The gravitas of our study of these letters is fashioned from a postbiblical moment when this small subcollection of Pastoral Letters (1 and 2 Timothy and Titus), probably already in limited circulation, was folded into the existing Pauline collection to complete it for subsequent use within the church. A "canonical approach" to biblical interpretation is naturally interested in this historical moment: When did the church recognize the final literary form of a particular collection of sacred writings? Such an interest is deeply rooted in a belief that God's Spirit guides the church's recognitions and related choices when forming its biblical canon; after all, the church is a community in which the Spirit dwells and works. In this sense, when we speak of Scripture as a literary "canon of sacred texts" or its performances within the church as "canonical," we do so in confessing that the persistent presence of God's Spirit is at work among Scripture's faithful readers of every age as they use these precious texts in

8. See Johnson, *1-2 Timothy*, p. 97.

drawing them into a more intimate and wakeful fellowship with the living God.

Naturally, there are all kinds of explanatory footnotes we need to add to this grand assertion to elaborate its meaning. For example, our claim suggests that God's word in Scripture is more clearly heard by a faithful reader who is brought to maturity by worship and study in the company of the other believers, whose habits and practices cultivate a robust life with God. We should also note that the reception of this word from Scripture is as ever-changing as is its ever-changing audience of readers. What properly constrains the church's reading of Scripture are those timeless theological agreements that bear witness to the apostles' testimony of the risen Christ, as well as the holy ends — courageous devotion to God and an active love for one another — for which Scripture is appointed by the church to help bring its members to maturity. In this sense, then, our interpretive approach to 1 and 2 Timothy is grounded in a particular conception of Scripture's "nature" as a whole book sanctified by God's Spirit in all its diverse bits and pieces to convey and clarify God's ongoing purposes for God's people in the world.

In any case, the effect of forming and receiving whole collections of individual writings for a single biblical canon creates another kind of literary aesthetic that is substantively and functionally different from those critical "collections" that scholars compose according to their historical-critical constructions of authorship and social location. The seven-letter Pauline canon accepted by most modern historical critics differs in shape and substance from the thirteen-letter Pauline corpus that was fashioned and fixed during the church's canonical process. Even though the canonical approach should not be considered a substitute for critical reconstructions (or deconstructions) of the Pauline Epistle collection, it places a premium on reading any of Paul's Letters within its canonical rather than historical context. At the very moment when the three Pastoral Epistles were added to the then extant ten-letter Pauline collection (toward the end of the second century), the church recognized that it had reached its final (or "canonical") form — a literary form that, upon its use in an array of settings, is found most effective in shaping a Christian congregation's understanding of Scripture's Pauline witness.

Think of the canonical process as a kind of evolutionary mechanism. New external threats that were present by the mid–second century, a change of audiences, and new responsibilities that arose to meet the internal pressures of an expanding religious movement — all of these forged an ecclesiastical environment different from Paul's original mission. Put positively, subsequent readers of Paul, about the time the Pauline canon reached its final canonical form — such as Irenaeus, and especially Tertullian — found the sweep of its concerns readily adaptable to this new environment. In our estimation, the addition of the Pastoral Epistles to complete the Pauline canon made it thus adaptable. Again, our thesis is that the church's preservation, canonization (even if in edited form), and continuing use of Paul's Letters, whether in its preaching or catechesis, is based on its adaptability to the social and religious exigencies facing the one holy, catholic, and apostolic church today.

While the formation of the Pauline canon is profitably studied as a historical phenomenon — what might be termed a "canonization from below" — this process should also be mined for what it implies for Bible practices in an ecclesiastical setting. Most scholars of canonization are not interested in explaining the choices that were made in forming the biblical canon theologically as a process of spiritual discernment led by the Holy Spirit — a "canonization from above." A canonical approach is interested in a careful reconstruction of the canonical process as a deep reservoir of important interpretive clues for using Scripture to inform the witness and form the faith of today's church. The church's discernment of the Spirit's leading role in the production of the biblical canon is not predicated on the identity of a text's author but on its effect in forming a congregation that is wise for salvation and mature for good works.

Most modern constructions of the canonical process follow individual books through their earliest history, whether in the West or East, and whether evinced in manuscripts, in allusions and citations of the earliest Christian writings, or in the various canon lists. While useful in helping track the sociology and theology that attend the canonical process within antiquity, this kind of work largely ignores the phenomenology of the process itself. Almost every individual book entered the biblical canon as an integral member of a whole collection (e.g., Torah, Psalter, Book of the Twelve, Fourfold Gospel, Pauline collection, Catholic Epistle collection, and so on). Therefore, the final form of a collection demonstrates an aesthetic that is maximally effective for performing the authorized roles of a biblical canon. In the Pauline idiom, these roles include making believers wise for salvation and bringing them to maturity to perform the good works of God (see our commentary on 2 Tim. 3:15-17 below). If readers recognize this theological dimension of the Bible's formation, they will examine the phenomena of canonization — and particularly the "canonical shaping" of discrete collections of biblical books and their placement within the final form of the biblical canon — for interpretive prompts that will continue to guide them in their faithful use of these texts as the church's Scripture.

In this sense, we contend that the final literary form of the biblical canon is a work of aesthetic excellence. That is, the formation of a canonical collection, or even of the biblical canon as a whole, was concluded, and its final shape was fixed, at the moment the church recognized that a particular literary shape of a collection or the canon had sufficient aesthetic excellence to function effectively as Scripture. While certainly related to what the church affirms about the Bible's authority and holiness, its formation into a textual analogue of the apostolic Rule of Faith is the ultimate result of a vast repertoire of choices that spiritual leaders observed being made when gathering individual texts into discrete collections and then putting these collections together to form a single biblical canon.

But this observation directs us to a more practical question that is more to the present point: What prompted the church to make those editorial decisions that put collections of individual sacred writings together into a particular shape and size? Even if we are to believe that these decisions merely recognize the Spirit's will, Adolf von Harnack observed that a century before the church discerned which way the wind was blowing, its various canon lists and manuscript traditions demonstrated multiple different possible shapes and sizes of this canon of sacred texts. This debate continues up to the present day: that is, whether to set aside the very idea of a biblical canon or to open it up to additional texts. The tenor of this debate points to another question: Why did the church settle on the biblical canon it did and, particularly, on a thirteen-letter Pauline collection that includes these three letters? Why this canonical shape and not some other?

From our routine experience as humans, we might allow that how objects are formed is an important factor of their utility. How individual bits work together as a whole, and toward what purpose, is a decisive measurement of an object's performance, whether it will be well received and well used by its future practitioners. In objecting to what he calls "high art," which is momentarily valued for art's sake but is unused in any practical way and thus soon forgotten as a passing fad, Nicholas Wolterstorff advances a more functional conception of the aesthetic excellence of an enduring work of art.[9] In his view, any work of public art should be shaped and sized in a way that makes it accessible to ever-changing audiences, constantly performing in ways that inspire them to do good work or to live more virtuously as a result. While defining aesthetic excellence in this more activist direction, Wolterstorff allows for inherent properties of color and texture, shape and proportion, that distinguish a good work of art from one of lesser quality. People are naturally drawn to a particular work of art or line of poetry or landscape not only because it inspires them but also because they are able to recognize the sheer excellence of its nature.

In applying Wolterstorff's definition of aesthetic excellence to the final literary form of the biblical canon, we would argue that, in addition to a deep sense of the Bible's completeness and coherence as a trusted witness to the word and ways of God, the Bible's shape may be appraised as an artifact of aesthetic excellence with the following implications.[10] First, the church discerned when the Bible got shaped into its particular literary form, which would more effectively enable the Spirit to use it in performing those religious roles that form a holy people who know and serve God. Every collection of texts was received and folded into the biblical canon on the basis of a résumé of ecclesiastical performances that would commend its future productivity according to the purposes of God. In this sense, the church's decisions were rational and based on solid evidence of a text's spiritual utility. It was first well used and widely so for congregational teaching, reproving, correcting, and training believers into the way of God before it was received into the biblical canon. Our point is that the enduring excellence of a particular form is recognized from among other possibilities by its capacity to perform the workload intended for a biblical canon. Scripture is a beautiful thing because it performs its public roles well.

Second, there are literary properties inherent in the biblical canon that might naturally draw readers to its wisdom or into its nar-

9. See Nicholas Wolterstorff, *Art in Action* (Grand Rapids: Eerdmans, 1980), pp. 65-174, esp. in his proposal of a distinctively "Christian aesthetic."

10. Christopher Seitz allows that the final literary form of the canonical text "bears the fullest witness to all that God has said and handed on within the community of faith." In *Dictionary for Theological Interpretation of the Bible,* ed. Kevin J. Vanhoozer (Grand Rapids: Baker Academic, 2005), p. 102.

rative world as advice or a story of higher quality. Are there norms of excellence that may be applied to the biblical canon that might help clarify the church's choice as one based on its aesthetic as well as religious excellence? Indeed, there are. For example, the Bible's diverse parts are noteworthy because of their rich texture. As a literary genre, the biblical canon is a collection of collections made up of artfully told stories, memorable lyrics, vivid poetry, exacting law codes — all of which aim us at ultimate meaning. Yet these diverse and discrete parts are nicely fitted together into whole collections and then into a single biblical canon whose internal unity of theological and moral content renders a more coherent — and perhaps for that reason, compelling — word about God. Moreover, the effects of reading Scripture in the company of the Spirit and the worshiping community enable the reader to experience God's holy presence, the joy and peace, and the conviction and judgment, that come from the divine word.

Finally, like the artist who changes the wording of a poem or a line of a painting because it makes the poem better or the painting's image more arresting, we might allow that the indwelling Spirit forms a community's capacity to recognize which particular bits (and in what form) are necessary in constructing a single biblical canon that is most effective in accomplishing its holy purposes. The church's decisions in forming the collections of the biblical canon, if they are directed by the Holy Spirit, will effectively help to accomplish God's redemptive desires for the world. In other words, if a loving God has created us for loving communion with God and each other, then the church's production of Scripture in its present canonical form and thus the church's practices of Scripture — carefully exegeting it, theologically interpreting it, and vibrantly proclaiming it — must target this same holy end.

The final edition of the thirteen-letter Pauline corpus, completed sometime toward the end of the second century by the addition of the Pastoral Epistles, may be understood in two different, yet complementary, ways. First, the Pauline Letters that were selected and collected together under the Spirit's direction provide the church with a complete expression of the gospel that Paul proclaimed to the nations, with the anticipated purpose of forging, with other canonical collections, a fully trustworthy analogy of the apostolic Rule of Faith. Second, the addition of 1 and 2 Timothy and Titus, with their distinctively pastoral materials, to the Pauline collection — which was prompted by the testimony from the earliest canon lists — completes its evangelical witness by supplying normative patterns of "ecclesiastical discipline." Not only does the exemplary Paul imagined by the Pastoral Epistles supply personal patterns of Christian ministry and character; his instructions regarding congregational life help to fashion congregations where his apostolic legacy is used to secure its future for the next generation of believers. These interpretive prompts will shape how we see these letters as "engaging congregational leaders" for a new day.

DISCUSSION QUESTIONS

1. Does it make a difference in how you view the importance of these letters for guiding Christian ministry if the historians say that Paul did not write them? Explain.

2. Review the reasons the ancient church included 1 and 2 Timothy in the Pauline collection. How does this "canonical intention" help shape the church's use of them today in a congregation's Christian formation?

3. How are "leadership" and "authority" similar and different?

4. What does Paul mean by "itching ears"? What forms does this phenomenon take in our own time?

What Is the Pastor's Most Essential Work?

1 Timothy 1:3-17

3 As I requested you to do when leaving for Macedonia: stay longer in Ephesus so that you may instruct certain individuals not to teach divergent doctrine, 4 nor pay attention to myths and unending genealogies. Their teaching only encourages idle speculation rather than faithfulness to God's way of stewarding the world. 5 The aim of instruction is loving relationships that come from a pure heart, good conscience, and earnest faith. 6 Some have rejected this and have turned to fruitless discussion, 7 wanting to be Torah teachers without understanding either what they are saying or what they are claiming. 8 We know, for example, that the law is good if used lawfully. 9 We understand a law is not for an innocent person but for the lawless and rebellious, godless and sinners, unholy and profane, for those who commit patricide and matricide, for murderers, 10 sexually unfaithful, homosexuals,[1] slave dealers, liars, perjurers, and anyone else who acts contrary to healthy teaching, 11 which agrees with the glorious gospel of the blessed God that has been entrusted to me.

---

1. We have translated the Greek compound *arsenokoitēs* as "homosexual." It may be Paul's own invention (cf. 1 Cor. 6:9; Lev. 20:13), in keeping with the literal meaning of *arsēn* ("males") and *koitē* ("having sex"). What homosexual practices are envisioned by the word are indeterminate, especially since Paul chooses not to use the more common word for homosexual practice, *androkoitē*. Almost certainly Paul has in mind behaviors that were widely considered shameful, which has led some to think he has in mind male prostitution or even pederasty.

12 I thank Christ Jesus our Lord who has strengthened me and considered me faithful, appointing me to a ministry 13 even though I was a former blasphemer and persecutor, a violent man who was shown mercy because I acted in ignorance and unbelief. 14 Our Lord's grace poured all over me along with the faith and love that are in Christ Jesus. 15 This saying is a core belief worthy of unqualified acceptance: "Christ Jesus came into the world to save sinners" — among whom I am first! 16 But I was shown mercy for this reason, that Christ Jesus might thoroughly demonstrate patience first in me as the role model for those who come to believe in him for eternal life. 17 Now to the King of the ages, to the immortal, invisible, and only God, be honor and glory forever and ever. Amen.

Part 1: Engaging 1 Timothy 1:3-17 as Scripture

Paul's departure from Ephesus requires that Timothy stay behind to lead the Ephesian Christian congregation in Paul's absence. Although we are not told why the apostle should give detailed instructions to his young protégé about matters that seem obvious to others, the charge to correct certain rivals seems to make Paul's absence more threatening to their fledgling congregation. Yet Paul rarely identifies his rivals by name (cf. 1 Tim. 1:19-20; 2 Tim. 2:16-18) and typically substitutes rhetoric for reality when discussing what they teach (cf. 1 Tim. 4:1-4; Titus 1:10-12; 3:9-11).[2] What seems clear is that whatever these faceless individuals teach, they do not represent Paul, and they may even exert a negative influence on his congregation in Ephesus. Paul's entreaty to Timothy to stay put and instruct them makes little sense otherwise.

But the theological crisis that occasions this letter is not the pesky presence of rival teachers; rather, it is Paul's departure from Ephesus

2. See Ben Witherington's balanced summary of scholarly conjecture about the identity and teaching of these opponents; *Letters and Homilies for Hellenized Christians*, vol. 1: *A Socio-Rhetoical Commentary on Titus, 1-2 Timothy and 1-2-3 John* (Downers Grove, IL: InterVarsity, 1993), pp. 341-47. He follows J. L. Sumney's methodology for identifying opponents in the Pauline letters, even though Sumney uses 2 Corinthians to illustrate and does not include the Pastoral Epistles in his analysis. Jerry Sumney, "Identifying Paul's Opponents," JSNTSup 40 (Sheffield, 1990).

and the threat to his mission in his absence. The difficult tasks of forming a Christian congregation in a pagan place are left to Timothy. While the mention of rivals may sound an alert, this letter's real aim is to guide his successor in forming a healthy Christian congregation according to the "glorious gospel of God" entrusted to the apostle Paul.

Ephesus was a cultural and religious center of the ancient world: the capital city of Roman Asia, it was among the empire's most prosperous regions. In due time the city would also become the headquarters of Paul's missionary organization and perhaps also the place where the first corpus of Paul's Letters was formed.[3] Within its canonical setting, the letter's Ephesian address cues the story of Paul's mission in Ephesus (found in Acts 19), which depicts an urban landscape rife with religious conflict provoked by Paul's identity as a Jewish teacher. Despite a mission that embraced both Jews and Gentiles (Acts 19:10, 17), the congregation's dismissal from the local synagogue (19:9) and the wider conflict over Paul's Jewish identity (19:34) form an important subtext that will shape our reading of the letter's instructions. Moreover, the passing mention of Paul's "departure for Macedonia" recalls the repeated forays Paul made with Timothy from Ephesus into Macedonia (see Acts 19:21-22; 20:1-6). More importantly, Timothy is among those who heard Paul's succession speech in Miletus (Acts 20:18-35), the echoes of which frame this Epistle's theological crisis: How will the congregation that Paul began survive his departure? This correspondence supplies the exhortation and instruction of a departed apostle to form the community left behind. In due time, and under Timothy's leadership, it will become the custodian of Paul's apostolic witness for the next generation of believers.

Paul's "request" (1 Tim. 1:3) sounds a note of irony, since an apostolic request presumes compliance: Paul gives instructions with the air of command. Yet the main clause of his initial request is lacking, and this has the rhetorical effect — perhaps purposeful — of elevating the importance of Paul's departure. That is, his departure signals a succession of pastoral leadership in Ephesus, but it also means that Timothy is left on his own with only his mentor's written instruction to school him for the important business at hand.

The purpose clause *(hina)* declares the first order of this business:

---

3. For the importance of Ephesus in the formation of the New Testament canon, see E. E. Lemcio, "Ephesus and the New Testament Canon," in R. W. Wall and E. E. Lemcio, *The New Testament as Canon* (Sheffield: JSOT Press, 1992), pp. 335-60.

"instruct certain individuals" (1:3). The meaning of *parangellō* ("instruct") in antiquity is quite elastic, and its use here has been translated in various ways. The preference of most commentators is "command" because of its sense elsewhere in the Pauline corpus when the apostle's instruction delineates a congregation's rule of faith and life (e.g., 1 Cor. 11:17; 1 Thess. 4:11; 2 Thess. 3:4-12). But the verb's repetition in 1:5, where it sets out the "aim of instruction," does not convey a strong-armed correction of non-Pauline doctrine but rather the catechesis of an entire congregation — a congregation that includes the false teachers. In a sense, Timothy's instruction not only defines the terms of Paul's gospel among those who disagree with it, but does so in a priestly fashion that seeks conversion as well as correction.

Paul says that the individuals in need of correction not only teach "divergent doctrines," but do so in a way that is without spiritual benefit. Paul's dismissal of a religious curriculum that specializes in "myths and unending family trees" (1:4a) is similar to concerns expressed by two of his contemporaries, Plutarch and Philo, both of whom described myths as "useless fabrications" (Plutarch, *Obs. Or.* 46) and "mistakes" that follow from inconclusive arguments (Philo, *Cong.* 53). The added adjective "unending" is a metaphor for the futility of targeting biblical genealogy (cf. Titus 1:14; 3:9) rather than Paul's gospel (cf. 1 Tim. 4:7; 2 Tim. 4:4; Titus 1:14), which is the source of a congregation's theological instruction. He later criticizes their ascetic lifestyle, which abstains from certain social conventions (e.g., marriage, certain foods, table fellowship) that make use of the good creatures of a holy God (see 1 Tim. 4:1-5).

In any case, a congregation's religious instruction is a practical matter, and the effect of instruction in life measures its theological clearness. For this reason, the reader is made alert by Paul's use of *mē* . . . *mēde* to construct a pair of prohibited practices: "Do not teach . . . do not pay attention." Timothy safeguards the Ephesian mission by combining the core beliefs of Paul's gospel with a pedagogy that pays attention to a congregation's spiritual life and ethical choices. It is significant that the summaries of Pauline teaching scattered across the letter are illustrated by personal example and punctuated by pointed exhortation. Christian instruction that sounds a Pauline note is a practical divinity. Yet the believer who follows Paul's lead is hardly a religious fundamentalist who makes a clean break from those considered heterodox. Paul calls for a redemptive strategy that engages those who disagree with him — "so that they may learn not to blaspheme" (1:20).

While obviously crucial in setting the table for this letter, the precise meaning of *oikonomia theou,* which we elaborately translate as "God's way of stewarding the world" (1:4), is notoriously difficult to pin down.[4] The meaning of *oikonomia* doubtless follows from its root, *oikos* ("house"), and is generally thought to refer to the mundane routines of managing any household, familial or otherwise. Perhaps one hears a resonance of a similar phrase, *theou oikonomos,* which Paul uses in Titus 1:7 concerning the congregation's *episkopos,* or "administrator" (see 1 Tim. 3:1-7), or again in Galatians 4:1-2 concerning the heir's relationship to his "trustees" (*oikonomoi* [NASV]) as an analogue of Christian conversion. The Galatians 4:1-7 text, in particular, has been a crux of interpretation for social historians who study the inheritance laws of antiquity. It is arguably the gravitas of the letter's argument. Various profiles of this transaction have been offered without a consensus emerging.[5] But if the one in view is the trustee of a young heir, the legal role of the *oikonomos* would include his supervision to maturity, at which time he would be able to assume the obligations of his inheritance. The catch phrase used here, *oikonomia theou,* is probably rooted in this same typological soil that envisions a kind of divine trusteeship by which God manages the outworking of salvation's history within the ongoing community of faith.[6]

If readers take it as a type of divine providence, then, they must determine the significance of the genitive *(theou)* and who or what the appended "faithfulness" targets. The later reference to the church as "God's household" (*oikos theou,* 3:15), which recalls *theou oikonomos,* helps us decide that *theou* is a subjective genitive: that is, God is the steward of creation, and the act of a believer's "faithfulness" to God's stewardship affirms trust in God's providential care of creation. Timothy now

4. Our translation and understanding are influenced by Luke Timothy Johnson's programmatic discussion of the catch phrase, which he considers thematic of the letter (Johnson, *1-2 Timothy* [Sacra Pagina] [Collegeville, MN: Liturgical Press, 1991], pp. 147-54).

5. J. Scott contends that the referent of these *oikonomoi* are the oppressive Egyptian slaveholders, employed by the government, from whom Israel is delivered by God through Moses. Accordingly, the text is part of a Pauline typology of Exodus: Israel is "heir" of God's promise to Abraham, whose inheritance is now realized because of Christ for those who believe. J. M. Scott, *Adoption as Sons of God: An Exegetical Investigation into the Background of ΥΙΟΘΕΣΙΑ in the Pauline Corpus,* WUNT II-48 (Tübingen: Mohr Siebeck, 1992).

6. See J. K. Goodrich, "Guardians, not Taskmasters: The Cultural Resonances of Paul's Metaphor in Galatians 4:1-2," *JSNT* 32 (2010).

realizes the astounding truth that his continuation of Paul's mission in downtown Ephesus is of a piece with God's overall management of the world!

This sense squares with the letter's wide-ranging instructions, which seek to form a congregation's life in the world as a public microcosm of *oikonomia theou.* Ancillary to this role, the "gospel of the blessed God" (1:11) is the curriculum of a Christian congregation's catechesis into an understanding of God's stewardship. Almost certainly, Paul means this to be at the leading edge of Timothy's ministry, and it suggests that Paul's exploration of the "household" metaphor for church orders is a significant political metaphor for a pattern of public life that is ultimately subversive of Roman rule. The images of suffering and imprisonment in 2 Timothy make clear that Rome and Christianity subscribe to opposite household visions.

The instruction of God's household trains its members in "loving relationships" (*agapē,* 1:5a): that is, whether people love each other is a test of their theological orthodoxy (see also 1 John 4:7-8). In Paul's thought, *agapē* is not an abstracted rule of life but is the principal characteristic of a congregation's life together and is formed in the company of the indwelling Spirit (Gal. 5:16-26). As such, neighborly love is a marker of the congregation's life in Christ (cf. Rom. 5:5; 8:35; 13:9). In the history of those interpreting this feature of Pauline ethics, it is well known that this is an implicit contradiction of the teaching of Jesus, who aimed his disciples at a loving God, which he sharply claimed is "the first and greatest commandment" (Matt. 22:38). Matthew's Gospel places the commandment in a context that is similar to the one in this letter to Timothy, that is, in an argument between Jesus and Torah teachers (the Pharisees) about the meaning of the law and the prophets (see Matt. 22:34-40; 1 Tim. 1:7). In fact, Aquinas (among others) interpreted *agapē* more broadly — that is, as humans' loving relationships with both God and neighbor to reconcile this purported conflict over the love command between Jesus and Paul.[7]

The triad of religious virtues — "pure heart, good conscience, earnest faith" (1:5b) — are marks of the congregation whose moral competence cultivates loving relationships, not only between its members but toward outsiders as well. This formulation of Christian existence is unique in the New Testament, and its Hellenistic resonance may well

7. *Nicene and Post-Nicene Fathers,* 1:3.275.

reflect the Pauline mission to the nations.[8] But its integration of inward affections and outward practices is central to Paul's definition of the Christian life and follows from the pattern of Jesus' moral instruction exemplified by Matthew's Sermon on the Mount (Matt. 5:17-48; 6:1-21). In fact, Paul undoubtedly agrees with other Christian readers of Israel's Scripture that observing the command of Torah is the moral marker of a covenant-keeping community: not to displace the singular importance of the Christ event in God's redemptive plan, but as an essential expression of God's victory over sin.[9]

The first quality is a "pure heart" (2 Tim. 2:22), which according to Jewish psychology is the epicenter of human existence: our "heart-felt" emotions, affections, and motives determine what we see and how we act. Added to this are the Jewish purity laws, which publicly expressed a community's covenant fellowship with God. Of course, the question of purity is central to the discussion and decision of the Jerusalem Council in Acts 15, which was prompted by the repentant Pharisee's question about purity and table fellowship, a question that Peter answered by defining purity as a matter of the heart (Acts 15:5-10).

The pivotal element of this triad is the "good conscience," which is central to a Hellenistic conception of the moral life. This belief that the Creator builds into every person an internal moral apparatus shaped Diaspora Judaism's (and thus Paul's) moral understanding. Even though it is unmentioned in the Old Testament, Philo lists the "good conscience" among his "special laws" (1:203) as the internal spiritual capacity to discern God's will with the intention of obeying it.

The final element of the triad is a "sincere faith," which adds a

---

8. Collins calls attention to the mixture of tropes, which draws from Judaism (heart), Christianity (faith), and secular Hellenistic culture (conscience) to draft an "interpretive triad" of religious life. By making "good conscience" the pivotal member of the triad, it is especially apropos for those struggling to adapt their Christian faith to their Hellenistic culture. Raymond F. Collins, *1 and 2 Timothy and Titus: A Commentary* (NTL) (Louisville: Westminster John Knox, 2002), p. 28.

9. In this sense, surely the criticism of a Christian theological interpretation of the Hebrew Bible raised by G. Ratheiser, *Mitzvoth Ethics and the Jewish Bible: The End of Old Testament Theology* (Edinburgh: T. & T. Clark, 2007), is misplaced. While his charge is true that a christological rereading of Tanakh is implicitly (and necessarily) supersessionist, which the New Testament itself suggests (see Acts 17:1-5), it does not follow that Christian interpreters have failed to pick up the importance of the moral life (i.e., "mitzvoth ethics") as an identity marker of a covenant community's loyalty to its God. See, e.g., W. Eichrodt, *Theology of the Old Testament* (Philadelphia: Westminster, 1961), 1:70-177.

distinctively Christian dimension to the kind of person who has the capacity for loving relationships. Different connotations have been made of Paul's use of "faith" in the Pastoral Epistles; however, its repetition in this passage (1:2, 4, 5) seems to imply the community's firm affirmation of God's way of stewarding the world (1:4b). Whether personified by the faithful actions it takes in life or in the profession of its core beliefs, the force of this virtue is the community's vigorous and rigorous embracing of the gospel truth disclosed in Christ Jesus.[10] Augustine writes that, "if our faith involves no lie, then we do not love that which is not to be loved, and living justly, we hope for that which will in no way deceive our hope" (*On Christian Doctrine*, 1:40-44).

According to the Pastoral Epistles, what conforms to "the glorious gospel of the blessed God" (1:11) in life and doctrine is considered theologically "healthy" (*hygiainō*, 1:10), a Greek medical term that provides an apt metaphor for the good effect of Christian instruction (cf. 1 Tim. 6:3; 2 Tim. 1:13; 4:3; Titus 1:9, 13; 2:1-2).[11] This word evokes the image of a vital congregation shaped by Paul's instruction, and it would have struck a responsive chord among its ancient readers, who were familiar with its use in moral discourse: good instruction is the moral foundation of all healthy relationships. Maximus of Tyre, writing a century after Paul, says that "truth and healthy understanding and morality and knowledge of the law and right cannot be acquired in any other way than by actually doing them, just as one can never learn the craft of shoemaking unless one actually works at it" (*Discourses* 16.3).

Sandwiched between these instructions about a church curriculum is Paul's curious reflection on the Torah in 1:8-10a. The reader need not be confused by its positive tone. In Romans, Paul admits that since Torah is revealed by God on Mount Sinai, it is inherently "good" (1 Tim. 1:8; cf. Rom. 7:12), and, when rightly used, is an impor-

---

10. Protestant interpreters since Calvin have struggled with this verse precisely because it seems to suggest a subordinate role for faith and even because it seems to displace a theological orthodoxy in which believers place their confidence for a moral orthopraxy of "loving relationships"; cf. *Calvin's New Testament Commentaries*, vol. 10: *2 Corinthians and Timothy, Titus and Philemon* (Grand Rapids: Eerdmans, 1996), pp. 191-92. Their struggle is misplaced when it is realized that this passage's contention is that love is the *telos* of Christian instruction only as the moral effect (and therefore religious test) of "healthy doctrine" — a central Pauline belief.

11. See Abraham J. Malherbe, *Paul and the Popular Philosophers* (Minneapolis: Fortress, 1989), pp. 121-36.

tant resource in understanding God's gospel. Following Jewish literary practice, Paul's use of moral catalogs like this one often has a particular situation or audience in mind. Perhaps the implied contrast is
that, unlike the rivals who engage in a "fruitless discussion" (1 Tim.
1:6) without bringing the "lawless and rebellious" to repentance, the
preaching of the "glorious gospel of God" produces the spiritual
healthy result of conversion (cf. 1:12-17).

The spiritual health of a Christian congregation and its leadership is the salutary effect of the orthodoxy of its instruction. The
leader's is a practical divinity, always expressed in terms that connect
the proclamation of truth with how truth performs in real life. For this
reason, those loving relationships to which God's purpose for people
springs forth from interior life are shaped by healthy doctrine; and an
"unlawful" use of the law (cf. 1:8) is that brittle kind of legalism that
substitutes a rigorous performance of the law's letter for a robust de-
pendence on divine grace.

The expression of thanksgiving for another is a standard, though
not uniform, ingredient of Paul's Letters. In most cases, epistolary
thanksgivings function much as a pastoral prayer does, in which
thanksgiving is given and petitions offered to God for the well-being of
the audience. In this case, however, Paul thanks Jesus for saving him
from ignorance and unbelief (1:13) and for a ministry of the gospel that
has been entrusted to him (1:11-12). He imagines this combination of
conversion and commission as a pouring out of divine grace (1:14) to
demonstrate to others not only that "Christ Jesus came into the world
to save sinners" (1:15-16) but also that such a salvation does not follow a
conventional pattern of human existence but is the merciful effect of
the one and only God (1:17).

Unlike in his other epistles, Paul's thanksgiving is biographical:
charin echō . . . me (literally "I thank . . . me"). Its purpose is to explain
the theological centerpiece of the gospel entrusted to Paul (1:10-11),
which is the religious experience of a sinner's conversion from ignorance and unbelief. If readers contextualize this biography of conversion via a prior reading of its narration in Acts, they will more easily
note that the drama of Paul's conversion (cf. Acts 9:1-9) is decisively
linked to his missionary calling (Acts 9:15-16; 26:15-18). Paul's conversion
is a teachable moment that not only shapes his gospel message about
the salvation-creating power of God's grace but underwrites Christ's
appointment of him to his apostleship as well (cf. Gal. 1:11-17). Here, as

in Acts, Paul's conversion stages his gospel commission and is, therefore, the most decisive moment of his ministry of the gospel.

The irony presented by Paul's biography is that these snapshots of an apostle's life are not really about Paul but about all those others whose similar experiences of a responsible grace frame their reading of the Pauline corpus. This biography, especially when contextualized by the conversion narrative in Acts, not only guides what the church should emphasize when using Paul's Letters, but it also personalizes a biblical pattern of the transforming effect God's grace carries into all of life (1:14).[12] The catch phrase translated "this teaching is a core belief" (*pistos ho logos,* 1:15), appears five times in the Pastorals (1 Tim. 1:15; 3:1; 4:9; 2 Tim. 2:11; Titus 3:8; cf. Titus 1:9) and nowhere else in the New Testament. In each case, the phrase either introduces or concludes a Pauline formulation of God's way of salvation. Regarding this saying, "Christ Jesus came into the world to save sinners" summarizes what is found in the "glorious gospel" entrusted to Paul (1:10-11) and is what one scholar has called Paul's "creedal cameo."[13] How these catch phrases originated is difficult to determine; but they were likely created as missionary "sound bites" — memorable yet dense phrases that helped converts conceptualize their experience of being initiated into the Christian faith.

The spiritual crisis that requires such a conversion is the sinner's ignorance of God's redemptive purpose, and thus agrees with how sin is routinely understood in Hellenistic Judaism (cf. Josephus, *Ant.* 3.231-32). The theme of human active ignorance of divine providence is also a narrative theme of Acts (Acts 3:17; 17:3). Reading Acts prior to this letter secures more firmly this theological point: God gives second chances to those whose prior rejection of God's Messiah is a matter of their ignorance of Scripture's messianic way of salvation rather than a matter of bad character. In this case, the attentive hearing of God's glorious gospel may dispel one's ignorance and open up one's heart to knowledge of God's truth (1 Tim. 2:4).

---

12. Acts does not present conversion as a personal transformation, even though this may be inferred from its triadic narrative of Paul's conversion. The keen emphasis on Paul's transformation in this biography is hermeneutical of a Pauline conception of salvation, which not only regards the forgiveness of sin in righting the sinner's relationship with God but also the freeing of believers from sin so that in Christ they sin no more (so, e.g., Rom. 5:12–6:23). What Paul exemplifies, then, is the transforming effect of grace, which turns an enemy into a champion.

13. Collins, *1 and 2 Timothy and Titus,* p. 43.

Even though "Christ Jesus" is the name used for Jesus in the Pastoral Epistles, here Paul adds "our Lord." The public profession that the risen Jesus is the church's Lord is a principal identity marker of Pauline congregations in the public square (see Rom. 10:9). By this public profession of faith, sinners admit their agreement with the central claims of Paul's gospel about Christ's atoning death: bodily resurrection, heavenly exaltation, and triumphant return (see 1 Tim. 3:16). That is, all believers share with the apostle the same core beliefs about Christ and experience the same realization that Jesus "came into the world to save sinners . . . for eternal life."

The concluding doxology (1:17) is characteristic of Paul, especially since it reflects on the apostle's own strategic role within the global economy of God's salvation (Rom. 11:36; Gal. 1:5; Eph. 3:20-21). The terms of his praise size up the character of the one who has the capacity to make good on the stunning promise to save sinners for eternal life through Christ Jesus. This general depiction of deity to underwrite his more particularly Christian claim about Jesus has a familiar ring in both Hellenistic and Jewish worlds, and this is precisely its purpose here, which envisions the formation of a Christian congregation — a microscopic form of the *oikonomia theou* — in a pagan world: to invite a conversation between these two worlds about God's manner of saving people from self-destructive sins through Christ.

Part 2: Engaging 1 Timothy 1:3-17 for Today's Leaders

What is a pastor? What is a pastor supposed to do? The various forms and expressions of church and Christianity in twenty-first-century North America provide an array — perhaps a bewildering array — of different options, models, and possibilities for understanding a pastor's work and core identity.

Among the many options, pastors might imagine their role and work as that of being entertaining, motivating, and inspiring public speakers. Such speakers would be engaging, attractive, and capable of drawing a crowd. Or, a second option, perhaps the role and work of the pastor is to be an able developer of programs that interest and attract people to a church. Some growing churches today offer an amazing menu of programs for diverse ages and interests. Entertaining speaker or program developer are two possibilities, and there are many more.

Many pastors manage complex institutions and budgets, which might lead one to conclude that they are managers with the skills, if not the degree, of a freshly minted MBA.

There are still more options and images of the role and work of the pastoral leader that compete for the attention of pastors and congregations. Some emphasize the role of community activist: leading the charge on a range of political issues facing the communities in which they are set, whether those issues be homelessness, gang violence, environmental stewardship, family health, or poverty. Another — and a different picture of the role of the pastor — is that of "church planter." As some denominations decline, others see opportunities to plant new congregations in the embers of old ones or in areas and among populations where no church has established a foothold.

Still other possibilities present themselves. For some, it appears, the work of the pastor is primarily that of the chaplain, one who provides a religious presence and services to individuals and families, as well as to an established congregation and its members. The pastor who is a chaplain to families and community is there to meet the religious or spiritual needs of people and communities particularly in moments of crisis or difficulty, such as illness, family crisis, or death. An analogue to the role of the chaplain who provides religious goods and services, but at the other end of the theological spectrum, might be the pastor as evangelist, one whose work is to win souls to Christ and to bring previously unchurched people to the church. If the chaplain focuses on individuals already in the fold, the evangelist seeks to reach individuals outside the fold and to bring them in. Both are, in some sense, focused on meeting the needs of individuals.

There are many possibilities and options facing pastors and churches. We can think of ourselves as inspiring — even motivational — speakers, program developers, organizational managers or administrators, community activists, church planters, chaplains, or evangelists. There is nothing intrinsically wrong with any of these roles or functions; depending on the context and circumstance, each one has value. And surely there are other possible understandings of the role and work of the pastor that could be added to this brief inventory.

What does the opening chapter of 1 Timothy add to the list? Or better, what does 1 Timothy and this text suggest is the essential work of the pastoral leader? Eugene Peterson suggested that there is a difference between the merely important and the essential, and that pastors are well advised to discern the difference. Given competing needs and interests, there is so much facing the pastor that seems, and is, important. But what is essential? If Paul's letters to Timothy are taken as a guide, what is the essential work of the pastoral leader?

To us it appears that the essential role and work of the pastoral leader is to be a teacher of the faith whose teaching orders are the "household of God" (the dominant metaphor for the church in 1 and 2 Timothy) in a way that is sound and healthy. This should not be taken to mean that the pastor finds her- or himself continually or only in formal instructional settings such as the classroom. Nor should it suggest that the pastoral leader is always or only functioning in a didactic mode, delivering instruction via lectures or sermons. It does mean that the pastoral leader is responsible for, in the words of the exegetical comments above, "the catechesis of an entire congregation." Moreover, the leader is to perform that task in such a way that the result is a healthy or sound congregation whose life and way of being in the world point to "God's way of stewarding (or ordering) the world" (1 Tim. 1:4). The measure of the effectiveness of a teacher of the faith is the life, health, and faithfulness of the congregation.

A slightly different way to put this might be to say that a pastor is to be a "center of theological integrity" for the life of the congregation, the church. As a center of theological integrity, a pastor reminds a congregation of its identity and its purpose, which derive from the core theological affirmations and convictions of the Christian faith. In claiming that the role and work of the pastoral leader is, in essence, to be a teacher of the faith and a center of theological integrity, whose teaching forms and orders a congregation's life and witness, we have introduced an ancient word and concept: "catechesis." From the Greek *katēchēsis,* it means the act of teaching catechumens. A catechumen is one who is being taught the core truths of the Christian faith, often at a basic or foundational level.

Some readers will be familiar with religious and Christian catechisms, usually short books formulated in question-and-answer format that seek to convey the basic principles or core convictions of Christian faith. For some this will call to mind a pedagogical method that is strong on memorization but without much room for unscripted questions, discussion, exploration, or analysis. We have nothing against memorization, which has its place; it is one mode of instruction, but not the only one. But we imagine catechesis to have a

34

more robust meaning than what is suggested by the memorization of older published catechisms. We see it as a larger process of forming people and a congregation in a particular way of life patterned after the way of life of Jesus and the apostles.

Nevertheless, the role and work of "the teacher" is, to judge by the social status and income of teachers in twenty-first-century North America, not perhaps the most arresting or impressive of roles or functions. To say "I am a teacher" does not carry the heft or clout of "I am a corporate executive," or "a doctor," "a CEO," "the president" (of this or that), or even "head coach."

Given the above, it may be useful to take a brief excursion to the Gospel of Mark (1:21-27) and an episode from the beginning of Jesus' ministry in order to redefine "teacher" and "teaching" in light of Jesus' own ministry. At first glance, this text is an account of an exorcism: Jesus casts an evil spirit out of a man whom he encounters in the synagogue in Capernaum. But what is particularly interesting about it is the frequency with which a version of the word "teach" is used in these seven verses: some form of the word "teach" appears four times here. What is perhaps most curious, given that, is that there is no mention at all of the content of Jesus' teaching. Not a word about what Jesus taught, only *that* he taught, that people were "astounded by his teaching," and that he cast out a demonic spirit. Indeed, at the conclusion of the incident the crowd does not say, "Wow, that was exciting!" They say, "What is this? A new teaching — with authority!"

By inserting an exorcism and not reporting on the content of Jesus' teaching, Mark succeeds in making a point that subsequent teachers of the faith may wish to remember and take to heart: that the teaching of Jesus had *power.* It had the power to exorcise demons, the power to change lives, the power to heal, and the power to liberate captives. Apparently, to encounter Jesus the teacher was to risk the possibility of conversion, of change of heart, change of mind, and change of life.

Often today, teaching — whether in the church or elsewhere — seems to suggest something of less consequence. But perhaps that says more about us than about the work or role of a teacher and of the teacher of the faith. We believe that teaching in the church should be informed and inspired by this Markan portrait of Jesus the teacher as one who changed lives. When Jesus taught something, a great deal was at stake.

Indeed, while this text from Mark is especially suggestive and illu-

minating, a portion of the text at hand, 1 Timothy 1:12-16, makes a similar point. Here Paul briefly narrates his own decisive encounter with
the risen Christ. Though he was a blasphemer and persecutor, "our
Lord's grace poured all over me," leading him to understand and pass
on, as a core conviction, that "Christ Jesus came into the world to save
sinners." This teaching is not a matter of abstract or speculative
thought; in fact, Paul cautions against such forms of teaching in 1 Timothy 1:4. As in Mark, so here with Paul, Christian teaching has life-
transforming and life-ordering effects. Indeed, Paul himself had experienced the saving power of God's mercy toward sinners, "among whom I
am the first!" (1 Tim. 1:15) His teaching is derived from experience.

Therefore, to claim that the role and work of the pastoral leader is
to be a teacher of the faith whose task is "catechesis of an entire congregation" is not to set a low bar, but a very high one. As teachers of the
faith, we are in the business of saving and changing lives. We are in the
business of forming congregations and communities that by their life
together point to the presence and power of God's Kingdom, God's
way of ordering the world (1 Tim. 1:4).

Recently, Quinn Caldwell, pastor of Boston's Old South Church,
made the following observation, which rings the changes on these
themes. Caldwell noted that his church, like many, is full of people who
wish to be "well-rounded." "Many," he said, "have time and resources to
take classes and seminars, attend lectures, and so on. They take opera
appreciation classes, kickboxing, sailing lessons, and they keep up on
current events." Then Caldwell added this:

> If we [pastors and churches] just present our Bible studies and ser-
> vice opportunities as more of the same (part of a well-rounded life),
> we're missing the point. Christian discipleship isn't a facet of a
> well-rounded life; it's the thing that will save your life. [NB: not in a
> save-your-life-from-eternity-in-hell kind of way.] If we aren't pre-
> senting it that way, we're failing. If we don't believe it ourselves as
> leaders, we ought to go home.

Something — a great deal, actually — is at stake here in teaching the
faith. This clarification from a twenty-first-century pastoral leader is
very much in the spirit of Paul's exhortation to Timothy in the first
century. If we aren't in the life-changing, life-saving business, we're not
in the gospel business.

It is important in this connection to take note, as we begin our exploration of the Pastoral Epistles and their implications for pastoral leadership, of both the occasion and setting of 1 Timothy. What is the occasion of this letter? Or, to put it slightly differently, what need or situation has produced this letter?

Verse 3 points to what has occasioned this letter: Paul's departure and current absence. Paul has left the congregation in Ephesus behind and has set out for Macedonia and the mission in Europe. Up to this point, Paul, the apostolic teacher, had himself been present as the authoritative teacher of the faith for the congregation in Ephesus. That is no longer the case. Paul has departed. With this letter he instructs and gives directions to his successor, Timothy, regarding the latter's work as a pastoral leader.

In a certain sense, all of us pastoral leaders are Timothy. We are all succeeding someone else and building on the work and ministry of someone else. Often we succeed generations of others. Even the pastor who starts a new congregation or plants a new church is building on the work of countless forebears, teachers and apostles, stretching back to Paul, Peter, and Jesus. Another way to put this is to say that we pastoral leaders are not independent operators, solo entrepreneurs, or freelance spiritual guides. Today there are many people in our culture who embody each of these roles. But these are not options for Christian pastoral leaders. Someone — usually many others — have gone before us. We do not invent our teaching. We are not called to be original so much as we are called to be faithful. We steward a tradition in which we ourselves have been shaped, saved, and formed.

Methodist Bishop Will Willimon makes this point in an essay for seminarians about making the transition from seminary study to church leadership.

> For example, Scripture, the tradition of the church, has a privileged place in the communication of the church. Pastors are ordained, ordered to bear that tradition compellingly, faithfully, quite unoriginally before their congregations, not primarily so that their congregations can think through the tradition, but rather so that they can in their discipleship incarnate Christian truth. We pastors are not free to rummage about in the recesses of our own egos, not free to consult other extra-ecclesial texts, until we have first done business with Scripture and the great tradition. Alas, too much of

today's theological training (arising out of the German university of the nineteenth century) places the modern reader above the texts of the church, assuming a privileged, detached, and superior position to the church's historic faith. The academic guild stands in judgment upon the texts, raising questions about the texts. Thus it comes as a jolt for the seminarian to graduate and to find him- or herself cast in the role of the ordained, the official who leads the church not in detached criticism of these texts but rather in faithful embodiment of the sacred texts.[14]

Paul's departure thrusts Timothy into the role of successor and teacher of the faith in order that a particular congregation in Ephesus may "in their discipleship incarnate Christian truth." Timothy is not called to a role as a spiritually sensitive individual, or to a fulfill a role as a member of the helping professions. He is called to a role — and to the work — of an official of a community, the church, and as a teacher of its faith in order to save lives.

It is also important to note the setting of Paul's letters to Timothy, the city of Ephesus in Asia Minor, what we now know as Turkey. A great deal can be learned about Ephesus and Paul's ministry there if we closely read Acts 19 and also Paul's parting words to the Ephesian elders (probably including Timothy) in Acts 20:17-38. That ministry in Ephesus was a colorful one, featuring engagement with disciples who knew nothing of the Holy Spirit and required further catechesis (Acts 19:1-7), confrontations with magicians (19:11-19), and a riot that was sparked by Paul's challenge to an economy based on the manufacture of idols (19:28-40).

All of this is to say that Paul, and Timothy following him, were not at work in a Christian — not even a nominally Christian — culture or society. They were out on the mission frontier. Paul left Timothy with, as our exegesis indicates, "the difficult task of forming a Christian congregation in a pagan place." This setting lends to the Pastoral Epistles — and, we hope, to our treatment of them — a particular relevance for pastoral leaders in North America today.

There was a time when Christianity had the status in North American culture of "most favored religion." Though not legally es-

---

14. William Willimon, "Between Two Worlds," in Allan Hugh Cole Jr., ed., *From Midterms to Ministry* (Grand Rapids: Eerdmans, 2008), pp. 279-80.

tablished, Christianity enjoyed a cultural establishment expressed in a variety of social supports and sanctions. These ranged from stores being closed on Sunday to publicly funded advertising that urged, "Attend the church of your choice this Sunday." A shorthand for this era is the word "Christendom," which combines the two words "Christianity" and "dominion." "Christendom" means Christian rule, establishment, or governance. In North America — in contrast to parts of Europe — this was not a legal but a cultural establishment of Christianity. However, the era of Christendom is now over. We find ourselves living in a culture that in some ways bears a greater resemblance to first- or second-century Ephesus than it does to, for example, nineteenth-century Boston.

Just as for Paul in Ephesus, there are alternative faiths and competing spiritualities for today's pastoral leaders. That cultural context is not necessarily friendly to the gospel, nor does it understand the gospel's nature and content. It is a pagan place where different faiths compete and where cultural patterns of materialism, consumption, nationalism, individualism, and violence are common. The situation of the church in North America today is increasingly "missional." That is, our congregations are not chapels to a Christian culture; they are outposts in a mission field. The Pastoral Epistles take on a new relevance in this atmosphere, for they represent apostolic instruction to a pastoral leader seeking to form and sustain a congregation set in the midst of a pagan culture. Both the occasion (Paul's absence) and setting (a pagan place) require clarity about the identity and task of the Christian congregation. These, in turn, require clarity in Christian conviction and teaching.

Up to this point in our engaging of 1 Timothy 1:3-17, we have paid attention to the overall topic, the essential work of the pastoral leader; to the occasion of this letter, Paul's absence; and to its setting in Ephesus. We have suggested some implications of each of these for pastoral leaders in the twenty-first century. I would like to add a fourth large category to this list, which is the thesis of this passage and, in a sense, of the larger body of 1 and 2 Timothy. What is at stake here?

The thesis is that there is an integral relationship between sound theological teaching and healthy congregations. Indeed, the Greek word *hygiainō* (1:10) is a medical term that can be translated as "sound" or "healthy." Not long ago I was invited by a judicatory of the United Church of Canada to give a series of presentations over the course of a year on the theme of "healthy congregations." In preparation, I spent time reviewing the literature that concerned itself with healthy congregations and what made them that way. I found that this literature came from four major schools of thought: family-systems therapy; conflict study and mediation; leadership studies; and from a business paradigm, including strategic planning and marketing. This is, largely, material that is quite helpful for pastors and congregations, ideas from which they can learn a great deal.

But I also noted a curious absence. I found nothing on healthy congregations that was particularly theological in nature. While an occasional biblical text or theological theme might get a reference in this literature, there wasn't anything that indicated that reasonable clarity about core Christian convictions and their significance also had an impact, perhaps a decisive one, on congregational health and vitality.[15]

A couple thousand years before I researched it and talked about it, Paul argued this same point — the importance of theology — and did it far better than I have. In his Epistles — and especially in 1 and 2 Timothy — Paul underscored the point. Time and again he urged Timothy to teach healthy doctrine that conforms to "the glorious gospel of our blessed God" (1 Tim. 1:11). This letter begins with Paul's concern that Timothy "instruct certain individuals not to teach divergent doctrines, nor pay attention to myths and unending genealogies" (1:3-4). Some commentators and preachers have taken these several brief references to "divergent doctrine" as the occasion to amount full-scale attacks on Gnosticism, Docetism, spiritualism, and other aberrant teachings or heresies. We are not sure that Paul really provides the basis for doing such a critique, nor that he is interested in doing so — at least not here. He doesn't give us much in the way of the content of the "divergent doctrine" that he is talking about, nor does he name either their schools of thought or exponents. What is clear, however, is Paul's concern for the effects of healthy (and unhealthy) teaching and doctrine.

"Divergent doctrine" has the effect of encouraging "idle speculation" (1:4) and "fruitless discussion" (1:6). In other words, one sign of divergent doctrine is that it doesn't strengthen faith, nor does it find expression in lives of discipleship and "loving relationships" (1:5). This

---

15. I have addressed this absence in my book *What's Theology Got to Do with It? Convictions, Vitality and the Church* (Herndon VA: Alban, 2006).

circles back to our initial contention that the essential work of the pastoral leader is to be a teacher of the faith who is responsible for the catechesis of a Christian congregation. The point is not sound doctrine in the abstract; nor is it simply to list propositional truths that are held to be correct. The point is that lives are shaped by those teachings and lived together in the congregation for the sake of the world.

Some religious, theological, and spiritual teaching, now as then, gives rise to little more than "idle speculation" and "fruitless discussion." From debates about the virgin birth, to disputes over whether particular words attributed to Jesus in Scripture were actually spoken by Jesus, to more arcane speculations about spiritual realms or forces — some teaching seems more an idle exercise than something that changes, shapes, and saves lives. Paul, in his instructions to Timothy, is after the latter. His point is that people should know the life-changing impact of "our Lord's grace poured all over me along with the faith and love that are in Christ Jesus" (1:14). Moreover, the point of sound teaching is that the life of a Christian congregation, set in the midst of a not always friendly environment, would be so ordered by sound teaching that it reflects God's own sound ordering of creation (1:4).

Therefore, 1 Timothy begins not only with the acknowledgment of a challenge posed by divergent doctrine, but with a summation (in 1 Tim. 1:14-17) of the core of sound teaching drawn from Paul's own experience. He sums that up in verse 15: "Christ came into the world to save sinners." In one sense this appears to be almost a slogan. But when we probe it more deeply, it is rich in content. It is, in John Wesley's words, "naked" teaching that points to the heart of the "glorious gospel of the blessed God." God is in the saving business. God seeks to save all people, especially the lost and sinful (a most inclusive category), and Christ came to us for precisely those ends. Moreover, Paul testifies to this truth because he has experienced it himself. His life has been transformed by the grace of God in Jesus Christ. This truth is not merely a concept — it is an experienced reality.

Arguably, a pastoral leader or a congregation that forgets this naked and essential truth has lost its core purpose and reason for being. The fact that not a few congregations today seem to have managed precisely that, and have displaced these essentials — their core purpose and reason for being — suggests the urgency of 1 and 2 Timothy for twenty-first-century pastoral leaders and congregations.

DISCUSSION QUESTIONS

1. Why might Paul's departure from Ephesus, and his appointing of Timothy to stay on as his delegate, occasion a crisis of confidence for both Timothy and his congregation?

2. How does Paul's conversion to Christ, as he remembers it, illustrate the centerpiece of his gospel?

3. Brainstorm a list of possible roles and tasks of a pastor. What, in your view, is the core task?

4. How do you react to the description of the pastor's role as being "a center of theological integrity" in and for a congregation?

Worship and the Missional Church

1 Timothy 2:1–3:1a

2:1 *First, therefore, I request that supplications, prayers, petitions, thanksgivings be offered for everybody — 2 even for kings and all those in positions of authority — so that we may lead a quiet and peaceful life in full godliness and holiness. 3 This is good and acceptable in the eyes of God our Savior, 4 who wants to save everybody and to come to a knowledge of the truth: 5 There is one God and one mediator between God and humankind, a man Christ Jesus, 6 who gave himself a ransom for everybody, the witness at the right time. 7 I have been appointed its preacher and apostle — I speak the truth and do not lie — and teacher of the true faith to the nations.*

8 Therefore, I want men to pray publicly with their holy hands lifted up without anger or argument. 9 Likewise, women should adorn themselves modestly and prudently with sensible attire, without braided hair, gold, pearls, or costly clothes, 10 but rather with good works suitable for pious women. 11 Let a woman learn quietly in complete submission. 12 I do not allow a woman to teach or to have authority over a man but to be a quiet [student]. 13 For Adam was formed first, then Eve, 14 and Adam was not deceived, rather the woman was deceived, became a sinner, 15-3:1a and yet she will be saved through childbearing — if they continue in faith and love and holiness with prudence. This teaching is a core belief.

Part 1: Engaging 1 Timothy 2:1–3:1a as Scripture

Paul's initial instruction to Timothy seeks to bring clarity to the theological motive and public manner of Christian worship. In this regard, Paul introduces prayer as the quintessential worship practice: the community's prayers are for everyone (1 Tim. 2:1-2) and are prompted by God's desire to save everyone (2:3-7).

Paul mentions two different and often competing human families: the one making up a political household led by "kings and those in positions of authority" (2:2; cf. Titus 3:1-2) as heads of the households, and the other a sacred household led by God. Paul's instructions partially recognize the tension often provoked by competing loyalties between rival households in which believers hold joint membership. In this case, the stability embodied by a congregation's political relationships serves the *missio Dei* rather than the empire: if God wants to save everyone from death (2:4) for eternal life (1:16), and Christ Jesus enters the world to mediate God's redemptive end (1:15; cf. 2:5-6), then the worship practices of the sacred household should have the same purpose that God does.

Paul's instruction regarding prayer is noteworthy, not only by placing it "first of all" (2:1), but by its sheer length: it is the longest discussion of prayer in the New Testament. The "therefore" that begins these instructions (2:1) may well assume that Timothy has in mind the vivid contrast made between the false teachers (1:3-11, 19-20) and the apostle, whose own conversion from falsehood imitates prophetic ministry (1:12-17; cf. 2:7). And there may be other divisions within the congregation as well, whether precipitated by the presence of false teachers or its cultural surroundings. But the plain sense of this passage indicates no such threat, and Paul's emphasis on the practice of congregational prayer is a means of peacekeeping with everyone (2:2).

Two brief observations about the importance of congregational prayers should frame any interpretation of this passage.

(1) God's household must be ordered to serve God's redemptive purposes. The prayers of the household are an essential worship practice by which its members grow in their spiritual understanding of God's purpose for them in all of life. In making this more general point, the interpreter should not make too fine a distinction between the four general terms used to describe the congregation's prayers: "petitions, prayers, intercessions, and thanksgivings" (2:1). Rather, Paul's

intent is to emphasize that the congregation's communication with God should seek what God seeks.

The catholic scope of the church's evangelistic concern is reflected by the phrase "rulers and all those in positions of authority." While the historical record has severe gaps concerning the persecution of earliest believers, most scholars agree that in certain regions believers had come under attack. Christians believe in the sovereignty of one God and the lordship of one Lord, Christ Jesus, and that challenged the central ideological tenet of the empire, the sovereignty of its emperor. The social friction between a powerless church and a powerful state is found everywhere in the New Testament (e.g., Acts 22–28; 1 Pet. 3:13-17; Rev. 13). Yet, even though it was counterintuitive of a Christian congregation, the religious sentiment to support those leading the secular household was widely shared in antiquity. Paul's Judaism practiced praying for one's pagan rulers and following the example of Daniel, who used prayer to ensure peaceful relationships with hostile pagan powers. Luke Timothy Johnson points out that Jews and Christians of the first century felt a deep solidarity with their sociopolitical world as a faithful response to the Creator's providential care for all things.[1]

(2) If the ultimate outcome of a congregation's worship is to testify to its membership in God's household, then the subject matter of its prayers and petitions must support the redemptive activities of God in the world. Worship gives public expression to a congregation's deepest religious commitments; worship is a verbal noun precisely because its practices demonstrate a community's loyalty to God. With a social setting where the two households, secular and sacred, are sometimes in conflict, public prayer may be seen as a radical, countercultural, and demonstrative activity. A people's worship practices are a principal means by which that group embodies its allegiance to God and its vocation to reorder the empire after God's will.

The use of the word *basileus* repeats the doxological refrain just heard in the letter's thanksgiving, where God is honored as immortal *basileus* (1:17), a trope that is repeated at the end of the letter, where God is declared "the King of the kings" (6:15). This repeated doxological refrain encloses the entire letter, not only to underwrite the church's confession of God, by which all the letter's instructions are read, but also

---

1. Luke Timothy Johnson, *Letters to Paul's Delegates* (NTC) (Valley Forge, PA: Trinity Press International, 1996), pp. 129-31.

to set the congregation's prayers for the empire's kings within the political boundaries of the economy of God. Within those borders the church's God is king over the nations' kings. The ambivalence of praying to the King of kings for the nation's kings is quite arresting, if only because petitions about kings and lords are received by a God who is one and thus fully wakeful to their job description. More critically, however, the doxology informs the instruction that the congregation's politics are ordered within the bounds of "God's way of stewarding reality" (1:4b), forged by faith and aimed at loving relationships (1:5).

For this reason, prayers must be coextensive with God's saving purpose and thus must include "everybody" (2:1b). The motive for doing so is not political, as though the church's mission is complicit in a program of social domestication and thus seeks to cultivate a peaceful working environment with outsiders. Paul's principal motive is clearly theological, because to pray for everybody is to pray after God's own desiring: "God our Savior wills everybody to be saved and to come to the knowledge of the truth" (2:4). Prayers for the emperor, which routinely offered petitions for his personal safety and political wisdom, finally were offered to God with the prospect of the emperor's conversion to the truth and the empire's salvation from its sins.

Much has been made of the purpose clause that follows the instruction to pray for kings, which some take as indication that such prayers are really a political strategy to keep the peace. Commentators correctly point out that the manner of life indicated here — "peaceful, quiet, godly, respectful" (2:2b) — could be read as an accommodation to the social order of the empire. But if the congregation's prayers are interpreted by the Pauline formula of *missio Dei* that follows, then not only are the prayers but their purpose moving in the direction of the salvation of kings and the sanctification of the public square over which they rule. The use of the adjectives *ēremos* ("peaceable") with *hēsychios* ("quiet") is not a redundancy, as is often suggested; rather, they are mutually glossing expressions that combine internal and personal with external and social experiences of God's shalom to indicate the entire sanctification of the public square.[2] In any case, this is how we

---

2. So while Paul's use of "acceptable" *(apodektos)* in v. 3 could allude to the OT liturgy of offering acceptable sacrifices in worship of God (cf. Lev 1:3-4; 17:4; *et al.*), the issue at stake is not that Christian prayers have replaced Judaism's priesthood as the normative medium for cultivating a godly presence; what pleases "God the Savior" are not cultic sacrifices but petitions that agree with God's desire to save everyone and everything.

view this dialectic in a nutshell: civil religion, no — missional church, yes.

The guts of the dense theological formula in verses 5-6 supplies a footnote to the final phrase of verse 4, which implies, in good Pauline fashion, that conversion is a coming to the "knowledge of truth." The crucial question that this formula evokes, of course, and the pivotal political question is this: Which narrative of salvation should the nations embrace as true? Which narrative should inform and form our political practices? The dialectic of this passage, followed in design by Titus 2-3 and elaborated by the Pastoral Epistle collection, makes it clear to the reader that the ongoing task of the Pauline apostolate to the nations is truth-telling, and this truth is set out in the essential elements of Paul's particular story of the *missio Dei.*

(1) "There is one God." This apt summary of Jewish monotheism serves to locate kings and presidents in their proper place within the economy of God. The singularity of God, of course, is an affirmation of the Old Testament *Shema* (Deut. 6:4) and held special importance in Paul's Jewish Diaspora, where Israel's God had competition from many deities, local and national. While monotheism is not a seditious claim in this setting, it certainly does disabuse the prayers for one's king as the practice of a domesticated church. Moreover, in contrast to the plurality of unnamed "kings," the singularity of "one God" challenges any counternarrative of salvation, whether promoted by Rome's Caesar or the rulers of lesser kingdoms. There is but one God, whose desire is to save everyone and everything.

(2) "There is one mediator between God and humankind." Paul's insistence that there is but one mediator, Christ Jesus, could have communicated a political message that would reject the king's role as the sole medium of the gods. One God, one messiah, one salvation — all form a particular and exclusive concept of the truth and how it arrives in the empire.

Although laden with christological freight, especially with inferences of the crucified Christ's mediation of God's new covenant (see esp. Heb. 8-10), Paul's primary meaning here is more diplomatic: God's offer of universal salvation is tendered by a single ambassador; to receive it from any other source on any other grounds is bogus. Paul's subsequent reference to himself as preacher and apostle (2:7), who is appointed by the command of God (1:1), suggests an ambassadorial motif: he is Christ's "undersecretary" in God's kingdom, and he is given the task of communicating God's gospel in Christ's absence. There may well be an even deeper implication: that in Paul's absence it is now Timothy who is given this crucial task to perform.

(3) "A man, Christ Jesus." The reference to Jesus' humanity seems awkward at first. Some suggest that it goes best with the next phrase that speaks of Jesus' death. Certainly Paul's Adam-Christology requires this connection to the Lord's humanity and his self-sacrificial death (cf. Phil. 2:6-8). But we doubt that this connection is intended here. In 2 Timothy 2:8, Paul exhorts Timothy to "remember Jesus Christ, raised from the dead, a descendant of David," which sums up his gospel. The mention that Jesus is royalty — a member of David's royal family — may be politically prompted, given that in the next line Paul says that this claim has resulted in his imprisonment (2:9). Nevertheless, we doubt that any of this is in play here in 1 Timothy 2, where Paul refers to Jesus' humanity as messianic broker of God's promised blessing for all the families of earth. Moreover, if an expansion of the prior claim that God desires every person to come to a knowledge of truth, then Christ's humanity includes an epistemological role: God's self-revelation in one of us — "a man, Christ Jesus" — makes clear God's desire to save every one of us.

(4) "[Christ Jesus] who gave himself a ransom for everybody." In Paul's social world, payment of a "ransom" freed slaves from indenture. Furthermore, perhaps the most important biblical typology of God's way of salvation is God's liberation of an enslaved Israel from its captivity to a pagan power to live in its land and freely worship its God. The politics of worship, which supplies an important subtext to the present instructions, is shaped not by Rome but by this Exodus story.

Yet the reader may well have expected a more traditional Pauline doctrine: "who gave himself a ransom for sin" (cf. Titus 2:14). Instead, Paul repeats "for all" (2:1), because under the present circumstances he is pressing for the global scope of God's salvation as the principal theological motive why the congregation should even pray for its pagan rulers. Sharply put, Christians pray for everybody because Christ died for everybody in agreement with God's chief desire.

Paul's mention of the Lord's payment of a "ransom" — one crucified Messiah in trade for all sinful humanity (1:15) — would have had special currency in an urban center like Ephesus, with its huge slave population, and it could have evoked images of a ransom price paid to free a slave. Moreover, the prefix of the distinctive word Paul uses for

ransom *(antilytron)* uses *anti-* ("instead") to add the nuance of a substi-
tution to the root word for "ransom" *(-lytron),* thus making decisive the
fact that Jesus exchanged his life as a man on behalf of everyone else.
The very idea of a person substituting his life for a community or nation is the noblest definition of covenant loyalty in the holy texts of
·Paul's Judaism (see 4 Macc. 6:29; 17:21-22; 2 Macc. 7:37-38; cf. Deut 32:36;
Mark 10:45).

(5) "[Paul] was appointed a herald, an apostle . . . and a teacher of
the nations in matters of faith and truth." The idea of Paul's apostleship
is a central concern of the Pastoral Epistles, not its defense but rather to
authenticate the canonical Paul, whose memory and message that have
been passed on by the collection of his Letters have enduring importance for the church. Nowhere else do we find this stunning claim that
Paul's apostolic appointment is to teach truth to the nations. The prior
reading of Paul's story in Acts would incline the reader to understand
"nations" in its most inclusive sense, to Jews first and then to Gentiles.
The Paul of Acts, a consecrated teacher of Israel, also aims his mission in
the same direction as the community's prayers: at bringing knowledge
of the truth about God's salvation "before Gentiles and kings" (Acts
9:15). Therefore, here the Paul of the Pastoral Epistles is teacher of the
nations, so that by his heralding of the good news about Christ, everyone may "come to knowledge of the truth" and be saved.

The collision, not collusion, between the apostolic herald and the
nations is about the instruction of those nations in faith and truth.[3]
While this pattern of mission follows Jesus' commission, recorded in
Matthew, to make disciples of all nations (Matt. 28:19), we note that the
following instructions aimed to praying men and prudent women, understood in context, are instantiations of Paul's mission to the nations.
In particular, the profile of the influential Christian woman, rooted in
the biblical story of Eve's salvation from sin (2:13-15a), supplies a pro-
foundly optimistic picture of the woman's role in exemplifying the
transforming power of God's grace in the public square. In fact, the
repetition of *hēsychios/hēsychia* in 2:11-12, which defines the prudent
woman's disposition in the classroom, relates her social manners to the
"quiet" life, which bolsters the prospect of God's sanctification of public places (according to 2:2b).

---

3. Conceptions of "faith" and "truth" in the Pastoral Epistles are battlegrounds of
modern criticism.

Paul's instruction for congregational prayers turns to more practical worship practices for Christian men (2:8) and women (2:9-15). In the case of an urban congregation, female converts sometimes came from Roman upper-middle-class households, and so their exemplary behavior was demonstrated in practices appropriate to their middle-class status, for example, their wardrobes (2:9), their philanthropy (2:10), and their schooling (2:11-12). In Paul's mission to the nations, however, the responsibility of influential women is prompted more by theological conviction than by social convention. God's desire to save everyone includes women (15a; cf. 2:3-6), who are saved from deception and sin (2:14-15a) for a life of "faith and love and holiness with prudence" (2:15b).

Paul's instructions recalibrate well-known caricatures of competitive men and modest women found in Greco-Roman literature of the time — to transform them into ideal worshipers. He nowhere refers to specific individuals by name or to problems that specific women are provoking within the congregation. The purpose of this instruction is to provide general patterns of worship that serve God's redemptive purpose.

The attentiveness of the congregation's influential women is cued by "likewise," intimating that they share in the congregation's public worship equally with men (cf. 1 Cor. 11:4-5). The images of the ideal Christian woman are enveloped within a rhetorical unit bracketed by the repetition of "prudence" *(sōphrosynē)* (2:9, 15), which was the most universally admired female virtue of the period. It is noteworthy, however, that although prudence — especially when qualified by "modesty" *(aidōs),* as it is here — carries a peculiar significance for Christian women, the same word is subsequently used in 3:2 more generally to characterize any Christian leader (see also Titus 1:8; 2:2, 5; cf. Acts 26:25). In this sense, the modesty of the ideal Christian woman is not exclusive to a particular gender but embodies the redemptive purpose of God for everyone, since it "abstains from whatever tends to sin."[4] Female modesty adorns religious existence and is the principal affection of a thoughtful, prudent outlook on all of life.

The contrast between secular and religious women is well known from antiquity. Secular women live a banal existence, lacking in moral scruples and religious devotion and typified by the trivial pursuit of

---

4. Tertullian, *On the Apparel of Women,* 2:2.

fastidious personal appearance. On the other hand, "pious women" are concerned with the well-being of their neighbors and exemplify "a life of productive virtue."[5] In modern parlance, prudence, like civility, seems to be a pale platitude. In classical culture, however, prudence did not connote shyness or coyness but a practical wisdom and savvy. If her prudent practices exhibit the self-possession and competent dignity of the influential woman who recognizes how her world works and has the know-how to act wisely in the world, then this word may lose some of its current Victorian distastefulness. Put differently, Paul may be drawing on the Wisdom tradition and its conception of *hokmah* — a skill for living well — in describing the competent woman.

The subject "pious women" combines the participle "promise-making" *(epangellomenais)* with the unusual noun *theosebeia* ("devotion to God") to form the image of a person who makes good on the public profession of faith by acting in a manner consistent with her theological claims. This image is consonant with Hellenistic (especially Stoic) morality, which placed a premium on a piety that translates religious talk into ethical walk. Paul's definition anticipates his concluding exhortation regarding the seductive power of wealth (6:8-10) and the obligation of wealthy members to care for those on the margins (6:17-19). Again, however, his motive does not appear to be provoked by a worry about conflict within the Ephesian congregation, or even by the self-absorption of the influential, but is illustrative of Christian women who have been saved from a banal existence to contribute to the congregation's welfare.

In this sense, a woman's public identity is linked to her dress. Even today a woman's relationships are symbolized by what she wears. For example, the first members of my own Methodist church refused to wear jewelry or expensive clothing so that they could identify with the poor and present an inviting image for those seeking after God: that is, they "dressed down" in order to form an unnatural solidarity with outsiders.

While doing "good works" is a social marker of the church's middle class in 1 Timothy (cf. 5:10, 25; 6:18-20), here it provides evidence of Christianity's positive effect on society — a persuasive societal standard for a newly introduced religion (cf. Acts 17:18-31) and reconceived in 1 Timothy as another concrete witness to the transforming power of divine mercy (1:12-16). At the same time, these are the worship practices of

5. For examples, see Johnson, *Delegates,* pp. 200, 204-8.

God's household and, while they are observed by outsiders, are actions that are not directed toward the latter but to "those who are of the household of faith" (Gal. 6:10).

A final contrast (2:11-12) applies female prudence to a theme of primary importance in this letter: which members of a Christian congregation are taught, and by whom. While this particular instruction has been extracted from its context and used in abusive ways to silence women, Paul's concern is of a piece with his formulation of the *missio Dei*. To a very large degree, the long history of the use of this particular passage, especially within male-dominated churches, to silence and domesticate Christian women is the result of bad exegesis. Not only do many fail to interpret the text's purpose and content within its compositional and social contexts; many also fail to follow the deep logic of Paul's argument within its canonical setting. To put the matter simply, how Christian women who are liberated from sin and have social influence learn — and from whom — facilitates their role as agents of God's salvation.

From whom does the prudent woman learn and about what? While inferences drawn from verse 11 may fairly respond to this practical question, Paul clarifies his intent by a subsequent injunction (2:12) and an appeal to Scripture's story of Eve, the archetypal woman of God's choosing (2:13-15a).[6] In fact, the shift in voice from third person voice to first person in verse 12, and from general exhortation to personal injunction (*ouk epitrepō:* "I do not allow"), sharpens this instruction. Many suppose that this abrupt shift in tone signals a more direct response to a real problem. But without clear evidence in the text of a woman problem in the Ephesian church, such speculation is unwarranted. In fact, readers may just as well understand Paul's motive in rhetorical terms: he sharpens his tone to clarify the general instructions for influential Christian women so that they can participate more effectively in the *missio Dei*.

The interplay of two infinitives ("to teach . . . to have authority" [2:12]) is of a piece — teaching authority — and prohibits women from having such a public role. Most interpreters assume that the meaning of the first (not "to teach") turns on the meaning of the second (not "to

---

6. Paul's midrash in 2:13-15 may illustrate a proper use of Torah in contrast to those misguided "teachers of Torah" who assert Torah's support for their false ideas "without understanding" (1:6-7).

have authority"). Some suggest that the unstated antecedent of *authentein* ("authority") is cultural and gender-specific; they claim that the use of this exceptional word envisions an exceptional problem of female rebelliousness that has gone viral and has provoked a problem of public perception for the church. Paul's instruction, the argument continues, seeks to tame these rebellious women and put them in their place, which one may infer from the earlier word *hypotagē* (v. 11b). Within this reconstructed setting, then, the use of *authentein* carries with it the sense of a bullying or coercive authority. That is, the ideal Christian woman is prohibited from exercising her authority in a brash manner, because modesty in all things is proper to the public square. The further implication of that reading of this text, of course, is that Paul would allow the prudent and modest woman to teach others.

But again, no such inferences can be drawn from a passage that does not speak of a specific problem! Rather, Paul's striking use of the indefinite *anēr* ("a man," 2:12) who has teaching authority reflects the social world of antiquity that comes with this letter. Teaching in Roman Ephesus was an exclusively male profession, and the culture of Diaspora Judaism was reluctant to advance women to positions of authority over men — and never under ordinary circumstances.[7] Moreover, the use of "authority" in antiquity did not carry a single "technical" meaning, but rather was used in various ways to denote one's superior role or social status.[8] Thus the principal use of "authority"

---

7. *The Hellenistic Commentary to the New Testament* (Nashville: Abingdon, 1995) notes Philo's midrash on Exodus 15 in *Life of Moses* 1.32.180, in which Moses divides a joyful Israel into two choirs, one male and the other female, to celebrate God's victory over Egypt!

8. See I. Howard Marshall's judicious discussion of the recent history of interpreting this word in *The Pastoral Epistles* (ICC) (Edinburgh: T. & T. Clark, 1999), pp. 456-60. See also George W. Knight, *The Pastoral Epistles: A Commentary on the Greek Text* (NIGTC) (Grand Rapids: Eerdmans, 1992), an important study summarized in pp. 141-42, demonstrating that there is no negative use of the word in antiquity, and that its use in 1 Timothy refers to the proper exercise of an ecclesiastical "office" — in this case to teach Paul's gospel to believers. Knight's conclusions have been vigorously challenged by Linda Belleville, "Teaching and Usurping Authority: 1 Timothy 2:11-15," in R. W. Pierce and R. M. Groothuis, eds., *Discovering Biblical Equality* (Downers Grove, IL: InterVarsity, 2004), pp. 205-23. We dispute, however, any rendering of this word that presumes its use here is determined by unspecified false teaching (cf. 1:3-11). Though we are deeply sympathetic with Belleville's desire to end the church's use of this text to silence women, we do not think her study is persuasive. See Andreas J. Köstenberger, "A Complex Sentence

need not be read as negative and more simply defines the exercise of one's higher rank or superior competence, while its secondary use recognizes authority as one's birthright. More simply, Paul's personal prohibition is aimed at Christian women whose learning should ideally exemplify the social values of the day: quiet submission to those tutors with the religious credentials to instruct them. In this way they cultivate public favor and participate more effectively in the *missio Dei*. We contend that this is good advice that extends to every member of the congregation (see 2:2b).

The word "for" introduces Paul's reading of Eve's biblical story in Genesis (2:13-15a), which helps to clarify the motive for his instructions. We should not simply see this midrash as a problem of idiosyncrasy, since it rehearses the plain sense of Eve's biblical story and agrees with contemporaneous Jewish interpretations of her complicity in humanity's first transgression. This is a familiar Eve: she personifies every woman's spiritual failure and her need for "God our Savior." This summary sounds yet another note of general disagreement with the recent history of using this text within the church. In fact, Paul's reading closely follows the biblical plot line, even if his application of it to the Christian congregation of ancient Ephesus is his own. Contrary to the more compliant Adam, who is not initially deceived by the serpent's mischief, Eve chooses an independent course away from God, is deceived, and thereby sins (2:14; cf. 2 Cor. 11:3).

Cued by the order of the creation of human life — woman from man — which hints at male priority (2:13; cf. 1 Cor. 11:8-9), the text has also been read as offering a straightforward justification of a woman's submission to a male mentor (2:12). In fact, many congregations, on the basis of this single text, silence their female members on implicitly ontological grounds: females are by nature out of control and need the male's strong hand to keep them from straying! But instructing Christian women to act prudently on the basis of fallen Eve's being deceived into sin is hardly likely in one of Paul's letters. According to Romans, for example, every believer has been made alive "in Christ" and has been liberated from deception and transgression as the powerful result of divine grace (Rom. 5:12–6:23). When glossing Eve's story by means of this

Structure in 1 Timothy 2:12," in A. J. Köstenberger and T. R. Schreiner, eds., *Women in the Church* (Grand Rapids: Baker, 2005). In any case, the relevant issue in adapting this text to today's church is primarily hermeneutical and certainly not merely exegetical.

theological argument, the reader should not assume that the unstated function of her story in these instructions is to check the regenerate woman's natural propensity toward deception and sin. Rather, we should assume that she can realistically aspire to live "with prudence" (2:15b) in the public square and as a result influence other women there toward God's love. If viewed from this more positive angle, Paul's interest in the pair of pedagogical contrasts he draws in 2:11-12 — learning but not teaching, submitting but not leading — shifts the reader toward a more evangelistic purpose that pertains to the community's regard of the female outsider and her prospective salvation.

This brings us to 1 Timothy 2:15, which remains "one of the strangest verses in the New Testament."[9] Paul's use of Eve's story from Hebrew Scripture turns on the question of whether Paul concludes its plot line with verse 14 or verse 15a. In part, the exegete's answer depends on a prior decision. If the reader supposes that the purpose of the injunction is to domesticate Christian women and allow men to take the lead, then biblical Eve is a likely exemplar for the subordinate, fallen, and inferior woman who keeps quiet and submits to a man's firm grip, whether in the classroom or at home. However, if the reader approaches this instruction as a worship practice motivated by the *missio Dei,* then the reader is more likely to regard the full story of biblical Eve as typological of God's way of salvation. In a canonical setting, it seems entirely plausible that Paul would conclude his version of Eve's story with an image of her restoration rather than her condemnation.

This second perspective follows from the most natural antecedent of the singular verb *(sōthēsetai)* in 2:15a, which must refer to a single woman, or the Eve of 2:13-14: "the woman" is the person who was deceived and who sinned but who then "will be saved in childbearing." If the grammar of the text suggests that 2:15a continues the plot line of Eve's biblical story narrated by Paul in 2:13-14, then to what scene might the reference to her "childbearing" refer? The phrase "yet [Eve] will be saved through childbearing" probably recalls the moment when the fallen Eve, now dismissed from the Garden, apprehends that her relationship with God has remained intact after all. That moment comes when she gives birth to her first child and exclaims that God (and not Adam!) is her partner in giving life to another (Gen. 4:1-2). This stun-

9. William D. Mounce, *Pastoral Epistles* (WBC) (Nashville: Thomas Nelson, 2000), p. 143.

ning reversal, which envisions the fallen Eve no longer under God's indictment but in a restored relationship with God, is picked up by the word "yet" in 2:15a and completes the Eve typology.[10]

In this reading, "childbearing" is understood as a metaphor for female salvation, since bearing children is a quintessentially and uniquely female activity. In this way, then, Paul's use of Eve's story is typological of every woman who, when giving birth to a new life, a uniquely female experience, is awakened to a realization of her partnership with God, who, because of the mediation of Christ Jesus, has not abandoned her. Eve's exclamation that she had created a child in partnership with God (Gen. 4:1) comes precisely at the climactic moment that she discovers the truth about God's mercy: God promises her a new life as well. This concept of female salvation subverts later Gnostic Christian female myths (e.g., in the Gospel of Thomas), which claimed that the redeemed women would finally be repristinated as Adam/male.[11]

In our view, the subsequent shift from singular to plural in 2:15b ("they remain . . . with prudence") also seems to lend support to this reading, since by shifting to a plural verb Paul evidently departs from his commentary on a particular woman, Eve, to conclude his general exhortation to Christian women that began in 2:9. The triad of virtues, "faith and love and holiness" (2:15b) recalls the biographical references in 1 Timothy 1:12-17, where Paul rehearses his conversion experience as an encounter with "the faith and love that are in Christ Jesus" (1:14). Christian existence is an experience of belonging to Jesus, of becoming like him as the confirmation of the gospel's claim that "Christ Jesus came into the world to save sinners" (1:15). Moreover, in the immediate context in which Paul instructs the reader on the manner of Christian

---

10. *Contra* Stanley E. Porter, "What does it mean to be 'saved by childbirth' (1 Timothy 2.15)?" *JSNT* 49 (1993): 87-105, who takes salvation in a physical sense: the promise that a virtuous woman will be saved from a difficult pregnancy or even from death when giving birth. Brian Winter suggests the opposite: wealthy women, preoccupied with other matters, did not want to have children (*Roman Wives* [Grand Rapids: Eerdmans, 2003], pp. 109-12). But Marshall is correct in arguing that the spiritual sense of salvation — salvation from sin — is uniformly in view in the Pastoral Epistles (p. 467). After all, it is Paul's conversion from sin and ignorance that defines the theological grammar of his apostolate (see our comments on 1:12-17).

11. See Pheme Perkins, "Gospel of Thomas," in Elisabeth Schüssler Fiorenza, Shelly Matthews, and Ann G. Brock, eds., *Searching the Scriptures: A Feminist Commentary* (New York: Crossroad, 1994), 2:558-60.

worship, this triad nicely summarizes the character of the worshiper, whose approach to God is made with "faith and love and holiness."

Paul concludes his instructions to Christian women as he began them, with a repeated appeal to prudence as the hallmark of the faithful woman (2:9, 15b). The rhetorical effect is to wrap the entire passage around this moral ideal. When competent self-control — or any other virtue relevant to a particular social location — comes to characterize the public manners of Christian women, it has the persuasive power to capture the attention of other women, who "come to a knowledge of the truth" (2:4). This is the expected effect of personal testimony in public life: good manners lend integrity to the gospel's truth claims. By such testimony, women "likewise" come to know that God desires to save them from the self-destructive results of deception and sin and to transform them into persons known for their virtue — "faith and love and holiness." We take it that this would have been a radical idea in a male-centered world.

Part 2: Engaging 1 Timothy 2:1–3:1a for Congregational Leaders

When congregations and their leaders think about worship or about mission, it often appears that they think of the two as compartmentalized and entirely separate from one another. Worship and mission are, it seems, quite different aspects of a congregation's life and ministry without any necessary or intrinsic relationship to one another.

Worship is one department, so to speak; mission is another. Church structures often reflect this separation by having a board of deacons or worship board focused on worship and a mission or community service board attending to mission. Church budgets also testify to this compartmentalization: they have line items for "worship," which may include corollary elements such as "music" or "the arts" listed under worship. "Mission" is a completely separate budget category or section, and under it one might find things such as "food bank," "tutoring," "ministry with immigrants and refugees." Sometimes, in fact, we encounter congregations that think and speak of worship and education, as well as ministries of care, as "what we do for ourselves," while mission or service is "what we do for others." While this may be understandable in one sense, it is also artificial and limiting. Furthermore, it reflects a period of nominal Christian establishment —

Christendom — and a culture that is now largely over. Ours is a new situation, one in which North America is a new mission field. This new situation invites and permits the church to (re)discover its essential missional nature and its relationship to the host culture.

In a new post-Christendom world, everything a congregation does is — at least potentially — mission. Who and what we worship makes ultimate claims that are at odds with the loyalties and commitments of the society around us. In worship we witness to who we believe God to be and what we believe God's purpose or mission *(missio Dei)* is in the world. Moreover, it is urgent to shift our thinking so that we imagine that, as some have observed, "it is not the church that has a mission in the world, but it is God's mission that has a church in the world." We worship a missional God. Who, what, and how we worship sends a message to the world and culture around us. This was true for Timothy's early Christian congregation in Ephesus, which was set in the midst of a pagan culture, and it is becoming true again for congregations in today's post-Christendom and postmodern culture.

When congregations conceive their life as divided into "what we do for ourselves (worship, education)" and "what we do for others (mission)," the church is in danger of morphing into an inward-looking club rather than an outward-looking community of transformation that participates in the *missio Dei*. The latter is what Paul describes here as God's plan for "saving everybody" (1 Tim. 2:4).

Nevertheless, after we have said that, 1 Timothy 2 is still a challenging chapter. Some have turned it into and used it as a "text of terror": a rationale for marginalizing and suppressing women in the church. We believe this to be a faulty interpretation. A more accurate and helpful way to approach this second chapter of 1 Timothy is to think of it as guidance for the public worship of a community that is a beachhead of God's radical new age in the midst of a culture that is in bondage to the twin ruling powers of sin and death. For a more vivid picture of the Ephesus setting, we urge the reader to closely reread Acts 19, where the congregation's worship is itself a sign and witness to God's redemption and a new creation. Here worship is mission and mission is worship. Here, in worship, the one God is enthroned upon the praises of God's people, and the emperor, who claimed to be the mediator between heaven and earth, is to be dethroned. Here is a church in ancient Ephesus that, insofar as it heeds Paul's teaching, seeks to keep God's mission — "to save everybody" — central to its worship and way of life as a community. In 1 Timothy 2, Paul reminds pastoral leaders of the centrality of worship to the church's life, of the theological core of worship, and of its missional nature.

Within this larger framework there are four specific matters that Paul raises in 1 Timothy 2: (1) prayer in general; (2) prayer for rulers and those in positions of authority; (3) the deportment of men in worship; and (4) the deportment of women in worship. All of these must be viewed through the lens of the core theological affirmation that is at the heart of the text and that announces the *missio Dei*, the mission of God. That theological core is found in verses 3-7, with the clear and "naked" (to again use Wesley's term) statement of God's mission in verse 4. As we have noted above, God is in the saving business: God "wants to save everybody" and wants all people "to come to a knowledge of the truth." The church — and specifically the congregation Timothy leads in Ephesus — is not an enclave that is to stay separate or stay within itself while awaiting Christ's return. Nor is it a club for the comfort and satisfaction of its members. Rather, the church is a mission outpost, a beachhead for God's mission that is for all people. Eugene Peterson's more colloquial rendering of verse 4 in *The Message* captures the spirit of it. "He (our Savior God) wants not only us but everyone saved, you know, everyone is to get to know the truth we've learned."[12]

This core theological affirmation also relates back to the previous chapter, where Paul describes his own experience of salvation: "Even though I was an ex-blasphemer and persecutor, a violent man who was shown mercy because I acted in ignorance and unbelief, our Lord's grace poured all over me along with the faith and love that are in Christ Jesus" (1:13-14). God wants to save all people from ignorance, from bondage, and from an aimless or inconsequential existence.

First Timothy 2 (once more in Peterson's colloquial rendering) begins: "The first thing I want you to do is pray. Pray every way you know how, for everyone you know." Of course, prayer can occur at all times and places, but in a chapter where worship is the lead topic, the emphasis that Paul places on prayer is striking. For most Protestants, the sermon is arguably the central act of worship, usually the single part of worship that takes the most time in a service and the most time in preparation. For Roman Catholics, the Eucharist has long held central

12. Eugene Peterson, *The Message* (Boulder, CO: Navpress, 1995), p. 443.

place, the priest's role reaching its most important focus in that celebration. But here Paul stresses the importance of prayer and the role of the pastoral leader as leading God's people into God's presence in prayer. Perhaps this emphasis on prayer, and its centrality, suggests a corrective for worship today that is often too little about prayer and too much about sermon, sacrament, and other priorities that may be entirely misplaced — for example, entertainment. Prayer necessarily puts God at the center of the church's worship. With this emphasis on prayer, Paul reminds pastoral leaders that a central part of their task as worship leaders is leading people into God's presence. All too often today, the focus of worship subtly shifts to us, to the congregation as audience. What do they/we like? Does worship work for us? Move us? The proper focus of worship, of course, is not us, but God. In the midst of a consumer culture, Paul's emphasis on prayer reminds us of this fundamental point about the nature of Christian worship.

Moreover, when we think of prayer, we often think of our (human) speech, our asking God for this or that. Insofar as it is prayer that reflects the spirit and priorities of Jesus, there is nothing wrong with prayer that lays our requests and needs before God. But prayer is more than seeking God's help by intercession or petition. It is even more than the prayers of thanksgiving, in which we give thanks for God's blessings and aid. Prayer is aligning our selves with God's will and God's ways. Prayer is less a matter of "give me, give me," and more a matter of "make me, make me," or "make us, make us." In this respect it makes perfect sense that Paul's call to prayer and emphasis on it are grounded in the central theological affirmation of verses 3-7, which emphasizes the Jewish conviction that there is one God, not the multiple and competing deities that were part of the pagan culture of Ephesus; that God's intent is the salvation of everyone, not just some people; and that the true mediator between God and humankind is not Caesar but "a man Christ Jesus, who gave himself as a ransom for everybody" (2:5-6). Prayer and worship are grounded in these core theological truths.

A second specific focus here is prayer for rulers: "For kings and all those in positions of authority — so that we may lead a quiet and peaceful life in full godliness and holiness." Today we are likely to read this through the lens of subsequent history, which includes the Holy Roman Empire and Christendom in its various forms. During those periods the church often practiced a civil religion, providing the "sacred canopy," the *cultus* that legitimated nation, society, and its rulers. The faith, at points, became subordinate to the state and nation and its designated leaders. While that history is undeniable, it is not the situation of the church described in 1 Timothy 2. Christianity did not enjoy the sanction or support of the state; nor did Christianity function as the state religion or cult. Rather, Christians and the church were regarded with some suspicion and at times were the objects of official harassment and repression.

While a cursory reading of 1 Timothy 2:1-2 may suggest a domesticated church that was subservient to the state and emperor, we discern a quite different possibility. To pray to the one God for "kings and all those in positions of authority" is to implicitly indicate that the authority of kings and earthly rulers, including the Caesar, is not ultimate. They are not divine, and their authority, while legitimate, is derivative. To pray to the one God on behalf of kings and others in authority is to relativize the authority of earthly rulers. They have their place and function, but they are not God. "There is one God and one mediator between God and humankind."

When the "confessing church" wrote the Barmen Declaration, the declaration of conscience and protest against the pretensions and usurpations of ultimate authority by the Nazis, they cited John 14:6 as their scriptural basis: No one comes to the Father but through Jesus Christ, who is alone "the way, the truth and the life," certainly not through Hitler, who presented himself as a new mediator. The confessing church might also have grounded its protest here in 1 Timothy 2:5, for it makes the same point. Governing authorities have a legitimate role and function. They deserve prayers and their subjects' respect in order to fulfill their appointed role and tasks properly; but they are not God, and their power and authority are not ultimate. Praying for "kings and all those in positions of authority," rather than being the act of the domesticated church, is the radical assertion of the limits of the power of all such authorities.

With verse 8 the focus shifts to the third and fourth specific concerns raised in 1 Timothy 2: the deportment in worship of men and of women. To recall our initial argument, worship is itself missional and is done in the awareness that the surrounding culture is watchful and aware. What, then, happens when the church gathers in worship? What does it look like? Does this radical community that does not worship the Caesar and actually includes women behave in ways that are alarming, promiscuous, and ostentatious? Or is their behavior restrained and modest? Paul's instructions to Timothy envision a radical community that does not unnecessarily provoke others by its immodest behaviors.

Perhaps because the attention given to women occupies more space in this passage — and because of its frequently repressive (mis)use — we may fail to note that Paul is giving instructions for the deportment of both men and women in worship. Men are to pray with "holy hands lifted up." His point here is not that proper prayer requires men to raise their hands; his point is its contrast to hands raised in anger. The holy hand is an open hand, in contrast to the hand raised in a clenched fist as a threat to enemies. We are all too familiar today with hands raised in anger and hate, whether in domestic protests against, for example, the integration of schools or against immigrants, or crowd actions in parts of the world where angry fists are often raised against America. Whether domestic or foreign, these fists raised in anger are often also raised in the name of God. We know what this looks like. The Christian men of Ephesus, who certainly did at times experience threat and repression, might well have been tempted to raise their fists in worship as a show of anger toward the merchants of the Diana cult. But Paul instructs them not to do it. He instructs men to raise holy, open hands in prayer.

In verse 9 and the verses following it, the focus shifts to the presence and deportment of women in the worshiping congregation and community. We acknowledge that these verses have been used to marginalize and repress women in the church; but we believe that their intent and significance is a different one altogether. First, recall the affirmation of verse 5, where God wants to save "everybody" (Paul does not say "every man" — but *every one*). Moreover, it is clear that the Christian community includes everybody: men and women, slaves and free, Jews and Gentiles (Gal. 3:28). We may not appreciate the radical nature of this in our life and time in North America. We find it perplexing or disturbing to read Paul's instruction that women are not to teach in the church but are to learn quietly from their male teachers. However, we might come closer to understanding this text in its context — and grasping its radical nature — if we imagine a community of worship and instruction, a school, in an Afghanistan run by the Taliban. There women were forbidden to attend school, to be instructed, or to learn at all. Here in Ephesus, as an expression of God's will "to save everybody," women are included in the congregation and are students there. Given the ancient social context and norms that we have noted in the preceding exegesis, this is properly understood not as a warrant for silencing women in the church or forbidding them from teaching roles. Instead, it is an indication that the Christian community in the ancient world, in stark and radical contrast to its surrounding culture, included women and considered it appropriate for them to participate in education.

We have discussed the final verses of 1 Timothy 2, in which Paul refers to the Genesis story, extensively in the exegetical section. These have also often been interpreted as a warrant for the marginalization of women in the church and for their subjection to male authority. Again, we believe that this interpretation is based on an erroneous reading of the Genesis text. The claim there — and here in 1 Timothy — is not that women are inherently inferior and thus must always be subjected to the authority of the superior male gender. Rather, the claim is that Eve, despite her previous failure, discerned in childbearing her full partnership with God and her participation in God's mission as an agent of God's redemptive activity of "saving everybody." The point is not that women, inherently out of control or a source of sin and temptation, must be kept in check by men in authority. The point is that women are God's partners in creation and redemption, both the objects and agents of God's saving work. The inclusion of women in the worshiping congregation — as well as in the instructional life of the church — was radical, not repressive.

To return, then, to our initial point regarding the missional nature of worship, Paul envisions a community whose participants are modest and restrained in their behaviors rather than ostentatious or provocative. The point of Paul's instructions for both men and women is the same one given to other radical, nonviolent movements: Do not give unnecessary offense, but behave in ways that are modest. Both men and women in the Christian community, and its worship, are to exhibit good judgment, prudence, and modesty. The world is watching. Worship is mission. And it is not the church that has a mission in the world, but God's mission — which is "to save everybody," that everybody "may come to a knowledge of the truth" — that has a church in the world.

In introducing this text, I noted that congregations have sometimes set up worship and mission in quite different and distinct programmatic compartments in a congregation's life and structures. Such

63

mechanistic organizational structures reflected the outlook and the Newtonian physics of the modern world. The result, good for its time, is less helpful today, because it does blind the church to the intrinsic relationships among the various parts of its life. An alternative to the modern, mechanistic, and static church organizational structure, one that may reflect our new missional situation, is to conceive of the church in a more systemic way. The church is a living system rather than a static machine.

What would that mean? Instead of a church's ministry or program being made up of separate departments, a congregation might conceive of itself as a disciple-making, apostle-sending system. A simple version of such a system would have three major components: inviting, transforming, and sending. *Inviting* extends welcome and hospitality to "everybody." *Transforming* deals with the practices of worship and instruction that engage people with the one God and God's appointed mediator for their salvation and knowledge of the truth. *Sending* is the directing of people out from the church into the larger world and community as instruments of God's grace and purpose — "to save everybody." In such a systemic reframing of the church, no part stands alone or separate. All are mutually dependent and related, requiring the others. Such a reframing of the church's life as a disciple-making system may help to reshape a church for a new time and for the worship of a missional church.

DISCUSSION QUESTIONS

1. Paul begins his instructions to Timothy with the practice of public worship. Why?

2. How does the Christian woman of 1 Timothy 2:9-15, who exemplifies prudence in her public life, embody Paul's conception of the missio Dei (2:3-7)?

3. How have you experienced the relationship of worship and mission in the church?

4. How do you respond to the picture of the church as a "disciple-making" system, made up of interdependent parts?

Lay Leadership in the Household of God

1 Timothy 3:1b-13

1b *Someone who aspires to become an administrator desires a good work. 2 Therefore, the administrator must be blameless: the husband of one wife, clearheaded, modest, respectable, hospitable, a skilled teacher, 3 not a drunk or a bully but gentle, peaceable, generous. 4 He must manage his own household well, holding children in submission with complete respect — 5 for if someone does not know how to manage his own household, how can he care for God's church? 6 He must not be newly converted so not to be arrogant and slip into the devil's condemnation. 7 He must have good references from outsiders so not to slip into disgrace, the devil's trap.*

8 Likewise, servants must be respectful: not duplicitous or imbibing in too much wine or in dishonest acquisition. 9 They should hold to the mystery of the faith with a clear conscience; 10 let those who serve first be tested and found blameless. 11 Likewise, women must be proper, not slanderous, prudent, faithful in all things. 12 Let the servants be the husband of one wife who manage children and their own household well; 13 for those who serve well acquire for themselves a good position and much confidence within the faith that is in Christ Jesus.

Part 1: Engaging 1 Timothy 3 as Scripture

This set of instructions profiles the ideal leaders of God's household. The household "administrator" must be able to manage a family household well (3:4-5), while at the same time must be blameless in his public conduct (3:2-3), mature in his faith (3:6), and must have good rapport with outsiders (3:7). Each contribution to this résumé of virtue envisions a particular competence of a leader who is able to safeguard the Pauline apostolate and its gospel for a new generation of believers. In the second pericope, Paul turns to the household's "servant staff." The catalog of virtues includes characteristics of ideal household servants (3:8, 12-13), whose faithfulness is tested and found blameless (3:9-10). Their spouses must be similarly qualified to serve others (3:11), since caring for members of the household is their principal responsibility.

Although undeveloped in 1 Timothy, Paul's passing comments about the ministry of a congregation's board of elders (4:14; 5:17ff.) suggest that those elders are collectively an important custodian of Pauline preaching and practices, and thereby are of indispensable importance for maintaining the spiritual health of believers. They provide leadership for those who meet together in Christian congregations for worship, instruction, good works, and fellowship. The reader may well puzzle over a biblical concept of Christian leadership drawn only by this passage, which seems to be in stark contrast to the more charismatic "body of Christ" trope that we also find in the Pauline canon (e.g., in Romans and 1 Corinthians).

For this reason biblical scholars put this text forward as evidence of a post-Pauline address in which the church had developed a more complex political structure to accommodate Roman society and safeguard the social institutions of Christian religion. Luke Timothy Johnson rightly objects to this construction, which would seem to suggest that the church of the Pastoral Epistles describes or even anticipates the more complex institutional episcopacy that developed much later within the early catholic church.[1] In any case, it bears repeating that "household" is the central metaphor for the church of the Pastoral Epistles. The "living God" is paterfamilias of the sacred household (cf. 3:15); and the political shape of this theological concept draws naturally

---

1. Luke Timothy Johnson, *The First and Second Letters to Timothy: A New Translation with Introduction and Commentary* (New York: Doubleday, 2001), pp. 74-76, 217-25.

on the experience of middle-class households in the urban centers of the Mediterranean world (see 1 Tim. 1:4-5; 5:1–6:2; 2 Tim. 2:20-21; Titus 1:5; 2:1-10).[2]

According to this household typology, those in charge of caring for the family household — from its administrator to its servant staff — had particular responsibilities to perform and social conventions to observe. As is true today, the progress of Roman society depended on maintaining the stability of its various households, civil and familial. While the outlook and the aim of those who lead God's household aspire to holy ends, the daily operations of any household require effective administrators and a competent servant staff. Paul's instructions regarding the political organization of congregations are roughly analogous to social and political practices, another example of missionary Paul's willingness to accommodate the outworking of Christian faith to those places where people actually live (cf. 1 Cor. 9:19-23).

Given the centrality of the household motif in the Pastoral Epistles, the terms we use in our translation — "administrator" and "servants" — do not refer to established church offices of a highly organized episcopacy (e.g., bishops and deacons); they are better understood as collective metaphors for a certain community's elders whose practices and roles are informed by the administrative or service practices within Roman "households." Paul's use of household as an ecclesiastical metaphor extends to the congregation's leaders, and so his instructions have added currency for those with experience in familial households or who met for worship and fellowship in a family's home (cf. Acts 16:40; 20:7-12). His subsequent references to elderly men (1 Tim. 5:1) and actual servants (6:1-2) create a purposeful ambivalence between sacred/transcendent and secular/historical households, which forms the impression that spiritual leadership is rooted in a realistic understanding of Paul's social world, where the appointment of virtuous persons to care for and lead its institutions was thought crucial to the well-being of the public square.

The word we have translated as "administrator" (*episkopē*, 3:1b) refers to one who oversees the business of a household; it is sparingly used in the New Testament (Luke 19:44; Acts 1:20; 1 Pet. 2:12). Acts 1:20

---

2. The literature that locates the "household" in the Greco-Roman and Jewish social worlds is enormous. For a fluent summary of both this background and its application to Pauline ecclesiology, see P. Towner, "Households and Household Codes," in *Dictionary of Paul and His Letters,* ed. G. F. Hawthorne and R. P. Martin (Downers Grove, IL: InterVarsity, 1993), pp. 417-19.

quotes Psalm 109:8 (Septuagint) and uses *episkopē* to refer to Judas's vacated position within the Twelve, which Matthias then fills at God's bidding. Although vague, the use of *episkopē* in Acts may provide a context for reading the aspiration of a qualified administrator as an inward desire prompted by God's calling rather than by self-promotion. The word is repeated in 1 Timothy 3:2 in slightly modified form *(episkopos),* which elsewhere appears with "elders" (cf. Acts 20:28; Phil. 1:1; Titus 1:7; 1 Tim. 4:14) in reference to those who share the responsibility for a community's spiritual and social well-being.

We have intentionally translated *episkopē* as "administrator" rather than the more familiar "bishop" to resist the anachronism of what the office of bishop later became within the church's episcopate. Our use of "administrator" also indicates our preference for understanding it as a collective metaphor for a council of elders that manages the mundane nuts and bolts of daily routines to ensure the congregation's well-being. In this sense, the catalog of virtues of this passage also corresponds to this practical role: they profile a manner of leadership that works behind the scenes for the common good of the household of God.

Although the administrator has singular importance with respect to these organizational tasks, Timothy alone is charged with those responsibilities that are normally associated with a congregation's lead pastor (see our comment on 1 Tim. 3:14–4:7 below). In distinction from those elders appointed to help manage the congregation's daily affairs, the administrator alone is called the "pillar and foundation of the truth" (3:15) and is singled out by "prophetic utterance" (1:18) and by the apostle (cf. 2 Tim. 1:6-7) as vested with the spiritual gifts and thus religious authority that empowers him to guide the congregation into its future with God our Savior (see 4:16). Neither the household's administrator nor servant staff is accorded similar legitimacy.

The moral philosophers of the day routinely condemned those who "aspire" to leadership positions, because ambition for public office was usually motivated by greed (6:3-10) or a "desire" for sexual conquest. Paul here challenges this more negative reading of human desire, suggesting that divine grace can transform the motives behind a believer's actions. What Acts suggests, however, is that the congregation has the responsibility to determine whether this is true of every candidate who aspires to a position of leadership (cf. Acts 6:1-7).

The run-on sentence (3:2-5) is structured to introduce "blamelessness" *(anepilēmptos)* as a virtue of principal importance. It provides cover for the entire catalog of sixteen characteristics that follow, nine positive and seven negative. In this sense, these virtues register a rounded "impression" of one's moral blamelessness. Paul's choice of this particular hallmark virtue is somewhat surprising, because *anepilēmptos* does not appear in Israel's Scripture, which defines political leadership after "the prophet like Moses" (cf. Acts 3:19-26) and thus in the language of Torah observance or practical wisdom rather than personal virtue. The "blameless" person, however, is well known in Hellenistic moral philosophy, and the holistic formula of virtue envisioned by this profile, especially with its pronounced concern for cultivating the respect of outsiders, is congruent with this ideal.

Scholars continue to debate whether this catalog of virtues is generic or whether each virtue carries particular significance for the reader. On the one hand, similar lists are found in the writings of Philo and the Stoics, who were concerned with the morality of public life. Epictetus, for example, defines the ideal citizen in terms of conduct related to "marriage, raising children, reverence to God, care for parents" *(Discourses* 3.26). Cicero adds that the character of those responsible for the community's welfare must "in the first place be honestly acquired by the use of no dishonest or fraudulent means; let it, in the second place, increase by wisdom, industry, and thrift; and, finally, let it be made available for the use of as many as possible (if only they are worthy) and be at the service of generosity and beneficence rather than of sensuality and excess. By observing these rules, one may live in magnificence, dignity, and independence, and yet in honour, truth, and charity toward all" *(De officiis* I.xxvi). That is, Paul's list of a competent administrator's qualities agrees with the moral criterion of the ancient world by which any household manager would have been assessed. These are stock qualities, then, of someone capable of sensible decision-making and a prudent lifestyle, a person who does not abuse his authority and can lead an organization well.

In fact, a few of these virtues are listed elsewhere in the Pastoral Epistles as indicative of every earnest believer. The effect of this repetition is to relativize the leader's persona as exemplary of the covenant-keeping community as a whole, where every believer shares equally and is equally obligated to attain these marks of discipleship. In any case, the rhetorical role of this list is to evoke general impressions of the kind of person who can effectively manage the household of God.

On the other hand, however, even a cursory comparison of the particular virtues cataloged here to comparable lists found elsewhere in Paul's writings — for example, Titus's profile of an *episkopos* (1:6-9) — shows modest differences that are probably related to different places and occasions. These lists, then, are not arbitrary or generic but reflect the particular concerns framed by the composition itself. For this reason, "the concept of 'good management of a household' provides the best access to the particular virtues of the supervisor."[3] This particular catalog really holds no surprises for the reader, because it includes qualities one might expect of a competent manager: an ability to manage others well, to handle finances fairly, to make clear-headed decisions, to represent the community's membership at the highest level. Marks of personal maturity ("not a drunk or a bully, but gentle, peaceable, generous") are coupled with those of a spiritually mature person (a "skilled teacher" who is not "newly converted") as appropriate for one who supervises God's household with competence, and especially a household that has been newly founded in a pagan place, Roman Ephesus (1:3; cf. Acts 19).

Yet this particular list is noteworthy because of its interest in a congregation's public life and in what outsiders think. For this reason, Paul's review of moral character concludes with an outsider's letter of commendation that supports a candidate's moral character. Collins points out that the repetition of *dei* ("must," 3:2, 7) forms an *inclusio*, a set of parallel bookends that emphasizes the importance of the principle that one reads between the bookends: a manager must have a good reputation among both those within and those beyond the congregation's membership. "Were an overseer not to have a good public reputation, he would likely fall into derision (and) along with him the community itself could possibly be derided."[4] Within 1 Timothy this pervasive interest in an outsider's opinion of the believer's social manners is theologically rather than politically motivated (cf. 2:8-15): the congregation's life together and its public practices embody for all to see God's will to save everybody (2:3-6). The motive for Paul's instructions is not a social program of domestication according to which the administrator is put forward as an exemplary citizen; rather, he is an

---

3. Johnson, *First and Second Letters to Timothy,* p. 223.

4. Raymond F. Collins, *1 and 2 Timothy and Titus: A Commentary* (NTL) (Louisville: Westminster John Knox, 2002), p. 86.

exemplary believer whose "good work" personifies the redemptive will of God for all to see.

Consistent with 1 Timothy's use of *household* as its primary metaphor of the church, Paul lists marital fidelity and well-behaved children as the marks of the excellent administrator. However, in the context of the Pauline canon, where a solitary life committed only to God is celebrated (1 Tim. 5:9-10; cf. 1 Cor. 7), the phrase "husband of one wife" might be understood more rigidly as the husband of *only* one wife: that is, as a signature of his commitment, the administrator of a Pauline congregation might well have been required to pledge to remain a widower in single-minded service to God's church should his wife die.

The objection is raised, especially by feminist readers, that this phrase also presumes the congregation's exclusively male leadership. But Paul later stipulates that the "truly needy" widow be "the woman of one man" (5:9) who qualifies for congregational support for the leading role she performs within the household. In this case, gender is not the relevant criterion of leadership but rather implies her fidelity to God and to God's church. By simple inference, the same is true here: that is, the virtue of "one spouse" notes compliance to the social norm of faithfulness to the household rather than to gender exclusivity.[5]

Significantly, hospitality is a hallmark of the covenant community. According to Acts, the host's good treatment of guests, a well-known characteristic of early Christian communities, is the expectation of any household in antiquity that was headed by a virtuous person (Acts 16:15, 34). To care for others, especially for their own (cf. Gal. 6:1-10; 3 John 5-8) and extended even to strangers (cf. Luke 6:31-36), reciprocates God's kind regard for everyone (1 Tim. 2:4). The administrator's own hospitality, then, inculcates this practice within the household of believers, where their obedience to God aims at love toward others (1:5).

Unlike the metaphor "administrator," the term we have translated as "servants" (*diakonoi*, 3:8) belongs to a word family *(diakonia/ diakoneō)* that has wide currency in Paul's writings and generally con-

---

5. Bassler admits that the transference to married men of an honor given to widows in antiquity who remain single out of respect for their deceased husbands should be considered "unusual." Jouette M. Bassler, *1 Timothy, 2 Timothy, Titus* (ANTC) (Nashville: Abingdon, 1996), p. 66. Although vague, the exclusivity of this phrase pertains to marriage and could also be read as excluding polygamy or a husband's sexual promiscuity. See also George W. Knight, *The Pastoral Epistles: A Commentary on the Greek Text* (Grand Rapids: Eerdmans, 1992), pp. 157-59.

veys the terms of a faithful servant's vocation. Paul considers all believers to be *"diakonoi* of the new covenant" (2 Cor. 3:6), whose competence in their common life and witness is a measure of divine grace mediated by God's Spirit (2 Cor. 3:3). Even though Paul sometimes attaches this word to specific tasks — such as carrying the Macedonian offering to the Jerusalem congregations (Rom. 15:25; cf. 2 Cor. 8:19-20) — his principal use of "servant" is metaphorical of a community that serves the interests of God in the "ministry *[diakonia]* of reconciliation" (2 Cor. 5:18). The members of such a community are called "servants *[diakonoi]* of Christ" (2 Cor. 11:23). Paul's use follows the witness of the synoptic Gospels to the Lord's definition of his disciples as "servant *[diakonos]* of all" (Mark 9:35; 10:43).

The use of "servant" here, however, is as a trope for a particular kind of spiritual leadership within God's household. Again, Paul is not interested in drafting a job description for those whose church office is "deacon"; rather, he wants to profile the characteristics of the council of elders, who collectively and faithfully serve God's household for Christ's sake. Perhaps for this reason, he says that this servant staff must "hold to the mystery of the faith with a clear conscience" (3:9) — a religious practice that distinguishes servant from household administrator. The servants must confess the "mystery of godliness" defined by the creedal formula of 3:16 (see Eph. 1:9; 3:4), since doing so ensures the fitness of work within the community. According to Hellenistic religious mores, beliefs linked to a "mystery" implied the use of magical formulae or esoteric teachings, or an initiation ritual known only to the membership. But in Pauline teaching, the "mystery of faith" is a public statement of what is believed, which marks out the confessing community as a people belonging to Christ. In this sense, then, the servant's responsibility within the household is to represent what is confessed to be true about Christ.

The structure of the catalog, which enlists four virtues before adding the "mystery" phrase, suggests that a virtuous life is a mode of conduct that is the effective yield of one who "holds to the mystery of faith with good conscience." To be sure, the virtues Paul lists — "respectful, not duplicitous or imbibing in too much wine or dishonest acquisition" (v. 8) — are appropriate to a servant's "domestic" work within the household. But a critical point should not be lost on the reader: the servant's character is forged by Christian faith for the work of securing the congregation's faith and life together.

Nothing stated would suggest that this role is subordinate to the administrator; rather, if both administrator and servants are roles assumed by the council of elders, the elder's household chores are simply *different* from those performed as administrator. The servant is less interested in the community's external affairs and more attentive to the spiritual formation of believers. (Perhaps for this reason, Timothy himself is called a "good *diakonos* of Christ Jesus" in 4:6.) Unlike the ideal administrator, whose public persona is best summarized as "blameless," the ideal servant's profile begins with "respect" *(semnos),* an adjective earlier listed to characterize the administrator's internal relationships with his own children (3:4). This earlier reading supposes that a servant's chores are internal to the "children" who belong to the household of faith and pertain to cultivating the faith of God's extended family.

Perhaps it is for this reason that Paul adds that the basis of such service is spiritual testing (3:10). "Let those who serve" suggests that such testing is ongoing with this service: the one funds and equips the other. Collins relates this spiritual testing to the embrace of faith's mystery "with a clear conscience."[6] If a "clear conscience" refers to one's internal moral apparatus and the source of loving relationships (cf. 1:5), then moral integrity must be seen as the complement of orthodox commitment, "holding fast to the mystery of faith." This formula of Christian existence, which views faith commitment and commitment to faithfulness as an integral whole, is central to the Pauline rule of faith.

The way the servant's "blameless" character is tested and then assessed by the congregation is not mentioned, only that a servant's character is tested as the necessary predicate of service. The adjective that we have translated as "blameless" *(anenklētos,* 3:10) differs from the earlier word, *anepilēmptos,* which concentrates the "blameless" character of the competent administrator (3:2). The word used here is a legal term for "innocence" (cf. Acts 23:29; 25:16), which, when used elsewhere in the Pauline collection, carries important theological freight: the believer who continues in the faith (Col. 1:22-23) is pardoned of spiritual crimes and thus participates with Christ in God's coming triumph (1 Cor. 1:8). The believer's faithful response to spiritual testing is the barometer of spiritual vitality.

6. Collins, *1 and 2 Timothy and Titus,* p. 88.

73

The central challenge we face in interpreting this passage is how to understand *gynaikas hōsautōs semnas,* which we have translated, quite literally, "Likewise, women must be proper . . ." (3:11). Because the phrase is sandwiched between two halves of a virtue list, the reader reasonably assumes some connection between these women and those who constitute the diaconate of elders. What remains unclear is the nature of their relationship, whether vocational (a discrete class of female servants) or marital (wives of servant-elders). Grammar alone does not settle the exegete's decision.[7] That turns on understanding the title *diakonoi* as a metaphor for elders, all of whom would have been male in this particular social setting.[8] These women, then, are most likely composed of the "one wife" of the elder-servants. Of course, in an ecclesiastical setting that allows for both female and male elders, this instruction properly targets "spouses."

The particular list that defines their personae is noteworthy by what virtues are mentioned, which correspond to those of their husbands. In particular, the concluding phrase "faithful in all things" parallels that characteristic featured in the earlier list, "mystery of the faith" (cf. 5:16). While, again, no description of tasks is added to this list, Paul's evident point is that faith is most effectively formed within households led by a faithful couple, perhaps the motive that lies behind verse 12, which otherwise seems out of place.

Part 2: Engaging 1 Timothy 3:1-13 for Congregational Leaders

For many contemporary congregations, the selection, recruitment, and equipping of lay leaders has become a challenge. "Time is," as one sociologist observes, "the new currency." People are less willing than they once were to serve on boards and committees. They often simply say, "I don't have the time." That's probably true in part. But sometimes the problem

7. For an analysis of the grammar of this phrase, see I. Howard Marshall, *Pastoral Epistles* (Edinburgh: T. & T. Clark, 1999), pp. 492-94, who, with most scholars, takes it as referring to female deacons.

8. Bassler follows others in providing a history-of-religions explanation for the lack of theological or religious justification for the appointment of church leaders. A pattern of virtuous life rather than theological orthodoxy was more important in a Greco-Roman world that was deeply suspicious of new religions. Bassler, *1 Timothy, 2 Timothy, Titus,* p. 71.

is that people do not perceive the experience of serving in this way as meaningful or consequential. Moreover, the tried and true processes like nominating committees don't seem to be working very well. Meanwhile, pastoral leaders wonder how well prepared and equipped the lay leaders they do have are for the needs and challenges they face. In this segment we want to engage the questions surrounding the preparation, selection, recruitment, and equipping of a congregation's lay leaders. How can this challenge become an opportunity? How does 1 Timothy 3:1-13 help us think in fresh ways about a congregation's lay leadership?

Yet, a reader may be wondering, "How did we get here? Isn't 1 Timothy 3:1-13 about ecclesiastical offices like bishops and deacons?" Translators and interpreters have pointed us in that direction for a long time, but we think that it is an erroneous direction. It perceives a more elaborate church and hierarchy than is envisioned or addressed in the Pastoral Epistles. More accurate, we believe, are terms such as "administrator" rather than bishop (with all the historical and contemporary connotations of that office), and "servants" in place of "deacons." As we have noted in the preceding exegetical section, "Given the centrality of the household metaphor in the Pastoral Epistles, the terms used in our translation — 'administrator' and 'servants' — do not refer to established church offices of a highly organized episcopacy (e.g., bishops, deacons, and the like), but are better understood as collective metaphors for a certain community's elders, whose practices and roles are informed by the administration or service practices within Roman 'households.'" Of course, this is not an exact parallel to what congregations today think of as "lay leaders" either, but it is closer.

There are two types of role and service considered here in 1 Timothy 3:1-13: both are, in a sense, "elders." The first (3:1b-7), "the administrator," is closer to what many congregations consider its elected lay leader, be it a president or a moderator. Or it might also be analogous to a church staff position: in some congregations that would be a business administrator; in others it might be an "executive minister" with administrative responsibilities. The second role and position (3:8-13) is analogous in many contemporary congregations to a body like the church council, session, or consistory. It might also be thought of as a congregation's elders or deacons. Different terms will be used in different congregations and church traditions, but this text provides insight for the selection and function of lay leaders, while the next one (3:14–4:16) fits the role and function of a pastoral leader.

When it comes to lay leadership roles and positions in contemporary congregations, many congregations today lapse into filling slots rather than calling spiritual leaders. While almost a cliché, it is nonetheless not far off the mark to picture an increasingly desperate member of the church's nominating committee, with a deadline looming, frantically calling members of the congregation in late November and saying something like the following: "Listen, can you help me out here? I have three more positions to fill before I can turn this in. I've asked all kinds of people and nobody is willing to do it this year. A couple of them said they'd do it next year. Do me a favor, take a term. It doesn't amount to much. The board just meets once a month. Will you do it?"

This is what I mean by "filling slots." Quite apart from the fact that asking someone to play a leadership role in the church by saying, "It doesn't amount to much," may not be the best approach, the caller is trading on personal connection and institutional loyalty to fill the slots for one more year. Really, such dynamics are the sign of an organization — a congregation — in decline.

Working with one congregation that had used this approach for yet another year, to no avail, I suggested a different approach. "Let's back up," I suggested. "Instead of filling slots, let's think and pray about whom you see as the spiritually mature members of your congregation. Let's ask ourselves, 'Who are the spiritual leaders, and those with the potential to become spiritual leaders in our congregation?'" That particular congregation had about 200 members. The group to whom I suggested this different approach was seeking people to serve on its ten-person governing board. In an hour of thinking and praying, they listed the names of forty persons they thought of as their congregation's "spiritual leaders." Next they called a shorter list of these people and explained their process. "We are seeking spiritual leaders to serve on the congregation's governing board in the coming year. It will be an important year for our congregation. Some of the challenges on the horizon include. . . . We have been praying about our leadership needs, and your name came to us as someone we think is called by God to this work. We'd like to talk with you about it and wonder if we can schedule an appointment." On that basis, all of the positions on the congregation's governing board were quickly filled. That congregation had moved from filling slots to calling spiritual leaders. Of course, the transformation cannot end there. The new governing board must also develop a new culture that reflects its call to be spiritual leaders of the congregation.

We believe that 1 Timothy 3:1-13 calls for such an approach. Let's turn now to our text in more detail to discover how it may inform and renew our thinking about the selection, recruitment, role, and equipping of lay leaders in the congregation. We will take the role of administrator first (3:1-7). As indicated, a contemporary analogy might be that of a congregation's elected lay leader, whether its president, moderator, or chair of the board. Or, in some larger congregations, this may be a role played by a member of the church staff, whether a church business administrator or an executive minister.

Four themes culled from the text are worthy of particular attention as they relate to this leader: (1) leadership is not only a matter of job skills or experience, but of faith and character; (2) how the leaders handle their own affairs and functions in their own family is an important indicator of their capacity for this role; (3) a faithful administrator has more of a behind-the-scenes than an always front-and-center position; and (4) the missional nature of God and thus of God's church is kept in mind, since this is to be a person who relates to people beyond the church and is held in high regard among "outsiders" (vs. 7).

1. *Faith and character.* Often when we think about leadership roles in the church today, we put a great deal of emphasis on appropriate skills and experience. So, for example, we may look for someone who has been in a leadership role in civic groups or in business. Or we may seek a person who has an accounting or a legal background for positions that entail financial responsibilities. These things are important, and there's nothing wrong with paying attention to skills and experience; but too often it is the only thing we consider. 1 Timothy suggests that character is crucial and spiritual maturity is central. Verses 2, 3, and 6 catalog virtues of character and faith. A person called to such a role in the congregation is to be "blameless," "clearheaded," "modest," "respectable," "hospitable," and "not a drunk or a bully, but gentle, peaceable and generous." These are virtues and attributes of character. Such a person is also to be "a skilled teacher" and "not newly converted" or "arrogant" in matters of faith. The point is that those who are considered for and called to such roles are called not just because they have held leadership positions elsewhere or possess a particular and relevant skill set, still less because they are wealthy, physically attractive, or tall, but because they are spiritually grounded and mature. They are people of solid character.

2. *How leaders handle their own affairs* and function in their families

or close relationships. As the exegesis notes, attention to such matters was ordinary in classical culture, where one philosopher urged: "Whenever you propose to consult with anyone about your affairs, first observe how he has managed his own. For he who has shown poor judgment in conducting his own business will never give wise counsel about the business of others." Consistent with this, Paul tells Timothy that someone "who aspires to become an administrator" in the church "must manage his own household well . . ." (3:5).

But this goes beyond a "background check" or looking for a person from a "good family." Congregations, which Paul describes here and in Ephesians with the metaphor of "the household," have some analogies to families. People who are able to put their own family together may be able to provide a similar service to the congregation. In the words of Rabbi Edwin Friedman, a family-systems thinker, "There is an intrinsic relationship between our capacity to put our families together and our ability to put ourselves together." Friedman develops this further by pointing out: "What is vital to any kind of 'family' is not knowledge of technique or even of pathology, but, rather, the capacity of the family leader to define his or her own goals and values while trying to maintain a non-anxious presence within the system."[9] It is less a matter of expertise than of character.

We live today in a culture that is dominated by ideas of expertise and specialization. We tend to look for experts who have data and information at their fingertips. These things can be helpful. But in families — as in congregations — faith and character, maturity and self-knowledge, are more to the point than expertise and specialized knowledge. Truly, neither parents nor church leaders can ever know enough. They can never master all the data or techniques. Nor do they need to do so. If leadership in a family or congregation is defined as being expert on all aspects of either parenting or marriage, or on church life and matters that touch on them, few if any will qualify. But if leadership in the congregation is more about maturity and self-definition, which Friedman defines as the capacity to "define one's own goals and values while trying to maintain a non-anxious presence in the system," then how one functions in one's own family and intimate relationships may be a very good guide to how a person will function in a leadership role in the church.

9. Edwin Friedman, *Generation to Generation* (New York: The Guilford Press, 1985), pp. 2-3.

The way people function in their own families and households is an indicator of how they will function in the church, the household of God. But this should not be turned into an expectation that the families of lay or clergy leaders will be "perfect." Such an expectation is neither fair nor helpful. Few if any families are "perfect." Often those that aspire to such an image or present such an image to others are simply masking real problems behind a facade. Better to be real than perfect.

3. *Leaders often work behind the scenes* and don't need to be out-front all the time. The exegesis notes that the leader or administrator (described in verses 1-7) "manages the mundane nuts-and-bolts routines to ensure a congregation's well-being." In this sense, the virtue catalogs of the present passage correspond to this practical role: they profile a way of leadership that works behind the scenes for the common good of the household of God.

My wife, who is a school principal, often observes: "When good leadership is going on in a school, people don't notice it. What they do notice is that the whole school is functioning well, that it works." Sometimes when people think about leaders, whether other people or themselves, they think of the person who is in the spotlight, who is front and center, who gets a lot of focus and attention. While there are times for leaders to be visible, my own experience confirms my wife's observations. Good leaders do the many little things behind the scenes that aren't always visible, until they aren't being done — and then things sort of fall apart.

If those who aspire to leadership only want public notice and group acclaim, or want too much of the spotlight, then being a congregation's president or moderator, board chair or business administrator, may not be for them. There is an element — perhaps more than an element — of sacrificial vocation here. It can't be an ego trip because it's a form of service to ensure the healthy functioning of the congregation, the household of God.

I recall a middle-aged man who wanted to serve as the chair of the congregation's governing board. He took me out to lunch to talk about the position, perhaps knowing I had some reservations about his candidacy. He told me, "I need this," by which he meant that he needed to be in this position for his own self-esteem and for what it would mean to his reputation in the community and congregation. I told him and the people charged with the nominations process that I didn't think he was ready yet. It was too much about him. Serving behind the scenes and taking care of the details for the common good of the church wasn't what he was about.

4. *The missional role of the church and rapport with outsiders.* In the previous chapter we noted the way in which the congregation in Ephesus, which Timothy was to lead in Paul's absence, was in a missional situation. They were an outpost of the Christian faith, story, values, and way of life in the midst of a pagan culture. As such, their way of life "speaks" to the wider culture and community of their God and of the Lord. So the household or congregational leader is to be a person who is held in high regard and respect by "outsiders." Such a person, writes Paul in 1 Timothy 3:7, "must have good references from outsiders so as not to slip into disgrace. . . ."

Such a person is selected with an eye to the missional nature of the congregation in its setting. Moreover, there is some basis for thinking that this particular position, a congregation's president, moderator, board chair, or business manager should have a particular capacity to represent the congregation externally and to the wider community, in contrast to the roles described in the following section (vv. 8-13), which are focused more internally. Congregations do and should interface with the wider community. The kinds of leaders described in these verses (vv. 1-7) have a role and responsibility to represent the household of faith in that wider community. They should have a capacity to function well in the public square, and to be trusted and respected by those whom they will encounter. This is based not simply on moral considerations, but on missional ones. This concern is rooted in the mission of God, which is to save everybody (1 Tim. 2:4).

When we turn to the second part of the text (3:8-14), the focus shifts from the administrator of the household of God to the servants in the household. These are elders in the congregation, something like a council of elders. Analogues to contemporary congregations might be a church council, a board of deacons, or a board of elders. In discussing the kinds of people suitable for such a role, one should not simply rely on the repetition of themes from the previous discussion of the administrator; there are several new themes and emphases.

Repetition of previous themes includes the emphasis on character and faith and attention to an individual's capacity to function well in his/her own family or household. So these servants/elders are to be "respectful," "not duplicitous or imbibe in too much wine or in dishonest acquisition" (3:8). They are "to be the husband of one wife who manage children and their own household well" (3:12). Once again, how candidates function in their own families, their capacity to "lead" and put a family together, is an indication of their capacity to put a congregation together. The exegesis notes the complexity of determining exactly what is meant in verse 12. It may be speaking of the wives of elders or of couples who serve as elders. What does seem noteworthy is that a significant criterion for leadership is how one functions in the domestic or family setting. By way of contrast — and often in contrast to our own situation — there is no priority placed on whether one is a success in business or a person of influence in the public square. That is not to say that these things are insignificant. It is to again note that success in the family augurs well for success in the congregation. Allow us to emphasize once again that "success" is not perfection. It does not mean an absence of struggles or problems, but the ability to face and address them.

I would also add that, in my own experience as a pastor, men and women who have been parents, and good ones, often seem to do well as congregational leaders and staff members. I suspect this is true for a couple of reasons. Knowing how to work with people of different ages, different levels of maturity, and in a complex emotional system like the family is good preparation for work in the household of faith. It also seems true that parenting is a sacrificial vocation where people learn to subordinate their own immediate desires or self-interests to the needs of vulnerable others and to the family as a whole. This does not mean, of course, that single persons cannot also be excellent leaders for the church. They certainly can be and are — after all, Jesus and Paul were both unmarried.

If there is, then, some repetition of criteria for leadership between the administrator and elders, there are also some differences. I note two in particular: one pertains to the "mystery of faith" (vv. 9 and 13), the other to the element of testing (v. 10).

Somewhat in contrast to the criteria for the administrator in verses 1-7, these verses place a greater emphasis on the role of elders as guardians or stewards of the core deposit of faith, which the apostle Paul has entrusted to Timothy and his community. So verse 9 says, "They [servants/elders] should hold to the mystery of the faith with a clear conscience"; and verse 13 says, "For those who serve well acquire for themselves a good position and much confidence within the faith that is in Christ Jesus." The greater emphasis here on faith commitment, a theological norm, and a responsibility to represent what is true about Christ, suggests that these elders, individually and collectively, have a special responsibility for the spiritual formation and spiritual health of the congregation.

This again suggests that some of the ways we tend to go about selecting and recruiting church leaders today may be off the mark. We sometimes see these positions as ways to get new people involved. Or we look for people based on their interests and past experience. A builder goes on the property committee. A teacher goes on the Christian Education board. A youth is asked to serve on a board for age diversity. None of these things is necessarily wrong, but 1 Timothy suggests the importance of spiritual formation and spiritual depth for a congregation's leaders. This, in turn, suggests a priority within a congregation that has been diminished or absent for many congregations: that is, a robust teaching ministry and emphasis on practices of spiritual growth for adults. Lacking these, congregations often find themselves choosing among people for leadership roles whose own spiritual formation has been deficient, not because they are bad people but because the church has not created opportunities and priorities for spiritual growth and maturity in faith. Also echoed here are points made in the two previous chapters: a congregation's health depends in large measure on sound teaching and doctrine.

A final point of emphasis drawn here in the discussion of servant elders is its reference to testing in verse 10. "Let those who serve first be tested and found blameless." It is somewhat unclear whether this means that potential elders should already have been tested or that they will be tested — or both. However we may come down on that, this theme is worthy of note and attention, because the plain fact is that those who are called to leadership within a congregation will be tested. They will sometimes find themselves dealing with difficult, angry, or hurting people. They may find that a pastoral leader is not as mature or grounded as one might wish. They may find themselves caught in a personnel issue or a congregational conflict, or they may be faulted when something unfortunate happens on the youth group's mission trip.

The point is this: those called to leadership in the church better not be naive people who believe that the church is just a bunch of wonderful people who are always nice and caring. There are a few people like that. But congregations are full of flawed people and are subject to stresses and challenges. The person who is called to and accepts a leadership role in the church cannot be naive about these things. He or she will be tested. People in the congregation will provide "tests" of faith and endurance. We do well to be honest and candid about this and to prepare the people we recruit for it. This underscores again the relevance of the familial household, where challenge and conflict occur and people at times disappoint one another, as a proving ground. It also underscores the importance for lay leaders in a congregation to be people of some spiritual depth and maturity.

In closing — and in preparing the transition to the next section and its emphasis on the pastoral leader — we simply note that leadership in a congregation does not rest exclusively with the pastor. There is a need for sharing leadership among clergy, lay leaders, and church staff members. It is equally necessary to rethink some past practices and norms for lay leadership. 1 Timothy 3:1-13 offers us a biblical setting for fresh thinking about such a prospect.

DISCUSSION QUESTIONS

1. How does Paul's missionary concern for the outsider's salvation shape the qualifications for congregational leadership?

2. Which of those qualifications seem to you least relevant for today's congregations? What new qualifications would you add for the twenty-first century?

3. How would you assess a potential leader's "spiritual depth and maturity"?

4. This chapter describes leadership in the church as a "sacrificial vocation." What does that mean? How would this affect the choice of people called to serve?

Pastoral Leadership in the Household of God

I Timothy 3:14–4:16

14 *While I hope to come soon to you, I write these instructions to you* 15 *so that if I am delayed you will know how you must behave as the pillar and foundation of the truth within the household of God, which is the church of the living God.* 16 *Indeed, the mystery of holy living we confess is important: He was revealed in flesh and confirmed by Spirit, seen by angels and proclaimed among the nations, believed worldwide and exalted in glory.*

4:1 *But in fact the Spirit says that in the latter times some will abandon the faith, adhering to deceptive spirits and doctrines of demons* 2 *because of the hypocrisy of deceptive liars and cauterized consciences.* 3 *For example, they forbid marriage and eating foods that God has created to be received with thanksgiving by those who believe and know the truth.* 4 *For everything God created is good and nothing received with thanksgiving is rejected,* 5 *since these things are sanctified by God's word and prayer.* 6 *If you instruct these things to believers you will be a good servant of Christ Jesus, apprenticed according to the teachings of the faith, the good doctrine, you have followed.* 7a *Have nothing to do with profane and silly myths.*

7b *Train yourself for holy living.* 8 *While physical training has some value, holy living has value for everything, holding promise for both this life and the life to come.* 9-10 *This teaching is a core belief and worthy of unqualified acceptance (for it is the aim of our work and struggle): "Our hope is set on the living God, who is the Savior*

84

of all people, especially those who believe." 11 Command compliance to these instructions and teach. 12 Let no one despise your youth, but until I arrive set a pattern for believers in speech, in public conduct, in love, in faith, in purity. 13 Pay attention to public reading, preaching, and teaching. 14 Do not neglect the spiritual gift in you, which was given to you through prophecy with the laying on of hands by the council of elders. 15 Practice these things; live by them so that your progress may be observed by all. 16 Tend to yourself and to your teaching; for by doing this you will save both yourself and your listeners.

Part 1: Engaging 1 Timothy 3:14–4:16 as Scripture

This expansive passage is arguably the gravitas of the Timothy correspondence. It is here, for instance, that the occasion for the letters is more clearly articulated: Paul provides instructions for Timothy to guide his work during the apostle's absence (3:14-15a; cf. 1:3). For this reason, Paul clarifies Timothy's pivotal role, as the apostle's delegated substitute, in forming Christian congregations. And he again does this by using household metaphors: Timothy is to be the "pillar and foundation of the truth within the household of God." The formulation of this foundational "truth" is expressed by the elegant christological creed (3:16), which is the lynchpin between the description of Timothy as the household's truth-provider and those apostates whose "doctrines of demons" pose a threat to believers (4:1-5). In this way the "church of the living God" (3:15c) is secured by the truth of the gospel.

After an interlude that sounds an apocalyptic warning about apostate interlopers, Paul returns to more practical instructions that present a "professional development plan" for his successor. Having already encouraged Timothy to ground his ministry in "good doctrine" (4:6-7a), Paul turns now to portray the kind of person who can effectively pastor those under his care. Paul establishes the overarching exhortation regarding the ultimate value of a holy life (4:7b-8) by means of a canonical saying that clarifies its eschatological benefit (4:9-10, 15-16). The pattern of holiness commended by Paul includes both personal virtues (4:12) and vocational practices (4:13-14). Timothy is to live a holy life that can be observed by all (4:15), so that the community may learn what is necessary for salvation from his example of faithfulness (4:16).

We doubt that this passage breaks the flow of 1 Timothy 3's definition of leadership, as some suppose; instead, it seeks to clarify the character of a congregation's pastor in functional terms apropos of a sacred household (rather than, say, by gender or social class). In particular, Paul now reimagines Timothy's role as the house's "pillar and foundation" (3:15): his role is to uphold "the truth" of the living God in a way that dispels the teaching of those who "adhere to deceptive spirits and doctrines of demons" (4:1).

Because Paul's purpose is to instruct his young protégé in the way of his religious practices and public life befitting the spiritual director of God's sacred family (1:18), the importance of his passing mention of a personal visit (3:14) lies well beyond the routines of polite discourse. In Paul's Letters, references to scheduled visits are vested with rhetorical importance in that they promise an "apostolic" house call that is laden with official importance.[1] Whether the promise is fictional or real, the very idea of an imminent visit implies the exercise of apostolic authority to fortify one's spiritual resolve (cf. Rom. 1:10-11; 15:20-22; 2 Cor. 13:1-2) or check on one's spiritual progress (cf. 1 Cor. 16:3-7; 1 Thess. 2:17–3:5; Philem. 22). Such apostolic visitations are typically anticipated following a protracted delay (3:15a), during which time letters become suitable substitutes for Paul's personal presence, an interim — even if inferior — measure of mentoring whose intention is to address problems until the apostle can return to handle the crisis in person. Read as a literary convention of Pauline letters, this reference to a personal visit suggests that Paul wrote 1 Timothy as a "virtual" substitute for his own personal presence.

Nonetheless, the relationship between delegated authority and the congregation must be more adequately defined. Paul defines Timothy's responsibility by appropriating the household metaphor, this time by appealing to its architecture: Timothy is the house's "pillar [*stylos*] and foundation [*hedraiōma*] of the truth" (3:15a).[2] Some may argue

---

1. The classic study of this motif is by Robert W. Funk, "The Apostolic Parousia: Form and Significance," in W. Farmer, C. F. D. Moule and R. R. Niebuhr, eds., *Christian History and Interpretation* (Cambridge, UK: Cambridge University Press, 1967), pp. 249-69.

2. See Luke Timothy Johnson, *The First and Second Letters to Timothy: A New Translation with Introduction and Commentary* (New York: Doubleday, 2001), pp. 231-32, where he argues that the referent of the phrase "pillar and foundation of the truth" is "how one ought to behave" rather than the more natural "the church of the living God" — a de-

that these architectural images are cued by the pagan temples of the various Ephesian deities, against which Paul posits the church as the actual dwelling place of the one God. More likely, however, "pillar and foundation of the truth" refers specifically to Timothy and suggests his role as guardian of the truth claims of Paul's gospel. In this regard, the text may well allude to the Old Testament idea of Israel as God's "household" and to Timothy's performance of a role analogous to that of Moses within Israel (cf. Num. 12:6-8; Deut. 31:30): to cultivate the people's understanding of God and God's law in order to ensure their covenant-keeping and thus their divine blessing (e.g., Deut. 4-6).

The placement of the christological confession here (3:16) is puzzling. But if Timothy's Moses-like role is to safeguard and transmit the truth about Christ to others, then its placement here makes sense: it elaborates Christ's role as the mediator of God's promised salvation (see 2:4-6) to clarify what truth Timothy is delegated to uphold.

The formula "great is the mystery of holy living [*eusebeia*]" introduces an agreed-on confession of the pious.[3] While it is plausible to suppose that these core beliefs about the exalted Christ comprise the revelation of a "great mystery" (Eph. 3:3-4), we should inquire about what way they constitute "holy living." Mary D'Angelo argues that moral philosophers since Plato considered *eusebeia* the Roman virtue that best combined religious observance with "family values." That is, the secular ideal of "holy living" presumed a profound devotion to one's family heritage, which was often expressed publicly by one's religious devotion to the deities and was thus a principal motive of one's religious practices. The pious person was religious for the sake of the family household's reputation.[4]

---

layed appositional phrase, then, similar to what the reader encounters in 1 Tim. 1:7. While we agree with Johnson that people more than place make better sense of the "pillar and foundation of the truth" metaphor in that people and not places transmit and uphold the truth, we do not agree that the referent of this metaphor is the entire congregation. The text addresses Timothy and not the congregation; and in this broader setting concerning leadership, the delayed apposition would seem best to refer to Timothy as the congregation's "pillar," whose instruction of the truth safeguards their faith and public conduct.

3. Cf. Raymond F. Collins, *1 & 2 Timothy and Titus: A Commentary* (Louisville: Westminster John Knox, 2002), pp. 106-7.

4. Mary R. D'Angelo, "*Eusebeia*: Roman Imperial Family Values and the Sexual Politics of 4 Maccabees and the Pastoral Epistles," *Biblical Interpretation* 11, no. 2 (2003): 139-65.

This ideal may lie in the background of Paul's use here in locating Timothy's ministry within the household of God, where two properties of Christian existence, a vital piety and sound doctrine, are mutually inclusive. Timothy's religious practices, including his public profession of faith, indicate that piety not only upholds the household's "foundation of truth" but also personifies its commitment to the Pauline legacy.

Paul often adorns his letters with confessions of faith (e.g., Rom. 1:3-4; 16:25-27; 1 Cor. 15:3-7; Phil. 2:6-11; Col. 1:15-20), though rarely are they as robust as this one. In most cases, he includes the lyrical line of a confession or hymn in a letter to remind its readers and hearers what they already know and believe. Sometimes such reminders respond to a spiritual crisis of some kind. In this setting, for example, a Pauline christological confession may remind Timothy what he is charged to instruct in order to secure the congregation's faith as its "pillar and foundation."

In any case, we doubt that the hymn's christological subject matter envisions a distinction that is sometimes made by modern commentators between an existential act of trust in Jesus (the real Paul) and a later institutionalized set of core beliefs about Jesus — "the faith" (post-Pauline church). Such a distinction is unprofitable because the decision to profess that Jesus is Lord is shaped by a commitment to certain core beliefs about his death and resurrection — a "justification by beliefs alone!" That is, to come to knowledge of the truth about Christ (1 Tim. 2:4-6) is synonymous with the act of trusting in him to save us from death and for eternal life.

The design of the confession, along with its placement at the letter's pivot point, declares its significance for the letter's recipient. The six parallel lines fashion three pairs that make three succinct claims about the risen Jesus, cast in spatial rather than temporal images. Each pair looks toward a dynamic interplay between heaven and earth, between what angels witness (what remains an invisible "mystery") and what the church witnesses, that is, what defines "the faith" (3:9). In other words, the subject matter of the congregation's professed beliefs about the risen Christ is confirmed by a second congregation of heavenly witnesses that rebounds throughout all creation, on earth and in heaven, in praise that the Creator's redemptive purpose is brought to realization by the Christ event. And this is the central truth claim that ·Timothy is charged to uphold (3:16).

(1) *He was revealed in flesh and confirmed by the Spirit.* The first cou-

plet introduces the church's most critical belief about Jesus. This affirmation is of a flesh-and-blood Jesus: his public life is nothing other than the presentation of God's redemptive purpose within history (cf. 2:5-6). The heavenly complement of this belief is that Jesus' messianic mission is confirmed by the Spirit at his resurrection (see Rom. 1:4; Acts 2:36). The odd use of the verb *dikaioun* here, which we have translated "confirmed," is similar to Paul's use of that verb in 1 Corinthians 6:11 in reference to the authenticating witness of "the Spirit of our God." Accordingly, we take it that the first line refers to the whole of Jesus' public mission and not just his post-Easter visitations, which is then validated as messianic by the Spirit who mediated God's power in raising him back to life, according to Pauline teaching.

(2) *He was seen by angels and proclaimed among the nations.* The second couplet reverses the spatial interplay by beginning with a belief about the witness of angels. Our translation of *angeloi* as heavenly "angels" (rather than as human "messengers") preserves the heaven-earth interplay of the creed. But why is there an interest in an angelic line of sight to the risen Jesus? Here a happy note is sounded and preserved in the Pauline canon: that an angelic host welcomes the risen Son of God, the Messiah, back into its heavenly embrace (Phil. 2:9-11; cf. Rev. 12:5-12). We suspect that the creed links the first two parallelisms by maintaining the resurrection subtext of the previous line. That is, this belief affirms the gospel's witness to the angelic pronouncement of the Lord's resurrection (see Matt. 28:5-7), whose confirmation is assumed by the apostolic proclamation of the risen Jesus among the nations (Matt. 28:16-20).

(3) *He was believed worldwide and exalted in glory.* This final couplet commends what Paul has already professed: God our Savior desires the salvation of everyone (2:3-6), a redemptive vision that shapes the prospects of those who believe in Christ, even as it is already and demonstrably realized in the heavenly exaltation of their risen Lord (see Phil. 2:5-11). While it makes perfect sense to link together the second line of the preceding parallelism, "proclaimed among the nations," and the first line of this one, "believed worldwide," the logical connection of this earth-heaven interplay is not immediately clear. We doubt that the doxology's final line is based on a prior reading of Luke, as some scholars suggest when they read this as a nod to Jesus' ascension as the ultimate proof of his resurrection (Luke 24:50-53; Acts 1:3-10). The accent here is Pauline and expresses Jesus' heavenly exaltation as creation's

Lord — and thus the utter logic of the church's trust in him and proclamation of him in the world.[5]

Although most commentators suggest that 4:1 marks the beginning of a new round of personal instruction, detached from 3:14-16, the connecting *de* is best understood as introducing a contrast between Timothy's pastoral role as the congregation's "pillar and foundation of the truth" (3:15) and those who seek to subvert this truth with a "doctrine of the demons" (4:1-3). In the first chapter of the letter there are vague references to the manner and motive of teachers of "divergent doctrine," who compromise the congregation formation by specializing in "idle speculation" rather than "loving relationships" (1:3-7, 18-20). Here Paul condemns what they teach as characteristic of the "latter times" (cf. 2 Tim. 3:1-9).

Paul's invective echoes Jesus' apocalypse (see Matt. 24, plus parallels in Mark 13 and Luke 21), which also predicts the arrival of false prophets in the last days, those who seek to subvert Israel's preparation for its messiah, even though they ironically herald the imminent triumph of God, whose coming will condemn their teaching and vindicate the gospel. The powerful trope "doctrines of demons" recasts the earlier expression "divergent doctrine" (1:3) in terms of a creation-denying asceticism that evidently disregards marriage and certain foods as the good creations of a benevolent Creator.

Paul's correction of this falsehood appears to follow naturally from his use of "household" in 1 Timothy as metaphorical of the Christian congregation. In this regard, the quality of a faithful marriage as a credential of spiritual leadership, or childbearing as the distinctive mark of God's keen interest in a woman's salvation (1 Tim. 2:15a), is of a piece with this household metaphor. Any opposition to marriage (and thus childbearing) or to certain foods, especially if received with thankful responses to the Creator's common grace, may signal teaching that is subversive not only to the sacred household's covenant with God but to its mission in the world.

Given the vagueness of this invective, however, scholars have found it difficult to identify these "doctrines of demons" with names or groups on a religious map of earliest Christianity. The James of Acts, for example, corrects Peter's myopic commentary on Cornelius's conver-

---

5. See I. Howard Marshall, *The Pastoral Epistles* (ICC) (Edinburgh: T. & T. Clark, 1999), pp. 528-29.

sion by arguing that the purity practices (Acts 15:20) that complement a "purity of the heart by faith" (15:9) are a sine qua non of covenant-keeping fellowship. According to Acts, the leaders of the church had gathered in Jerusalem to discuss issues of table fellowship, presumably prompted by an earlier conflict within the Antiochene church (Acts 15:1-2). James is deeply concerned particularly about the initiation of repentant Gentiles into the Diaspora church where Moses is preached (Acts 15:21). Most of these were not Jewish proselytes but were converted from paganism to Jesus, and James thinks that this might threaten the Jewish legacy of the church's faith. Appealing to Israel's Scripture, his solution concerns food and sexual practices (perhaps linked to pagan rituals), and the fact that it is repeated three times in Acts emphasizes its importance (Acts 15:20, 29; 21:25). Indeed, religious practices related to food, marriage, and sex in antiquity often defined the sometimes difficult social relationships between repentant Jews and Gentiles (see 1 Cor. 6-7, 8-10). Perhaps Paul's harsh words about the "hypocrisy of liars" and his appeal to God's good creation (1 Tim. 4:4) and to the alternative religious practices of "the word of God and prayer" (4:5) have a similar setting in mind in which a world-denying asceticism is mandated by false teachers for converts who have recently left their pagan religions for membership in God's household. And James, the Lord's brother, follows the pattern of Jesus, who allows for (but does not require) a celibate lifestyle as a property of a disciple's kingdom vocation (Matt. 19:12) and considers all foods kosher (Mark 7:19).

The thankful reception of material things (such as good food) or healthy social conventions (such as a covenant-keeping marriage) is sanctified for holy outcomes by the church through "God's word and prayer (of thanksgiving)" (4:4-5). In this compositional setting, the consecrating agent is not the Holy Spirit but the holy household. Even these mundane activities — eating good food around a table with one's extended family and friends — carry religious importance for believers, especially when contrasted with non-Christian "households," whose use of food (or not) during religious rituals framed a different natural theology than did the Christian households. In continuity with the Jewish tradition, table fellowship is consecrated by prayers of thanksgiving that recall the biblical story of creation, in which "God's word" brings forth a creation (Gen. 1:31), and in which food (Gen. 1:29-30) and marriage (Gen. 1:28) are given strategic roles that serve the Creator's way of stewarding the world.

The later conditional of 1 Timothy 4:6-7a continues from Paul's correction of a creation-denying Christianity rather than introducing the personal charge that follows in 4:7b-16. *Tauta* ("these things") is frequently used in this Letter (3:14; 4:6, 11, 15; 5:7, 21; 6:2, 11), but often without a clear indication of its referent. In this use, a case could be made that "these things" anticipates what comes next, and particularly the canonical saying found in 4:10. We think that it more plainly concludes the implied contrast between those teachers who seek to influence a sacred household with "doctrines of demons" and Timothy, whose instruction follows the "healthy doctrine" of Paul's legacy with respect to his vocation as the household's "pillar and foundation of the truth" (3:15).

The adjective *graōdēs*, which we translate "silly," refers literally to "old women," which some ancient philosophers used as a trope for a person who promulgates household remedies instead of profitable teaching. While it is sexist at face value, this word is typically used in antiquity to denigrate the "profane and silly myths," no matter what the rival's gender was. Lucian, for example, used the expression against other schools of philosophy, calling their arguments "stories consisting of old wives' *[graōdēs]* fables" (*Philopseudes* 9). Paul's exhortation is aimed at a congregational leader tempted to substitute teaching contrary to the core beliefs of the Pauline gospel in a futile effort to sustain a more relevant Christian faith.

The final pericope of this passage (4:7b-16) opens with an exhortation to follow the habits of a well-trained athlete: "Train yourself for holy living" (4:7b; cf. 2 Tim. 2:5). The word for training, *gymnazō* (from which "gymnasium" derives), envisions the practices and habits of bodily self-control. Paul, of course, is interested that Timothy develop spiritual self-control (cf. 2 Tim. 1:7), which is decisive in securing his and his congregation's future with God (4:16).

"Holy living" translates the most distinctive catchword for Christian existence in the Pastoral Epistles, *eusebeia*, which Paul uses to characterize both the ideal congregation (2:2) and those who provide for its spiritual leadership (6:3, 5-6, 11). He likely is trading on a well-known belief in his world that religious manners are important within the general population — much like his earlier reference to a woman's "modesty" (2:9-15) or an administrator's "blamelessness" (3:2). While knowing the public regard for the pious person in his world, Paul surely understands that the source of personal rectitude is the inward effect of God's righteousness-producing grace (cf. 1:12-16).

The combination of personal discipline and the holy life targets the coming age. Not only does holy living benefit "everything" (i.e., internal and external things), its effect transcends time and extends into the coming age (4:9). Although "promise" is undefined here, when it is read within the Pauline corpus, its antecedent is likely the promised blessing God made to Abraham: the blessing of a people and a place (Gen. 12:1-3; cf. Rom. 4:13-20; Gal. 3:14-29), which is now realized for the community of believers baptized into Christ for the coming age (Rom. 4:17).

Paul supports his exhortation for holy living by an appeal to another canonical saying (4:9-10) that summarizes his theological legacy for his successors (see also 1:15; 3:1a). Most commentators agree that these five sayings, which are scattered across the Pastorals, formulate a Pauline way of salvation. In fact, the saying makes better sense of Paul's concluding concern: that Timothy "will save both yourself and those who listen to you" (4:16b). Perhaps no other text in the Pastoral Epistles more clearly connects the expectation of future salvation with the present performance of one's sacred calling than this one does. To put it bluntly, if Timothy were to neglect "the spiritual gift in [him]" (4:14), which includes the practices of a holy life (4:12, 15) and the Bible practices delegated to him (4:13, 16a), he would also neglect a "hope set on the living God," and the personal cost of doing so would be eternal.

This pointed and personal definition of salvation's future may explain Paul's parenthetical elaboration of the introductory formula, which anticipates that "struggle" accompanies the hard "work" of spiritual discipline (4:10a; cf. 4:7b). This same pairing of "work and struggle" is frequently found in Paul's writings to describe an apostle's missionary labor (cf. Rom. 16:6, 12; 1 Cor. 16:16; 1 Thess. 5:12; Col. 1:29), and that is the sense here. In other words, the truth of the canonical saying is confirmed by the sacrifice motivated by it. The "work and struggle" of ministry, analogous to the hard work required by physical discipline, is endured by its promissory note: the victory of salvation in this life and for the life to come.

Such a definition, of course, is predicated on one's belief in a particular kind of God: "the living God who is the Savior of all people" (4:10b; cf. 2:3-4). The combination of "living God" and "Savior" emphasizes one of Paul's core beliefs: that God enlivens "especially those who believe" as the promissory note for the life to come. Even though the universal reach of God's benefaction to "all people" continues an important theme of this Epistle (see 2:3-4; cf. 4:4), the use of the superlative *malista,* ("especially") restricts the present experience of God's promised salvation to those who have believed "the teachings of the faith" (4:6). Towner rightly concludes: "[T]here is no division here based on limited and unlimited atonement, and no need to posit two shades of meaning for the term 'Savior'."[6] The plain sense of this core belief is that God has offered salvation to everyone, though not everyone has embraced it, since divine grace does not coerce an unwilling acceptance of the gospel.

Paul introduces a portrait of the youthful Timothy in this cautionary exhortation: "Let no one look down on your youthfulness" (4:12a; cf. 1 Cor. 16:10-11). In this light, the prior instruction to "command compliance to these instructions and teach" suggests that Timothy's curriculum offers more than a congregation's catechesis into Pauline doctrine, indeed includes a demythologizing of those cultural biases that may have engendered age discrimination. We cannot determine Timothy's precise age; perhaps Paul's use of "youthfulness" refers to a lack of work experience, especially when compared to the absent Paul or even to the elders of the congregation. The Roman world considered apprenticeship and field experience to be requirements of mature instruction. Rather than a reference to chronological age, then, Paul's exhortation may reflect a people's concern for an incomplete or inadequate résumé of their congregation's leader. Even the catalog of virtues, which earlier had concentrated the reader on what kind of person leads a sacred household (rather than on his expertise), would have assumed a level of real-world experience; virtue is not formed in a vacuum. In any case, the clipped allusion to a future apostolic visit (4:12a) doubtless assumes that Paul's spiritual authority extends to the congregation even when he is absent, and on that basis he will examine its response to Timothy and his instruction upon his arrival (see our comment on 3:14-15a).

To ensure a good visit, then, Paul sets out a series of five sharply worded phrases of well-regarded credentials that transcend age and job experience (4:12). In his public speaking and social manners Timothy should demonstrate a virtuous life consisting of the triad of "faith, love and purity" (probably sexual; cf. 5:11-15). As with most virtue/vice lists in the Pauline corpus, this one is no doubt created with the letter's recipient in mind, not necessarily because Timothy is lax in any one of

---

6. Philip H. Towner, *1–2 Timothy and Titus* (Downers Grove, IL: InterVarsity, 1994), p. 312.

the moral practices but because, when taken together, this initial triad supplies the sine qua non of effective ministry.

A second triad catalogs standard worship practices (4:13) that are instrumental in cultivating a Jewish way of life (cf. 2 Tim. 1:5; Acts 16:1-5). Rather than finding opponents hidden behind these instructions, these two triads together provide a thick definition of the congregation's spiritual leader: the worship practices (4:13) of the virtuous leader (4:12) will have a maximum effect on shaping the saving faith of the worshiping community (4:16).

Not only the congregation's but Timothy's recognition of his spiritual authority is predicated on personal and public experiences of charismata, which, according to Paul's teaching, are supernaturally apportioned by the Spirit according to the congregation's need and for the common good (1 Cor. 12). Timothy knows that he has such a gift because prophecy (or revelatory speech) confirms the particular charism that is "in you" (4:14a; cf. 2 Tim. 1:6-7). Nowhere is the nature of Timothy's gift defined; but the reader should assume a logical — perhaps even causal — connection between the different parts of this unit of instructions. In this sense, the spiritual gift enables the performance of the prior worship practices.[7]

The congregation's acceptance of Timothy's divine authorization, however, is publicized by a liturgical gesture: the imposition of hands. This gesture by the congregation's elders is not the effective means of Timothy's ordination (see 2 Tim. 1:6 and the phrase "through the laying on of my hands"); rather, this particular use of the phrase "with the laying on of hands" indicates that the elders provide public testimony to the prophecy's expected fulfillment (1 Tim. 4:14b; cf. Acts 9:17-18; 13:1-3). Especially within an apostolate shaped by Jewish tradition (cf. 2 Tim. 1:3), the responsibility of the most revered (and typically most senior) group of leading men would include public recognition of those charged with administering the congregation's affairs, which is reminiscent of Moses' laying his hands on Joshua as a symbol of the

---

7. If Acts introduces and 1 Cor. 12 glosses this text within its canonical setting, readers should assume that the spiritual gift is given to Timothy by the Holy Spirit (see 2 Tim. 1:6-7). The alluded connection between the spiritual gift (v. 14) and the worship practices (v. 13) is similar to the effect of the Spirit's reception especially in Acts where Spirit-filling enables the community's leaders to interpret Scripture, preach and teach others with greater skill and more positive effect. See John R. Levison, *Filled with the Spirit* (Grand Rapids: Eerdmans, 2009), pp. 347-65.

transfer of authority to one's successor (see Num. 27:18-23; Deut. 34:9; Acts 6:6; 13:3). The "presbytery" (*presbyteroi*, "council of elders") corresponds to the leadership council of the synagogue (called the *gerousia*), who made appointments within the congregation.[8]

The final piece of Timothy's spiritual résumé gathers evidence of his moral progress (4:15). Paul's exhortation to "practice these things" *(tauta meleta)* contrasts with his prior instruction "not to neglect" *(mē amelei)* his spiritual gift. Consistent with the shape of Paul's general concept of the mature Christian, the formulation of Christian character includes doing and not doing certain things. Relevant evidence of progress concerns what is observable by others, which may include outsiders as well as insiders (cf. 3:7). Moral practice (rather than inward virtue) is a hallmark of Stoic philosophy, following Aristotle, for whom inward virtue is more like a habit developed in a person only over time by a routine of moral practices (e.g., Plutarch, *Moralia* 75b-86a). In his famous essay "On Progress in Virtue," Plutarch extols the virtue of the person who stands up under his own scrutiny rather than is disdainful of himself as an incompetent "witness" (81a), which may help one appreciate Paul's concluding charge for Timothy to "pay close attention to yourself and to your teaching" (4:16a).

The concluding reminder is variously understood. Its plain sense clarifies Timothy's payoff when he follows Paul's prior exhortation: his future salvation from God's future judgment depends on the careful exercise of his charismatic leadership within the congregation (cf. James 3:1). To this point of the letter, Paul repeatedly confesses God as "our Savior," and salvation is realized according to God's desire and because of Christ's death (1:15; 2:4). In what sense, then, is Timothy responsible for his and his congregation's salvation? Human responsibility in working out God's salvation agrees with Paul's teaching, which stipulates that the believer is responsible to "work out" (*katergozomai*) her salvation in God's company and the fellowship of believers (see Phil. 2:12-13; 2 Tim. 4:1-7) and calls for self-examination (e.g., 2 Cor. 13:5; 1 Cor. 11:27-32) along with the dire consequence of failing to pass the test, which extends even to the apostle (1 Cor. 9:27). Moreover, the covenant-keeping shape of a community's salvation forces a distinction between the divine source of humanity's salvation and its future realization, which is based on works (cf. Rom. 2:6-11; 2 Cor. 5:10).

---

8. Johnson, *Letters to Timothy*, p. 253.

Paul's exhortation to Timothy assumes that it is also human performance that complements divine grace, which brings the living God's redemptive plan and thus "our hope" to realization (4:10; cf. 1 Cor. 10:32-33; 9:22). What is distinctive and perhaps confusing about this text is that the pastor cooperates with God's saving grace by engaging in ordained practices (4:14). This more vocational (as opposed to moral or religious) formulation of human agency is an important elaboration of Pauline soteriology, and it sets the stage for 2 Timothy, where this idea is given rich texture, especially by the worship practices and holy persona of Paul's faithful successor, whose responsibility is to safeguard and transmit the memory and message of Paul's apostolate.

Part 2: Engaging 1 Timothy 3:14–4:16 for Congregational Leaders

Not long ago I attended a service for the installation of a pastor. In my denomination this is a service in which a congregation and its newly called pastor make covenantal promises about their relationship as pastor and people in the household of God. The presiding body for such a service in my denomination is the regional judicatory, conference, or association, and the presiding officer at this service was the conference minister.

A high degree of informality and levity marked the entire service. The unspoken message seemed to be, "No solemnity here, folks!" When we came to the portion of the service that is described as the "exhortation," the conference minister played it for laughs, larding the words of the exhortation with sarcasm. She said, "We urge you, our brother, to warn the idle, encourage the timid, help the weak, and be patient with all" in such a way as to suggest that the words themselves were either hopelessly antiquated or simply ridiculous. If the tone wasn't sufficient to convey the trivializing message, facial expressions ("wink, wink") provided further punctuation.

As I listened, I was both bewildered and saddened. I wondered what kind of pain this church official had experienced that led her to articulate words such as "be patient with all" with such obvious sarcasm. I wondered what the laity who were present made of a conference minister treating — mistreating, really — the rites of installation of a pastor in this way. It does seem that we live in a time when solemnity is readily confused with pomposity, and formality is equated with lack of personal expression — and yet this was somehow wrong. What message did it convey to the congregation and guests from other churches about the ordained ministry and the church itself?

If this installation service conveyed a message, as I think it did — that there really isn't anything terribly serious or particularly important at stake here — the text before us in this chapter conveys precisely the opposite message. From the standpoint of a focus on pastoral leadership, this passage is the center of gravity, the pivot point, of 1 Timothy. Here Paul, against the backdrop of a pending "apostolic house call" (3:14), lays out for Timothy the heart of pastoral leadership, the challenges to be encountered, and the disciplines necessary for a faithful and fruitful ministry as a pastoral leader in the household of God. Far from being trivial or a laughing matter, Paul says that Timothy's performance of his office has eternal import and lasting consequences (4:16). If pastors have sometimes erred in the past by taking themselves too seriously, the antidote is not — as it was in the installation service I attended — to diminish the office with silliness. Perhaps pastors do need to take themselves a little less seriously; but they also need to take God, the church, and their calling far more seriously.

A brief summary of the exegesis and synopsis of the text may be helpful to readers at this point. Again, Paul sets the stage by referring to a pending visit, and this reminds readers of the occasion for the entire letter: Paul's absence and thus his instructions to Timothy as pastor and teacher of the congregation at Ephesus. Paul then describes Timothy's role in architectural images that are appropriate to his overall operative metaphor for the church as a "household." Timothy's role as "pillar and foundation of the truth" is grounded in another of the epistle's core faith affirmations regarding Jesus Christ in 1 Timothy 3:16.

This affirmation paves the way for a contrast between sound teaching and deceptive teaching, an indication of the consequences of such teaching, and an urging of Timothy toward faithful teaching to ensure the health of the household of God. In the final portion (vv. 7b-16), Paul exhorts Timothy to maintain a disciplined spiritual life and to give priority to essential tasks of ministry, leading to the conclusion in verse 16: "Tend to yourself and to your teaching; for by doing this you will save both yourself and your hearers."

In engaging this text for today's leaders, I want to begin here — at the end. I begin with the words "tend to yourself and to your teaching."

In some respects, this seems odd counsel for contemporary pastoral leaders. It may appear to be at odds with conventional wisdom about the nature of leadership, and pastoral leadership in particular, which emphasizes caring for others in their need and distress. Are not pastoral leaders those who by definition "tend to others"? Are they not those who have heard the words that Jesus directed to Peter in John 21: "Feed my lambs" and "Tend my sheep"? Aren't pastoral leaders those who, like Jesus himself, seeing the crowds, have "compassion for them, because they [are] harassed and helpless, like sheep without a shepherd" (Matt. 9:36)? Are not leaders other-oriented servants and shepherds of others, people who feel the pain and need of their human flock, and as such are characterized by their acute sensitivity to others? Yes and no.

Yes, compassion for others and for their needs is important in those who would be pastoral ministers and pastoral leaders. Martin Luther King Jr. was certainly right when he said, "Those whom we would change we must first love." And yet sometimes love, compassion, caring, and tending to others — like all virtues — can be taken to improper extremes. A genuine love of people is elemental to ministry, but self-knowledge, self-awareness, and what Edwin H. Friedman and others have described as "self-differentiation" is also crucial to pastoral leadership.

Paul's words "tend to yourself and to your teaching" resonate remarkably well with the insights of Friedman and Peter Steinke and others, whose work with congregations and pastoral leaders has been shaped by their study of social systems and groups and leaders' functioning. In his posthumously published work *A Failure of Nerve: Leadership in the Age of the Quick Fix,* Friedman, himself an ordained rabbi, writes of a "major shift" in his work with leaders. Instead of focusing on their expertise, their communication technique, or their skills in motivating others, Friedman began to look — in families, congregations, and work systems — for the person "who could express himself or herself with the least amount of blaming and the one who had the greatest capacity to take responsibility for his or her own emotional being and destiny." "I began," says Friedman, "to coach [that person] to be the leader. . . . I stopped trying to get people to 'communicate' or find better ways of managing their issues. Instead, I began to concentrate on helping the leader to become better defined and to learn how to deal adroitly with the sabotage that almost invariably follows any success in this endeavor. . . . It is the integrity of the leader that promotes the integrity or prevents the 'dis-integration' of the systems he or she is leading."[9]

In other words, Friedman discovered that it was crucial to the health of any system, including a congregation, to encourage the leader toward behaviors that may seem counterintuitive, that is, "tending to yourself." This does not mean a preoccupation with one's self; still less does it mean the kind of narcissistic behavior that characterizes some pastors. It does mean developing a capacity to "self-manage." One of Friedman's students, Peter Steinke, writes:

> The capacity to self-manage is sometimes referred to as being a "nonanxious presence". . . . The nonanxious presence is a description of how a person works to keep the center of control within oneself and as a way to affect relationships in a positive manner. To be a nonanxious presence, you focus on your own behavior and its modification rather than being preoccupied with how others function.

It's a bit like the admonition given to parents on airplanes: "Put on your own oxygen mask first, then assist your child." Or Paul's words to Timothy: "Tend to yourself."

For pastoral leaders, "tending to yourself" and "tending to others" are not matters of either/or, but of both/and. A good pastor not only does notice what is going on with others, but he or she wants to be attentive. And yet attentiveness to others and their needs cannot — should not — turn a pastor into someone who is overly reactive to others, a people-pleaser, or a need-filler. Capable pastors are those who are clear about their own values, identity, and calling. "A positive outcome will emerge," writes Steinke, "if the leader's presence and functioning is centered in principle, based on self-regulation, and anchored by taking thoughtful positions. Principle provides clarity; self-regulation helps to avoid extremes; thoughtful positions lead to necessary action."[10]

One might note how illuminating in this regard are the stories of the temptation of Jesus (Matt. 4:1-11; Luke 4:1-12). At a decisive point early in his ministry, following his baptism but before beginning his

---

9. Edwin H. Friedman, *A Failure of Nerve* (New York: Seabury, 2007), p. 19.

10. Peter L. Steinke, *Congregational Leadership in Anxious Times: Being Calm and Courageous No Matter What* (Herndon, VA: Alban, 2006), pp. 31, 65).

public ministry, Jesus was tested on precisely these issues. Who was he and who was he called to be? What does it mean to be the Son of God? Does he have the capacity to manage himself in the face of pressure and anxiety? Is his ministry centered in principle and in God? Leaders cannot eliminate or escape anxiety, whether it be their own or that of others. This is indicated by Satan's attempt to evoke anxiety in Jesus by asking, "If you are the Son of God, command these stones to become loaves of bread." Jesus locates his identity and ministry in God's calling, in principle, and in Scripture. "It is written, 'One does not live by bread alone but by every word that comes from the mouth of God'" (Matt. 4:3-4). Thus does he "tend to himself and to his teaching" (1 Tim. 4:16).

Throughout this particular text and the Pastoral Epistles, Paul's approach to pastoral leadership and his counsel to Timothy are consistent: Timothy is not to be preoccupied with others and their functioning. He is to be aware of deceptive teachers (4:1-2); he is to be aware of the needs of the most vulnerable (5:1-16) and of unruly members of the congregation (5:17-6:2). But, most of all, he is be focused on his own functioning, his way of life, his spiritual disciplines, and his teaching. Contemporary pastoral leaders are also wise to tend to themselves, to know themselves, to manage their own anxiety, to ground their ministry in principle, to examine their own teaching, and to base action on reflection. One is reminded of the Jesuit ideal for clergy: "Contemplation in action." A slightly different way to put this is to say simply that pastors are called to be leaders. Leaders are people who know themselves well, who are animated by core convictions, and who are capable of being sufficiently distinct from a group that they may help the group to gain clarity and make progress.

Today, sometimes Paul's exhortation "tend to yourself and to your teaching" has been reduced to what has almost become a cliché of "clergy self-care." Lillian Daniel has written recently of this subject:

> I do not think clergy need more lectures about self-care. It seems that at every ordination or installation service I attend there is a charge given about clergy self-care. One minister stands up and tells another minister that they know they are about to work themselves to death, so resist the temptation. "Take your day off . . . set boundaries . . . don't try to be all things to all people." All this is done in front of an audience of lay people who are supposed to be impressed that we clergy would need such a lecture. It has become a

cliche, and seems to have trumped prophecy, theology and the love of Jesus. . . . I would personally like to declare a moratorium on all clergy self-care conversations, in the interests of clergy self-care.[11]

"Tend to yourself and to your teaching" goes far beyond the tired and predictable admonitions of self-care! Having begun at the end of this text and pointed to a central theme and explored it in reference to Friedman and Steinke's work on leadership, let us then go back to the beginning of the text and note some of the other most urgent themes and insights for today's pastoral leader.

In an era when the ordained have been urged to be humble servants, wounded healers, enablers, and facilitators, Paul's call to Timothy to serve as the "pillar and foundation of the truth within the household of God" is striking. The tendency for several generations has been to downplay the role, power, and authority of clergy. In some respects, this is not only understandable but correct. Too often authority has been expressed in authoritarian and autocratic ways. Moreover, in many well-publicized cases, clergy have misused and abused their authority and the trust placed in them. Nevertheless, the answer is not to flee from proper authority or to disclaim all power. Rather, it is to exercise both authority and power wisely, judiciously, courageously, and temperately.

While it is certainly true that other members of a given congregation have important insight into the truth of the gospel and its implications, it is also true that the pastor-teacher of a congregation has the responsibility to pay consistent attention to a congregation's norms and its direction. If we play the metaphor out a little bit, we would note that a building that lacks either a solid foundation or a sturdy central pillar is fragile and subject to collapse in the event of storm or earthquake. So too, a congregation that lacks norms and center is fragile and vulnerable to both external and internal storms. In this respect, capable pastoral leadership provides both stability and orientation. It reminds us of the living tradition of which we are inheritors and stewards. It orients a congregation in the face of contemporary needs and challenges, providing a sense of direction, without which a congregation flounders. Performing these tasks in a time when people do not

11. Duke Divinity School, "Call and Response Blog," Center for Faith and Leadership, Feb. 12, 2009.

readily accede to external authority (and perhaps rightly so) is both challenging and delicate. Wise pastoral leaders manage to provide the foundation and central pillar in a way that supports the life of the whole congregation and enables its ministry. Paul did not tell Timothy, "You are the main stage or the star act." His role is a foundational and supportive one for the entire structure, for the entire household of God.

Paul does, however, move then to the one who is the focus, the featured attraction, and lead actor, Jesus Christ, "revealed in flesh and confirmed by the Spirit, seen by angels and proclaimed among the nations, believed worldwide and exalted in glory." As this hymnic acclamation moves back and forth between heaven and earth, flesh and spirit, it weaves a holistic Christology and not a dualistic one. It is not either heaven *or* earth, flesh *or* spirit, believed worldwide *or* exalted in glory — but both.

Why does Paul insist on such an emphasis, and with such repetition? Apparently because some were teaching "divergent doctrine" (1:3). Moreover, some were "adhering to deceptive spirits and doctrines of demons" (4:1). Such teaching, in need of correction, was dualistic. It invited its adherents to hold ordinary life and its expression in eating and food, marriage and sex, at a distance and with suspicion. "For example, they forbid marriage and eating foods that God has created to be received with thanksgiving . . ." (4:3). This kind of dualistic, world-denying spirituality seems to be a persistent threat to Christian faith and teaching. In a time when people are using the language of "spirituality" more frequently and comfortably, it may be important to remind congregations that ours is a "this-worldly spirituality," an "incarnate faith."

In his wonderful recent novel, entitled *Jayber Crow,* poet and Christian Wendell Berry points to the way such dualism has seeped into Christian teaching. Young Jayber, an orphan who has been sent to various schools, reflects on what he has heard:

> I took to studying the ones of my teachers who were also preachers, and also the preachers who came to speak in chapel and at various exercises. In most of them I saw the old division of body and soul that I had known at The Good Shepherd. The same rift ran through everything at Pigeonville College. . . . Everything bad was laid on the body, and everything good was credited to the soul. It

103

scared me a little when I realized I saw it the other way around. If the soul and body really were divided, then it seemed to me the worst sins — hatred and anger and self-righteousness and even greed and lust — came from the soul. But these preachers I'm talking about all thought the soul could do no wrong, but always had its face washed and its pants on and was in agony over having to associate with flesh and the world. And yet these same preachers believed in the resurrection of the body.[12]

Such theological dualism tends to send the church out of the world, trying to find a more spiritual one, rather than into this world in service to "the Word [that] has been made flesh and dwelt among us, full of grace and truth" (John 1:14).

In verses 4:7b-16, Paul addresses himself to the spiritual practices or disciplines of the pastoral leader, beginning with the words "train yourself for holy living." Again, he provides Timothy with a core theological teaching, a "you can take this one to the bank" kind of affirmation: "Our hope is set on the living God, who is the Savior of all people, especially those who believe." Here again, he emphasizes the *missio Dei*. God seeks to save everyone. The God who seeks this is a living God. And this God respects human freedom, for not all will believe. But the referent of Timothy's teaching is God, a God who is living, active, and at work in the world, a God who is up to something. And that something is spelled out: saving all people.

What follows then are a string of exhortations, all framed in the imperative, one after another: "Command," "Let no one despise," "Pay attention," "Do not neglect," "Practice," and "Tend." Taken together, these six provide both job description and way of life for the pastoral leader.

"Command compliance to these instructions and teach." In our time — depending on particular churches and denominations — "command" in its normal or implied meaning may be neither easy to pull off nor even advisable. Few pastors can simply give orders. But one can teach with a certain sense of confidence, with an air of command, while still embodying appropriate humility. In 2 Timothy we shall see that Paul is concerned that Timothy is perhaps overly restrained and timid. Indeed, many clergy today seem to fall prey to such a tentative

12. Wendell Berry, *Jayber Crow* (Washington, DC: Counterpoint Press, 2000), p. 49.

voice. Rather than a ringing declaration of faith, a "This I believe, here I stand, I can do no other," these clergy intone: "I think it might be possible, could be true, might be so." In preaching, the genre of proclamation, the bold declaration of what God has done, is doing, and promises to do seems to have vanished — at least in some quarters.[13] My perception is that many in congregations long for pastors who are passionate, who actually do believe something deeply and passionately. There are dangers here, of course. Passion is not a substitute for sound teaching. But without passion and conviction, sound teaching is unlikely to compel or convince — or perhaps even get a hearing.

Sometimes, but not always, such tentativeness is amplified by a particular personal characteristic that flies in the face of culturally established patterns of authority, whether age (as in Timothy's case) or gender (in the case of some women in ministry). Such culturally established markers, Paul indicates, are not to be heeded, because the work and the way of life of the pastoral leader are what matters. "Let no one despise your youth, but until I arrive set a pattern for believers in speech, in public conduct, in love, faith, and purity." In other words, pay attention to yourself and to your own way of being in the world. Again, Paul's emphasis is on self-management, self-awareness, and Timothy's controlling what he has control over — that is, his own behavior. Sometimes we clergy members get wrapped around the axle concerning the behavior of others. We can point it out. We can offer sound teaching. But we can't often change other people's behavior, at least not directly. But what we can change and pay attention to is our own behavior. And sometimes that is our very best point of leverage for supporting change in the congregation: taking responsibility for our own behavior, setting "a pattern for believers in speech, in public conduct, in love, faith, and purity."

Not only is a pastoral leader urged to a morally sound life and conduct, but Paul urges Timothy to give major attention to the major subjects of pastoral ministry. "Pay attention to public reading, preaching, and teaching" (4:13). There are many, many things one can do as a pastoral leader and minister. It is important early on to sort out the major from the minor subjects, and to avoid "majoring in the minors." The majors are public reading and interpretation of Scripture, preaching and teaching. Some have pointed to the so-called "80/20 rule," ac-

---

13. Paul Scott Wilson, *Setting Words on Fire* (Nashville: Abingdon, 2008).

cording to which 20 percent of what a person or group does yields 80 percent of the results, while 80 percent yields 20 percent. The trick is to focus on the 20 percent that produces 80 percent of the results. For most pastoral leaders, the 20 percent will be preaching and teaching. This is where you reach the most people. This is where you form the congregation's identity and mission and help people grow in the faith. This is not to say that pastoral work, board work, and community ministry are unimportant. They are not. But they do not substitute for a robust ministry of preaching and teaching.

It is my conviction that many preachers do not preach and teach enough, nor do Christians worship and study enough. Often preachers preach but once a week, and then for ten to twelve minutes. Some church members worship weekly, but many much less often. For congregations in a missional situation, this is too thin a diet. Think of Augustine preaching daily. Think of Wesley preaching five to six times on the Lord's Day. At some point in my ministry I made a shift from preaching the same sermon two times on Sunday, to preaching on Sunday and then a different sermon on Wednesday, as well as also teaching Bible studies twice a week. Rather than seeing that deplete me, I found more frequent preaching and teaching actually gave me more energy and material. Moreover, I felt that I was giving more time to the "majors" (the essentials) and less to the "minors."

"Tend to yourself and to your teaching; for by doing this you will save both yourself and your hearers." This entire text amplifies and underscores our core theme and thesis, which we introduced in chapter 1: that pastoral leaders are teachers of the faith, and that sound teaching is essential to healthy congregations. The subject of our teaching is the nature and purposes of God. The consequence of such teaching is "holy living" and congregations characterized by loving relationships.

DISCUSSION QUESTIONS

1. What relationship does Paul draw between the moral integrity of Timothy's character and the practices of his congregational ministry?

2. Compare and contrast Paul's advice, "Tend to yourself and your teaching," with the contemporary emphasis on "self-care."

Order (and Disorder) in the Household of God

1 Timothy 5:1–6:2

1 *Do not rebuke an older man harshly. Encourage him as though he were your father, younger men as though brothers, 2 older women as though mothers, and younger women as though sisters, with complete purity.*

3 *Care for widows who are truly needy. 4 But if a particular widow has children or a relative, they should first learn to practice their piety by taking care of their own household and so repay their parents; for this pleases God. 5 If truly needy and completely on her own, the widow puts her hope in God and pleas and prays continually night and day. 6 But the one who lives extravagantly dies even though alive. 7 Instruct these things so that they will be blameless. 8 Especially if someone does not care for a member of his household, he repudiates the faith and is worse than an unbeliever.*

9 *Enroll widows older than sixty, wife of one husband, 10 a reputation for good works — she has raised children, practiced hospitality, washed the feet of believers, helped those during difficult times, accompanied by all kinds of good works. 11 But decline [to enroll] younger widows, for when they are distracted from Christ and choose to marry, 12 judgment results because they invalidate the prior confession of faith. 13 Moreover, by going from house to house they learn laziness, and not only laziness but how to gossip and meddle, saying things they shouldn't. 14 Therefore, I prefer that younger widows marry, raise children, keep house, to give the oppo-*

nent no opportunity to slander us; 15 for some have already turned away to follow Satan.

16 If any female believer has widows, she should care for them and not burden the church in order that it can help other widows who are truly needy.

17 Request a double honorarium for elderly men who lead well, especially those who labor in public speaking and teaching. 18 For the Scripture says, "Do not muzzle the ox that is threshing" and "The worker is worthy of his wages." 19 Do not respond to an accusation leveled against an elder if not confirmed "by two or three witnesses." 20 Discipline those who sin before the entire congregation in order to provoke fear in those present. 21 Bring testimony before God, Christ Jesus and the elect angels in order that you will discharge these instructions without prejudice and without making a biased claim. 22a Do not ordain anyone hastily.

22b Do not share in the sins of others. Keep yourself pure. 23 Stop drinking just water but use a little wine for your upset stomach and frequent illnesses! 24 The sins of some folks are blatant, leading to judgment, while others follow close behind; 25 on the other hand, the good works of still others are obvious and cannot remain hidden from view.

6:1 Those who carry the yoke of slavery must respect their own masters as deserving every honor so that the name of God and the Teaching may not be reviled. 2 Those who have believers as masters must not despise them because they are brothers; rather, they must serve them more faithfully since the recipients of good work are beloved believers.

Part 1: Engaging 1 Timothy 5:1–6:2 as Scripture

Paul's next instructions to Timothy codify rules of engagement that order household relationships "with complete purity" (5:1-2). In agreement with biblical tradition, Paul pays attention to the welfare of those widows who are "truly needy" and require financial support (5:3-10, 16), and to those who are young and vulnerable to spiritual disaffection.

They require the support of a family household or patron to concentrate their talent and energy (5:11-16).

From elderly widows, the next instructions concern the household's elderly men *(presbyteroi)* — "who lead well." These instructions also elaborate the organizing principle introduced in 5:1. Those engaged in ministry should be fairly compensated (5:17-18), and those accused of malpractice should be fairly judged (5:19-22a). Negotiating the congregation's law court is tricky business, especially for someone viewed as inexperienced — as Timothy might have been viewed. Spiritual and physical health is good preparation (5:22b-23), even though sometimes the wisest course of action is to wait patiently on the consequences of another's action before passing verdict on it (5:24-25). The final group — and perhaps most controversial to today's readers — regards the slaves of a Christian household, who are to be treated as "brothers," even as they "must respect their own masters," as regulated by "the Teaching" (6:1-2b).

These instructions are of a piece with other household codes found in this letter that arrange human relationships according to the "economy of God" (see 1:4b). Significantly, central to the political ideology of antiquity is the well-run family household, which is a necessary condition of civil and competent society. Likewise, an orderly congregation of believers is a necessary condition for maintaining a covenant-keeping relationship with God. Such cooperation with God envisions a keen sense of responsibility toward other members, like that mapped out in the prior passage, in which Timothy's faithfulness is a measure of his future salvation (4:16). Relatives who fail to care for needy widows are as good as unbelievers (v. 8), and younger widows whose devotion to Christ is displaced by self-interest lose their religion and presumably their salvation (vv. 11-12).

Moreover, the manner of responsible care for the household's membership has a salutary effect on outsiders who find the virtuous widow "blameless" (v. 7; cf. 3:2, 7), and the younger widow who remarries rather than reject Christ squelches the opponent's slander (v. 14). This mixture of responsible care for insiders and conscientious regard for the opinion of outsiders (v. 10) is characteristic of Paul's household code, which reflects extraordinary sensitivity to people of all ages under the banner of God's desire to save everyone (1 Tim. 2:3-4).

The repetition of purity (5:2, 22b; cf. 4:12) in reference to the young indicates a core emphasis of these instructions. Most commentators think that the call to purity indicates that there was a particular threat to the congregation's reputation, probably sexual, and the likely source was the congregation's youth.[1] "With complete purity," therefore, is a code phrase for chastity. One might well understand that the subtext of Paul's subsequent instructions about younger widows who pursue new husbands without any thought of Christ (vv. 11-15) is anticipated by this charge. But that hardly means that the subsequent exhortation for Timothy to "keep yourself pure" (5:22b) is similarly motivated. The particular application in Timothy's case is purity of discernment in administrative matters. Purity, then, is what safeguards responsible decisions, whether those decisions are about marriage or management of a congregation's jurisprudence.

Paul prefaces his instruction regarding widows with a general principle of social manners within God's household (see Titus 2:1-6). The principle is a departure from the more intimate codes of Ephesians and Colossians, which order spousal and parental duties. In his moral instruction, Paul targets various age groups of both genders that would make up a household (rather than parts of a "body," the principal metaphor of a Christian congregation elsewhere in the Pauline canon). The word for "older man" *(presbyteros)* is translated with respect to age and gender, even though the ecclesiastical sense of a congregation's ruling "elders" is in play in 4:14. This repetition of *presbyteros* does imply an interpenetration of household and ecclesiastical social structures and roles, which substantially thickens its metaphorical use. In both cases, order is maintained via mutual respect rather than via abusive force. In this regard, the force of contrasting injunctions — sharp rebuke and exhortation, a quintessentially Pauline formula of pastoral care — shapes every working relationship within the household.

The members of primary concern for an orderly congregation are its widows (5:3-16). In part, this concern reflects Paul's scrupulous attention to the Jewish Torah (cf. 1:8-10), which demands that the faithful community take special care of its widows and orphans, those most vulnerable to the vicissitudes of life (cf. Exod. 22:22; Deut. 14:29; Zech. 7:9-10). The Letter of James, which reflects this same concern, considers the care for widows in distress a hallmark of the religion approved by God (James 1:27; cf. Acts 6:1-7). James's concern for the treat-

---

1. Josephus, *Against Apion* 2.198.

ment of widows adds another layer to the household motif. Roman law declared that, if a dowry was paid at marriage, the widow would be provided for by the new head of her deceased husband's household — usually her son. If there was no son or the household was dissolved, then the proceeds of its sale would repay the dowry, and the widow would be returned to her parents. Of course, if there was no dowry paid, and there was no family to which a widow could return — as evidently is the case for the "widows indeed" — then a subsistence stipend was to be provided to the widow by the city-state (in this case, Ephesus). Essentially, the code we have here in 1 Timothy is Paul's attempt to structure the congregation's welfare system according to Judaism's Torah rather than Roman law (cf. Acts 6:1-6; 9:39; James 1:26-27; see also Luke 7:11-17).

The congregation's widows are divided into three groups: (1) those who are "truly needy," whose age precludes remarriage, who lack the financial support of an extended family, and whose piety is exemplary (5:3, 7, 9-10); (2) those who should expect financial support from their children (5:4, 8, 16); and (3) those who are still young and can expect to remarry (5:11-15). We have translated the initial word as "care," which frames this entire passage: the congregation shoulders the responsibility to *care for* these widows. This same word is often translated "honor": it is welfare for an honorable reason. In this first case, widows supported by the congregation are financially needy, and caring for them is a sign of an "honorable" congregation's "good works" (v. 10) and religious devotion (v. 5). In fact, because her "hope is in God," to whom she continually prays, the widow's welfare is not viewed as exploitation but as an answer to prayer.

The practice of putting people "on a list" (5:9) is well known from Hellenistic literature: mercenary soldiers signed on to wage Rome's wars by adding their names to a general's list (Herodotus, *Persian War* 1:59; 7:1). Likewise, new initiates were added to the rolls of a religious group (*Oxyrhynchus Papyrus* 416), or newly elected members to the Senate's roster (Plutarch, *Life of Pompey* 13:7). This registry of widows in need of the congregation's material support has less to do with keeping a public record of who are really "widows indeed" than with encouragement to follow the protocol of discernment that Paul stipulates.

In this regard, among a widow's qualifications are her age and faithfulness: she is "not less than sixty years old" and "the wife of one man" (5:9; cf. 3:2), an evidence of fidelity. Paul is appealing to contemporaneous actuarial tables for defining an age beyond which women could not remarry or be expected to do hard work. Moreover, in Roman society the ideal of one marriage for women was honored (Livy, *Roman History*, 10.23.9); this was also true of Judaism, in which a widow's not remarrying would provide additional evidence of marital fidelity to her now deceased husband and of devotion to the Lord (cf. Judith 8:4; 16:22; Luke 2:36-38). Paul is concerned that the congregation, whose vocation is to engage the wider culture with the gospel, not be at odds with social convention. At the same time, his concern is that widows supported by the congregation be known for their Christian character, which is indicated by their piety (5:5) and "good works" (5:10). The catalog of virtues found in verse 10 is bracketed by "good works," which is thematic of the Christian life in the Pastoral Epistles and characteristic of the public operations of divine grace.[2] The presence of the exemplary widow within the congregation not only occasions the congregation's hallmark activity but is also a personal reminder of God's "great grace" that resides in its midst (cf. Acts 4:32-35).

Even though the social convention of Paul's day — very nearly into the modern period — was that "younger widows" did not seek to remarry, the verbal mood of verse 14 is active: "I prefer that younger widows marry." His exhortation is for widows of marriageable age to actively seek a Christian husband as a necessary good. Paul supposes that this kind of remarried widow will be more likely to avoid the unseemly behaviors described in 5:11-13, and that would "give the opponent no opportunity to slander us." The "opponent" in this case is probably Satan (v. 15), God's principal antagonist, whom Paul borrowed from his Jewish apocalyptic background. Rather than being a reflection of his world's misogyny, his instruction is set against idlers (v. 13; cf. Titus 1:10-12), who are easily perceived by outsiders as morally lax (cf. Aristotle, *Nicomachean Ethics* 1097b). As for the reference to the "idle" younger widows, this almost certainly would have carried a sexual connotation in Paul's world (5:11; cf. Dio Cassius, *Roman History* 47:15.4; 53:2.4), which would have subverted the integrity of the gospel.

The chief threat to the spiritual vitality of younger widows is expressed by a compound verb, *katastrēniasōsin*, whose meaning is very difficult to determine (v. 11). The prefix *kata-* aims the reader toward

---

2. I. Howard Marshall, *The Pastoral Epistles* (ICC) (Edinburgh: T. & T. Clark, 1999), pp. 227-31.

practices that are "against" Christ, and then to an earlier "confession of faith" that these believers had made to or about him (v. 12). The verbal root *strēniaō* denotes a strong compulsion or inclination toward some desire, in this case to get married. We have translated the verb as "distracted" to convey a relational sense: pursuit of a marital relationship is at the expense of a relationship with Christ. If this is the case, then "Christ" in this passage refers to the living Christ rather than to "Christology," or a body of beliefs about Christ (such as found in 1 Tim. 3:16) that are jeopardized by a different preoccupation. What is imperiled is a prior confession of faith in Christ, which must have included a vow of single-minded devotion similar to that embodied in the older widows (v. 10). This concern is similar to what Paul expresses in 1 Corinthians 7, both in its preference to remain unmarried to better serve the interests of Christ, but also in allowing those to marry rather than to be distracted by sexual desire (1 Cor. 7:8-9). Against the backdrop of this earlier Pauline text, the subsequent and apparently contradictory instruction to marry (v. 14) must be understood as the pastoral solution for the believer whose pronounced desire to find a husband now imperils her life with Christ (vv. 11-12).

Finally, the vague reference to the believer who "has widows" (v. 16) has been variously interpreted, despite the efforts of scribes' additions to the text to make its intent more clear. Paul uses the feminine form of "believer" *(pistē)*, which indicates that the instruction is aimed in particular at the Christian woman. Most interpreters qualify the widows as her relatives, extending the earlier injunction that families should take care of their own. In this sense, to "have widows" in the family implies a responsibility toward them. While this reading is certainly plausible and continues the letter's interest in the financial responsibility of middle-class Christian women (cf. 2:10; 6:17-19), it does not explain why this instruction is necessary, since it repeats a point made earlier (v. 8), nor why it focuses exclusively on female disciples.

Perhaps it is better to assume the most common sense of "have" as "to possess" or "to own" something. That is, this instruction is directed at wealthy female Christians (cf. 2:9), and not their husbands, whose personal servants are widows for whom they are directly responsible as members of their extended household. The scope of the earlier rule is here expanded to include nonfamilial relationships within the household. This is consistent with Paul's *paraenesis* (a genre of literature specializing in practical instructions), in which the traditional hierarchy of household relationships in the Jewish-Roman world is reset to embody the mutuality that exists in Christ (Gal. 3:28; Col. 3:11) as a real-world microcosm of the economy of God, whose aim is love (cf. 1:4-5), especially in those social relationships where abuse is likely. It would also seem to bring balance in the subsequent instruction aimed at household slaves in 6:1-2.

Just as Paul's earlier instructions concentrate on widows, presumably because of the community's special responsibility toward them, here, too, he has a particular group of older men in mind: those who lead the congregation and especially those who have assumed important and sometimes difficult public roles (v. 17). Leadership within middle-class households of antiquity was typically determined by gender (male) and age (elderly), and this social norm here extends to God's household, even if Paul is probably less concerned about chronological age than spiritual maturity (3:6; 4:12).

Payment of a "double honorarium" is consistent with the congregation's policy of the financial support given its older members. The formula "for the Scripture says" (5:18) introduces Deuteronomy 25:4 (Septuagint): "Do not muzzle the ox that is threshing," which, when combined with "the worker is worthy of his wages," probably recalls instructions regulating the fair compensation of priests (cf. Num. 18:31 [Septuagint]). Paul uses a well-known device of rabbinical rhetoric, first appealing to Scripture's lesser claim — in this case the use of a farm animal — to prove Scripture's ultimate claim, in this case a fair wage for a person laboring in the gospel ministry. That is, if we generally treat beasts of burden fairly, then how much more should we treat fairly those teaching elders who labor in God's behalf. Significantly, Jesus uses a similar wisdom when instructing his disciples for mission (see Luke 10:7). The resulting intertext between 1 Timothy 5:18b and Luke 10:7b lends Christ's support to the principle of fair compensation for those who "labor in public speaking and teaching" (5:17).

The support of the congregation's teaching elders is of a piece with its support of teaching widows of a similar age, who were added to the welfare roll in part because of their "good works" (see 5:10). In this next case, their good works are "public speaking and teaching" (v. 17). Not only would competence in public speaking be considered a sine qua non for effective leadership in antiquity; the distinction between the two activities regards their different audiences and intentions, the first directed toward outsiders and the second to the church. And this is hard work! The word used for "labor" *(kopiaō)* portrays the kind of sweaty exertion that exacts a physical toll on a daily laborer.

While nothing is said about a list of elders approved for financial support (5:9), a similar scrupulousness of attention is required of Timothy that concludes with a sparse warning against the hasty ordination of an unfit elder (v. 22a). As before with the widows, Paul's instruction not only concerns the quality of work performed but also the elder's character: those guilty of sin are unfit to lead a congregation (v. 20).

In a protocol of jurisprudence (5:19-22), Paul sets out guidelines for determining the congregation's financial support of its elders (5:17-18). Again, following Scripture's injunction regarding the gathering of credible evidence (5:19; cf. Deut. 19:15), Paul instructs Timothy not to "receive an accusation against an elder" in the absence of multiple witnesses (5:19). If the evidence proves him guilty, such a verdict would presumably disqualify him from congregational leadership and financial support. The purpose of this procedure is not the spiritual repair of a guilty party (as, for instance, with Jesus' protocol of discipline set out in Matt. 18:15-17) but a spiritual doctrine of deterrence in which the public shame of a disgraced elder provokes the congregation's fear of a similar fate.

The appropriation of a familiar Old Testament trope — in which God's prophet cross-examines Israel before a heavenly court that includes God, who renders a guilty verdict based on the evidence before executing a fair punishment — functions as a cautionary note to Timothy not to preside over a kangaroo court. A trial before an impartial God, who fairly considers all relevant evidence (cf. Sir. 35:12 [Septuagint]; Rom. 2:11; 1 Pet. 1:17), requires an impartial handling of the evidence. The presence of "the elect angels" in this heavenly court is a curious detail but perhaps trades on the connection in apocalyptic literature (which Paul knew) between the angelic guardians of God's elect people and their perseverance into the coming age. In this case, Paul's implication is that Timothy's attentiveness to this sacred jurisprudence helps to ensure the congregation's salvation (see 4:16). To blithely ordain (literally, "lay hands on") an elder (5:22a), or to exonerate him in a careless fashion, is subversive of a congregation's perseverance to the end.

Timothy's most urgent responsibility as the apostle's delegate is to monitor the application of the economy of God to the congregation's loving relationships (cf. 1:3-5). Since this vocation requires character as well as competence (cf. 1:5), a public protocol that ensures the selection of effective leaders melds naturally into more personal instruction headed by the exhortation "keep yourself pure" (5:22b; cf. 4:12; 5:2). Paul juxtaposes the two for good reason. Timothy's youth is no doubt perceived by some in the congregation as inexperience or lack of wisdom. Perhaps even Paul sees the perception of Timothy's immaturity as a liability in gaining the congregation's confidence during the sometimes tricky negotiations of a disciplinary proceeding where the sin of an accused elder was not self-evident (cf. 5:24-25). And if the issue is Timothy's nerve (cf. 2 Tim. 1:6-7), the "use of a little wine" would have been viewed as medicinal. Greco-Roman physicians prescribed wine for a "nervous stomach," and the Talmud stipulates wine as the "first among medicines" (b. B. Bat., 58b; cf. b. Ber. 35b).

Timothy's reluctance to drink wine, even if for medicinal reasons, has been widely attributed to the cultural setting: drinking "too much wine" is a mark of those who lack the virtue to lead (3:8). But the reason could be theological. Indeed, the asceticism that Paul has already demonized (4:1-4) may be a subtext here: perhaps Timothy's anxiety is not the point at all, but rather that Paul is once again reminding the congregation — or those misguided teachers who are eavesdropping on Paul's letter — that wine, like food and marriage, is the good gift of a benevolent Creator.

But there is yet another possibility set within canonical context. If the canonical Paul — the Paul whose memory and message support the tradition Timothy is to safeguard for the next generation (see 6:20; 2 Tim.) — shapes the portrait of the Paul of Acts, who enjoins the practices of the Nazirites (which include strict abstinence from wine) to demonstrate his faithfulness to his Jewish heritage (Acts 18:18; 21:26; cf. Num. 6:1-21), perhaps Timothy is inclined as faithful protégé to follow his example. Paul's exhortation, then, intends to grant Timothy a dispensation from his Nazirite vow of abstinence for reasons of ill health.

But even with a glass of wine in hand to settle an upset stomach, the best test of Timothy's fitness is to discern between the sinner who needs rebuke and repair and the saint who needs support and encouragement. Assessing people is the truck-and-trade of Timothy's job description. Appropriately, then, Paul gives the final instruction (vv. 24-25) in the third person as though it were axiomatic. The contrast between obvious and hidden, whether regarding sin or good works, would seem to suggest that Timothy must wait on the consequences of behavior before assessing it. What is blatantly sinful or conspicuously good is not difficult for people to measure; however, the full effect of what is hidden from public scrutiny is more difficult to discern. Rather enigmatically, Paul reminds Timothy that the consequences of what one does "cannot remain hidden from view"; perhaps they could be hidden from Timothy, but not from the heavenly tribunal of "God, Christ Jesus and the elect angels" (v. 21; cf. Heb. 4:12-13).

Since most middle-class urban households of the Roman world included household slaves, moral codes typically included instructions to govern their responsibilities and conduct. Paul does not include additional instructions about the congregation's or Timothy's responsibilities toward slaves, and some think that this is because the membership of urban congregations like this one consisted mostly of slaves. I doubt that Paul intended to imply this, especially since the letter also includes instructions for its middle-class members (e.g., 6:17-19). What is remarkable about this version of the traditional household code is the motive for good conduct: slaves are to serve their masters well so that "the Teaching" may not be reviled (6:1), and believing masters are to be served even "more faithfully" (6:2).

For some Christians, this passage, with its vivid image of "the yoke of slavery," has made it a "text of terror"; indeed, few others in the Pauline canon evoke the inward, even visceral, conflict that this one does. While we approach this text as one sanctified by the Spirit for sacred ends — and thus refuse to decanonize it — we do so with full recognition that it has been used throughout its history to support slave practices that dehumanize fellow humans and prevent loving communion with them, in disobedience to Christ's command. The fact that no reciprocating virtue is demanded of slave masters, who are in fact viewed as roughly analogous to God in this instruction, may lead readers to use this text to endorse a social hierarchy that sanctions the oppression of other humans for God's sake. We consider that blasphemous. At the very least, before offering a theological explanation that elaborates certain aspects of the Apostolic Rule, we must seek first the plain sense of its particular prescription.

Because most middle-class households in the Greco-Roman world included slaves, traditional conduct codes included rules that reflected their duties. The congregation that Paul addresses with instructions in 1 Timothy evidently included household slaves, which the reader should expect, because slavery was integral to the economy of

Roman urban society. Slaves were often well educated, were tutors, and exercised enormous influence in shaping the daily routines of the household. At the very least, Paul seems alert to the effect the gospel might have on working relationships between household slaves and their masters, which might in turn undermine the congregation's influence on the wider culture. In fact, the reader may allow that this instruction in particular reflects, perhaps uncritically, a missional concern for the outsider referred to throughout the letter.

Paul addresses two different slave-master relationships. In the first case (v. 1a), some slaves belong to a nonbelieving "master." Once again, Paul begins with an exhortation for the congregation to give "honor" to a social group (cf. 5:3, 17). In this case, however, some of those honored do not belong to the congregation, but they own slaves who do: that is, they are the pagan masters of Christian slaves, an awkward social relationship. The honor due them, in this case, is not financial, since they are outsiders with no evident need of support. Nonetheless, the extravagant description of a working relationship with such a master is striking and is suggestive of an ironic subtext.

The master is called *despotēs*, a word used elsewhere in Scripture to refer to God's sovereign rule over the world's affairs (cf. Luke 2:29; Acts 4:24), whether of God's providential care of creation (a motif in the Wisdom literature) or to justify the severe consequence of disobedience (cf. Isa. 1:24; 10:33). In addition, the layer of the adjectives *pas* and *axios* added to the noun for "personal honor" (literally, "every worthy honor") creates the allusion to a master with absolute power — negatively, a "despot" — whose exalted status deserves the respect of those under his authority. But the true motive of the Christian servant's regard is loyalty to the world's real *despotēs*, who is the one and only God (cf. 1:4b, 17). This irony is implied by "the Teaching," which in combination with "the name of God" refers to Paul's teaching about God: "healthy doctrine," which is considered the community's norm. This doctrine is succinctly set out in 1 Timothy 2:3-6: the Christian's master is the one God, who is "our Savior." To discredit this teaching by careless or unprofessional conduct is to subvert the gospel and thus the means by which the world is put to rights.

A more surprising concern is reflected by a second kind of slave-master relationship (in v. 2), one that stands outside a traditional household code. The situation in which "familiarity breeds contempt" between a Christian slave and Christian master is hardly sociological;

rather, the problem is theological. It is roughly similar to what Paul works out in his letter to Philemon: What is the nature of a slave-master relationship within the household of God? To what extent is the institution of slavery undermined because of Christian faith? Surely the radical egalitarian significance of Paul's gospel, memorably articulated in Galatians 3:28, would unsettle things when applied to a hierarchical arrangement. Slaves might naturally come to despise their Christian masters if the latter refused to emancipate as a Christian practice, and would prefer to be treated with honor by the pagan master of verse 1.

But the use of the intimate "brothers" reverses the move found in Philemon, where the master is pressured to resist the societal norms and to treat his runaway slave as a "dear brother." The present instruction is so shocking to the modern reader precisely because Paul is asking the slave to regard his master as a dear brother in order to maintain a cultural norm that seems antithetical to "the Teaching" and to transform one's faithful servitude into a Christian practice. It is not the honorable master who is responsible for righting a broken relationship, even though he would be in a position of power to do so legally; rather, it is the powerless slave who is to take responsibility for a ministry of reconciliation.

Perhaps a way forward is guided by the literary shape of this passage, which sandwiches the cautionary note about reviling Christian teaching about God (v. 1b) between parallel instructions regarding a Christian slave's relationship with two different kinds of masters, pagan (v. 1a) and Christian (v. 2). That is, the congregation's witness to "the name of God and the Teaching" is located at some risk in a believer's most difficult social relationships, whether with other Christians or unbelievers.

The odd reference to "the Teaching" is crucial for negotiating this social practice. The "name of God," which is a trope for God's reputation in the world, is linked to the community's religious curriculum, probably consisting of the "healthy doctrine" that supplies the working grammar for Paul's gospel of God (cf. 1:10-11). That is, what is most worrisome about disruptive relationships within the household of believers is not only that God's reputation is slandered by such behavior but that they are corrosive of a Pauline apostolate, which is the custodian of right teaching about God. And it is this worry that grounds the catholicity of this sacred text rather than a particular prescription shaped by the social institutions of a Roman world that is far removed from its current readers.

A final cautionary note must be sounded. Twomey's description of the slave catechisms in antebellum America, composed by Christian masters to support a profitable social institution, included this text for its biblical justification, and illustrates the danger of applying biblical prescriptions to every social location.[3] Surely the use of an interpreted text must be avoided when its effect subverts Scripture's performance in cultivating loving communion with God and all other humans. For this reason, the catholicity of this sacred text is better placed not on its address to those under "the yoke of slavery," which too easily misses the irony of Paul's injunction and is transformed into a political reason for one to control another, but on the subsequent purpose clause, "that the name of God and the Teaching may not be reviled." Herein lies the real purpose of this letter for every reader and every working relationship.

Part 2: Engaging 1 Timothy 5:1–6:2 for Congregational Leaders

I had never concerned myself much with a congregation's bylaws, those documents that prescribe what each board or committee of the congregation is for, who can serve on it and for how long, and generally how a church is to do its business. All of that — committees, terms, officers, meeting dates, quorums, and on and on — seemed somehow pedestrian to me when I was a young pastor. I was into the important stuff: preaching, teaching theology, community ministry, and pastoral care. Who cares about the bylaws? I didn't. Moreover, it seemed to me that those who did care a great deal about church bylaws were far more enthusiastic and knowledgeable about the bylaws than they were about Scripture. The bylaws were often trotted out as a way of quenching the Spirit, or so it seemed to me as a young pastor.

As time in ministry went on and I had the opportunity to work with other congregations as a consultant or teacher, I developed some different perceptions about church governance and bylaws. I noticed that bylaws, the rules of the road for congregational life, became important, by and large, when there was a crisis. The pastor has resigned — what do we do now? Check the bylaws. The senior minister and the organist are at each other's throats, each insisting they are in charge of

---

3. Jay Twomey, *The Pastoral Epistles through the Centuries* (Chichester, UK: Wiley-Blackwell, 2009), pp. 93-94.

worship — what do we do now? Let's see if the bylaws are of any help. There's conflict because the board of trustees has told the church council that, though there is money in the bank, they can't spend it on what they deem a crucial mission initiative because it isn't theirs to spend. What do the bylaws say about the jurisdiction and authority of the trustees and the council? You get the idea. We mostly pay attention to the bylaws when there is a crisis. This may not be the only or even the best way forward at such times, but it does provide some guidance and direction that is impartial, and as such, helpful.

Not only did I notice, as time and experience gathered, that congregations often paid attention to their bylaws when problems or crises developed. I noticed something else: congregations that paid little heed to their bylaws were in a state of perpetual crisis, chronic conflict, and steady decline. I remember one congregation that was all in a tizzy about the kind of music that was being used in worship — and thus about the music director. Everyone, it seemed, had an opinion on the matter, and most were strongly held opinions. Moreover, every person seemed to think that it was his or her business to be in on the decision of what the music should be, who the music director should be, and how the situation should be handled. Meeting with the congregation's board, I tried to determine who actually employed the music director and to what person or group that person was accountable.

"What do your bylaws say?" I asked. From the looks on people's faces, it was clear no one had thought to look.

"Well, we don't really take the bylaws seriously here," someone said. "We're much more informal. We're like a family." She said this with some pride, as if their church were too free-spirited, special, or unique to need "rules of the road."

I thought to myself, *Yeah, you're like a family all right — a highly dysfunctional family.* I suggested that they might be suffering from "sloppy agape" — love and good intentions that were disordered and without clarity or accountability — and that they would do well to determine who had what role and responsibility (and authority) in the situation they were now facing.

To use a different metaphor, I have noticed that congregations that are not clear about how their households are ordered, or do not respect the given patterns of order, often function in a way that is similar to six-year-olds playing soccer — better known as "bunch ball." Everyone runs to the ball, creating a scrum in which kids flail away in the direction of the ball. What happens is that shins get kicked a lot, kids start to wail, and the ball doesn't move much. If the ball happens to squirt out of the pack, there's no one out there to pick it up because everyone is bunched up. My mantra as a soccer coach became, "Play your position." When a soccer team's members play their position, they are much more effective at moving the ball down the field. But playing your position requires that there are known and assigned positions (by-laws) and that there is discipline. Discipline means that, instead of rushing to the ball, you play your position and trust your teammates to play theirs. When kids get this and see that it works, it has the quality of a revelation.

Often in congregations, particularly ones that are stuck or declining, people have bought into the idea that everyone needs to be in on every decision or that everyone has a right to put her or his oar in the water (to mix in yet another metaphor) about every big or little thing. We may sanction this with appeals to participation, inclusion, and equality, but the result is often bunch ball — with its sore shins, little progress on the issues, and frustration. There is no order in the household of God. It's a mess.

Christian ethicist Larry Rasmussen has addressed himself to the matter of the importance of order in the household of God this way:

> Governance is a crucial part of our life together for at least two reasons. One reason is simple: life is a mess. It is not only a mess. Some of it is a mess all the time, all of it is a mess some of the time, and disordered houses do not stand. Just as our bodies do poorly without food, bodies politic do poorly without governance. Communities, in order to be communities, must be ordered, cared for, fed. The other reason is equally noted: governance is necessary for the positive flourishing of life.[4]

"Disordered houses do not stand." As we have pointed out, the "household" is precisely the metaphor that 1 Timothy uses for the church. This text is "household code": it is about ordering the household of God. It provides direction for Timothy and the congregation on how to order their life together so that the mess of life doesn't take

---

4. Larry Rasmussen, "Shaping Communities," in Dorothy C. Bass, ed., *Practicing Our Faith: A Way of Life for a Searching People* (San Francisco: Jossey-Bass, 1997), p. 120.

charge and so that there is a positive flourishing of life in loving relationships — to the glory of God.

Order is important. Rules of the road are important. Governance matters. Bylaws matter insofar as they help us have order, avoid disorder, and function fairly and openly. If all of this sounds a bit too old-fashioned and uptight, then consider the newfound popularity of the concept of "boundaries" with respect to congregations, and particularly pastors. Having "good boundaries" means that persons or groups understand their role and responsibilities. Persons with good boundaries know where they stop and others begin. They take responsibility for their own words, feelings, and actions. They know, for example, the difference between being a pastor and being a friend. They know the difference between being a pastor and being intimate in ways that are inappropriate and abusive. People — and pastors — who do not know and mind their boundaries are a source of confusion and pain. When people in a congregation do not understand and respect boundaries, they not only feel unsafe, they *are* unsafe. "Boundaries" is simply another way of talking about order. Pastors, church staff members, congregational leaders, or officials — or even church members — who do not understand and respect their role and responsibilities, the given boundaries that come with it, cause confusion and havoc that hurts people and may, in extreme situations, destroy a congregation.

But let's put it positively: Where there is *good* order, reliable governance, clarity about roles and responsibilities, and attention to appropriate boundaries, a congregation and its members tend to flourish. There is a sense of reliability and safety that allows a congregation to feel confident in the face of challenge and change. In this sense, good governance and administration is very much a form or aspect of pastoral care.

Sometimes pastors, preachers, and congregations have discounted the Pastoral Epistles because these Letters do pay attention to order, church discipline, roles, and responsibilities. Like me when I was a young pastor, this has all seemed a little pedestrian, unimaginative, prosaic. Give me the great biblical stories, creativity in worship, innovation in mission. Indeed, all of those are important. But so are governance, boundaries, clarity of roles, and responsibilities — even bylaws. These are, to use a metaphor from Friedman and Steinke, crucial parts of a congregation's "immune system," which protects the body (the congregation) from infection and sickness.

Several predictable kinds of infection or illness do beset congregations frequently today, especially when there is a deficiency of order, clarity, or "rules of the road." I've mentioned one already: "sloppy agape." In the name of concern and compassion, all members make everything their business. Decisions made by one authorized group are unmade by another — unauthorized — group because, well, "We don't do things that way here," or "This would hurt so-and-so's feelings."

If "sloppy agape" — not paying attention to order and boundaries in the name of caring — is one common disorder, another might be termed "pastor master." That inelegant phrase (by which we do not suggest that the behavior is limited to male pastors, because female clergy can do this as well) means that the only order is whatever the pastor says it is. Everything must be done that person's way, and often in order to make that person feel needed, flattered, or appreciated. No one can question the pastor; otherwise, they become an "enemy." No one can exercise authority except the pastor. There are no "rules of the road" to which to appeal — just the personality and dictates of the pastor. If the disorder that causes the house to fall is sometimes care or concern run amuck, other times it is the congregation where the pastor's needs are so great that it is only about the (often charismatic) leader — the "pastor master." The results are the same: the household is disordered. The body is sick.

Based on my experiences and observations as a pastor and congregational consultant, two other forms of disorder or illness need to be noted. One is the unruly, even toxic, member or small group within the congregation that is not held accountable. Usually because of some personal problems or personal spiritual disorder of their own, such members or small groups demand constant attention and take advantage of, even bully, other members of a congregation and the pastoral leaders. Like malignant tumors, such persons require the attention and enabling of others, which implicates the congregation as a system. When a congregation lacks clear behavioral expectations and the capacity for reasonable church discipline, the "unruly member" can be like a tumor in the body, growing out of control and impeding the proper functioning of other body parts.

Finally, and sometimes in response to experiences of the other three types of disorder — "sloppy agape," "pastor/master," or "unruly member(s)" — a congregation can become legalistic and rigid. All flexibility and suppleness are lost, and there is no spirit of discernment, no testing of the spirits. Whoever has the best mastery of the bylaws or *Robert's Rules of Order* or *The Book of Discipline* runs the show, and a hardening of the arteries sets in. Fear, not love, rules.

I have noted all of these relatively common types of contemporary congregational illness and disorder in order to underscore the importance of the spirit and the intent of 1 Timothy 5:1–6:2. Today these precise "rules of the road" may not be a good fit for our context and culture, but the point is that, if it lacks sound governance, appropriate bylaws, and good boundaries, a congregation is terribly vulnerable to one of these four forms of congregational illness — or to others I have not named. On the other hand, sound governance, bylaws, and boundaries create a situation in which congregations and their members may flourish in loving relationships and in a community of faith as "salt to the earth" and "light to the world," to use the missional images of the church from the Sermon on the Mount.

This focal text draws our attention to several specific topics under the broad rubric of ordering the household of God. These are (1) how a congregation cares for its most vulnerable members (e.g., widows, 5:2-16); (2) unruly members who have influence (e.g., elders and members, 5:22b-25); and (3) employment relationships that are susceptible to problems (slaves and masters, 6:1-2). It is important for readers to carefully study the prior exegetical material for each of these sections, because here we will assume that readers will have examined that material in order to generalize from the treatment of these specifics.

How a Congregation Cares for Its Most Vulnerable Members

Paul's instructions to Timothy call for the exercise of discernment in the way that a congregation cares for its most vulnerable members. Widows are both a specific focus of concern for the church and symbolic of those at the margins of society and of a congregation. In some congregations the vulnerable will include single persons, young men, single parents, the elderly, and those experiencing mental illness or disabilities. How a congregation notices and treats all such vulnerable people is a test of its profession of Christian faith. Congregations that send a subtle message to such persons, "You aren't really welcome here," or "You don't fit in with us," have failed that test. But to judge from this text, congregations also fail this test if their concern or aid in some way communicates to a person who is more than usually vulnerable, "Your only role is to be a receiver; you have nothing to give or contribute." Paul insists that those widows and vulnerable people who are given aid and shelter by the congregation also have gifts to give and are expected to exercise those gifts for the good of the church. Positively, the vulnerable are to perform good works, practice hospitality, and help during difficult times (5:10). Negatively, they are to avoid laziness, gossip, and meddling (5:13-14). The congregation offers something, but it also expects something. The vulnerable are not simply objects of charity or care, but are subjects of whom character and contribution are expected.

Unruly Members Who Have Influence

Here Paul addresses himself to the care and discipline of church elders or persons of influence. These elders practice some form of ministry within the congregation and have a certain status because of their age. In contemporary congregations, these may be "persons of influence" for a variety of reasons. They have been called to serve as church officers, leaders, or teachers. They may have served as such often in the past. Perhaps their family has played a particularly prominent role in the congregation, or they are members of long standing. Others may contribute liberally and significantly, whether financially or with their time. Sometimes they are former ordained ministers within the congregation or former pastors of that congregation.

Persons of influence can use their influence for good or for ill. They can support or sabotage current leadership. They can set an example of responsibility, or they can regard themselves as entitled to something. They may stick to an appropriate role in times of conflict, or they may insert themselves where they should not be.

With respect to persons of influence, Paul's instructions to Timothy have several dimensions. They are due their wages, whether in a monetary honorarium or in another form — such as recognition and thanks. If accusations are brought against such a person by others in the congregation, the pastor must not rush to judgment without basis or corroborating testimony. But in the event of genuine wrongdoing or betrayal of trust, the leaders are to confront such an individual, and that confrontation is to be public, for the benefit and edification of the congregation. This sounds harsh, but note two things. One such public rebuke is for leaders. We are not talking about chastising a pregnant teenager in front of the congregation. We're talking about someone who is in a leadership role in the church. Tolerating malfeasance on the part of those entrusted with leadership undermines a congregation's health. In conclusion (5:22a), Paul reminds Timothy not to ordain anyone hastily. Take your time, be deliberate, be discerning.

Second, while pastoral leaders will certainly have to be very thoughtful and cautious about church discipline that is public, it is also true today that in instances of, for example, clergy sexual abuse or financial failure by a staff member, it is important that the congregation be informed and that such matters not be kept a secret among a very small group in a congregation. Too often failures on the part of leaders have been swept under the rug rather than being dealt with openly and honestly.

The larger point — whether with church leaders, persons of influence, or unruly members — is that such behaviors must be verified and confronted, and then an appropriate discipline must be enacted. This is crucial for the twin reasons of the soundness or health of the congregation and its missional vocation, as a sign of God's presence and mission of salvation in the world.

Employment Relationships That Are Susceptible to Problems

These verses on the master-slave relationship are tough ones. The exegesis earlier in this chapter acknowledges that they have been seen and (mis)used, at times, as "texts of terror." They must be viewed in both cultural (Roman household) and canonical (e.g., Galatians and Philemon) context and not in isolation. We do not view these as a sanction for slavery today, even less as a rationale for harsh or inhuman treatment of any person employed by another.

We do understand this passage as a reminder that complex or multifaceted relationships in the church deserve special care, "so that the name of God and the Teaching may not be reviled." We note, in particular, that the relationship envisioned here has at least two dimensions. Two people may be in an employment relationship, one as employer and the other as employee. And at the same time, they are (in one instance) also both believers and members of the church, and thus brothers — or brother and sister — in Christ.

Something analogous is common in contemporary congregations when a member of the congregation is also an employee of the church or a member of the church staff. Such relationships are complex and frequently difficult. They call for discernment, maturity, and thoughtfulness. The church office manager who is also a member faces this challenge. The pastor who is both supervisor and pastor to a particular person may find that a real challenge. The youth minister may not know where the line is between a church member who is a youth and that person as friend. Or two people may be church members and in a business relationship as well. There are no easy answers in such complex relationships, especially when employment is part of the mix. Some churches simply do not hire church members as a matter of policy. That covers some of these challenges, but not all of them. Suffice it to say, the complexity of these relationships merits special care and intentionality so that God's name and the gospel do not come into ill repute because we have failed to manage these relationships wisely.

While order and good governance can, like all virtues, be taken to such an extreme that they flip over and become vices, that does not often seem to be our problem in the contemporary church — or for its leaders. More often, we need to practice good governance, pay attention to the rules of the road, ensure openness and transparency whenever possible, and mind our boundaries. With such practices a congregation is a safe place where faith, hope, and love may flourish. Without them, distrust grows, relationships are destructive, and we are poor witnesses for Christ to the world. As Rasmussen puts it, "Disordered houses do not stand."

DISCUSSION QUESTIONS

1. Does your worshiping community care for its most vulnerable members? How does its leadership team decide who gets care and how much to give them? In what ways does this passage provide a moral compass for your community's ministry to the poor?

2. Discuss the pattern of church discipline Paul sets out in this passage. Compare it with the pattern described in Matthew 18:15-22.

3. How would you describe your congregation's policies and practices of governance? Are they clear, open, and reliable? Or are they better described with other words, say, "confusing," "ignored," or "ad hoc"?

The Challenge and Opportunity of Having Money

1 Timothy 6:2b-19

2b *Teach and encourage these things:* 3 *If someone teaches differently and does not come to agree with the healthy teachings about our Lord Jesus Christ — teaching that accords with godliness — 4 he is arrogant, understands nothing, but has an unhealthy interest in contesting the meaning of words that provoke envy, dissension, slander, evil suspicion 5 and persistent argument among those who are corrupt and deprived of the truth, who think that piety is profitable. 6 Indeed, there is great profit when piety is combined with self-sufficiency! 7 For we brought nothing into the world and so are able to take nothing out: 8 we shall be satisfied with food and shelter. 9 Those who are determined to be wealthy, however, are tripped up into temptation and a trap — many foolish and harmful desires — that plunge them headlong into ruin and destruction. 10 For the love of money is the root of all kinds of evil. Some who have aspired for wealth have wandered from the faith and have impaled themselves with many pains. 11 But you, O man of God, flee from all this! Instead, pursue moral rectitude, piety, faith, love, endurance, gentleness. 12 Fight the good fight of faith! Lay hold of eternal life for which you were called and have confessed the good confession before many witnesses! 13 (I exhort you before God who dispenses life to all things and before Christ Jesus who made the good confession when testifying before Pontius Pilate.) 14 Obey this command without fault or failure until the appearing of our Lord Jesus Christ, 15 whose timing God alone determines — God, the blessed and only Ruler, the King of kings and Lord of lords, 16 who alone has immortality, dwells in unapproachable light, whom no human has seen or is able to see, to whom is honor and everlasting sovereignty, amen.*

17 To the rich of the present age: tell them not to be arrogant, or to count on the uncertainty of riches but on God who richly offers us all things for our enjoyment; 18 to do good — to be rich in good deeds — and to be generous communicants, 19 storing up for themselves a good foundation for the future in order to lay hold of what is truly life.

Engaging 1 Timothy 6 as Scripture

The repetition of the letter's familiar exhortation for Timothy to in-struct the congregation "about these things" (6:2b; see 4:11; 1:3; 2:1; 5:1; cf. 3:14-15) brings up a familiar problem: the presence of false teachers who need to be corrected by Paul's young successor, Timothy. The sharp contrast between true and false teachers (6:2b-16) forms a re-peated parallel with 1:3-17, a passage that also sets out the crisis that oc-casions this letter's instruction and exhortation: that is, Paul has de-parted Ephesus, which requires Timothy to do the apostle's work in his absence, ready or not. What this correspondence makes clear is that congregational leadership not only concerns the substance of what is taught but also the sort of person one is, especially when measured by the "healthy teachings about our Lord Jesus Christ" (6:3; cf. 1:15-16; 3:16; 6:13). Thus the content of "healthy teachings," which continues what Jesus began to say and do (cf. Acts 1:1), forms the integral criterion of effective Christian ministry.

The rule of faith is not Pauline orthodoxy as stipulated earlier (1:10-11, 12-16; 2:4-7) but "the healthy teachings about our Lord Jesus Christ" (6:3b). Perhaps this phrase recalls the earlier formula about the exalted Christ found in 1 Timothy 3:16, which provides incentive for a godly life and also a qualification for congregational leadership (cf. 1 Tim. 2:9). Moreover, the repeated use of "healthy" (see 1:10) again cre-ates a link between what one believes and how one behaves. Put posi-tively, the material effect of orthodox faith is spiritual vitality.

The identity of the "someone who teaches differently" is not given; nor is a particular heresy identified. The catalog of evil characteristics and unprofitable practices, carefully fitted into this setting, emphasizes the unhealthy effect any sort of bad theology will have within any Christian household. This religious axiom is set out in a single, elaborate conditional statement, consisting of stock polemical expressions and vice catalogs from familiar philosophical writings of the day (6:3-5). The main clause of this conditional statement introduces the contrary example of an ineffective teacher who does not follow the "teachings about the Lord Jesus Christ" (6:3a). It is practically impossible for such a person to embody a pattern of "godliness." Instead, the hallmark virtues of spiritual health are replaced by a malformed intellect and "an unhealthy interest in contesting the meaning of words" (6:4; cf. 1:6-7). Stupid does as stupid is! And the terrible consequence for a congregation under the influence of such a teacher is a house divided by "envy, dissension, slander, evil suspicion," which is the cumulative effect of a people "deprived of the truth" (6:5). The ancient world generally did not judge the soundness of speech merely on the basis of what was said but also on its salutary effect on the way a people lives (Homer, *Iliad* 8.524).

The haunting refrain that such a teacher fakes godliness as a money-making scheme may have in mind the Lord's contrarian teachings about wealth, which is one of the most important themes of his instruction of the disciples. Money attitudes (6:10) and practices (6:17-19) are among the most evident ways in which a Christian way of life challenges and perhaps even destabilizes the cultural norm. Yet the reader should also recognize that the danger implicit in acquiring wealth was a part of the conventional wisdom of the time. Aristotle, for example, taught that "the life of money-making is limiting, and wealth is surely not the good we seek after for it is at best only the means to something else" (*Nicomachean Ethics* 1.5.8). Paul's instruction agrees wholeheartedly with Aristotle, even if for different ends.

The repetition of "profit" in superlative dress — "great profit" — cues a move back to a definition of "godliness" that is grounded in "teachings about the Lord Jesus Christ" (6:3b; also 3:9, 16). However, rather than appealing to a christological formula, as we might expect, the form of godliness that yields "great profit" is marked by the philosopher's ideal of "self-sufficiency" *(autarkeia)*.[1] In 2 Corinthians 9:8,

---

1. Luke Timothy Johnson, *The First and Second Letters to Timothy: A New Translation with Introduction and Commentary* (New York: Doubleday, 2001), p. 294.

Paul posits that "self-sufficiency" comes from the overflow of divine grace, which enables the congregation to give generous gifts to the poor. This concern for a practical divinity, glossed by Paul's missionary vocation, routinely compels him to reinterpret secular ideals, in this case the Cynics' idealization of the simple life that empties the "self" from self-sufficiency (and self-centered envy). Of course, while we take nothing of material value out of this world at death (6:7), the true believer can certainly bring valuables of a spiritual kind from this world into the next (6:19). In this sense, godliness is the way of wisdom because its profit has eternal purchase.

The gravitas of the spiritual leader's struggle is over inward affections. Paul emphasizes this point once again through poetic resonance that would occur when this passage was read aloud (as would have been the case in antiquity), with the use of a series of p-words to create a keen impression of a person who desires to be "wealthy" *(plouteō),* but who is then "tripped up" *(em-piptō)* into temptation *(peirasmos)* and a trap *(pagis).* In his translation of this verse, Luke Timothy Johnson translates *epithymia* as "cravings" instead of "desires" in order to capture the central deception revealed in this exhortation: that financial security defines sufficiency (cf. James 1:13-16).[2]

Although the kind of "ruin and destruction" that awaits those who are trapped by their love of wealth is not specified, the image conjures up other biblical texts about God's final judgment to create a terrifying intertext (see, e.g., 2 Pet. 2–3; Matt. 7:13; Phil. 3:19-20; 1 Thess. 5:3; 2 Thess. 2:3; Rev. 17:8-11). Its contemporary Jewish background may be reflected in the Rule of the Community, in which the day of God's judgment is described as a "glut of punishments . . . for the scorching wrath of the God of revenge, for permanent error and shame without end with the humiliation of destruction by the fire of the dark regions" (1QS 4:11-13). The sense of the ruination of those who advance theological falsehood for love of money is eschatological, even when their immediate success might suggest otherwise.

On this basis, Paul can reasonably conclude, with the consensus of ancient philosophers and Jewish moral teaching, that a crass materialism is the source of every kind of mischief (see James 4:1-2). In fact, the placement of "root" at the head of the proverb — "the love of money is the root of all kinds of evil" — only intensifies the truth that greed is

---

2. Johnson, *The First and Second Letters to Timothy,* p. 295.

the source of every destructive power. Yet Paul's sense of this remains eschatological and practical rather than existential and abstract: the "many pains" of those who foolishly pursue wealth at the expense of genuine piety are the "ruin and destruction" experienced at the final judgment of God.

Paul repeats the same verb here that he used earlier ("aspired") to refer to the mature leader whose aspiration is to manage the congregation's spiritual affairs with competence (3:1), but he uses it here to portray the failed leader who aspires only to prop up his own fame and fortune but only achieves personal ruin at day's end (cf. 1:19-20). The reader cannot help but recall Paul's stunning conclusion to an earlier exhortation, where he bids Timothy to obey his sacred calling to save both himself and his congregation (4:16), presumably to save them all from this unhappy end.

The contrast between the previous profile of the false teacher and the profile of the virtuous "man of God" is signaled by a characteristic conjunction: "But you . . ." (6:11). What follows is a series of exclamations that indicate the kind of piety required by God and demonstrated by Christ. In placing them here, Paul plots the movement toward a very different kind of destiny than awaits the false teacher, whose avarice tempts and traps him into a manner of life that leads to eschatological "ruin and destruction" (6:9). The "man of God" will appear before a tribunal headed by God, who alone "dispenses life" (6:13-16), and Christ Jesus, who exemplifies "the good confession" with faultless testimony that assures his eschatological reward (6:13).

The solemn idiom of this passage is less liturgical than it is juridical. The emphatic "man of God" recalls an important Old Testament title of the prophet (especially Elijah in 1 and 2 Kings), who is identified as God's witness to Israel, a carrier of God's word (cf. 2 Tim. 4:17), and a prosecutor of God's case against Israel and the nations. This "man of God" is, of course, Timothy, the ideal Pauline successor. His prophetic ministry is to carry God's word that was given to Paul (cf. Titus 1:3) so that the nations may come to an understanding of the truth (cf. 1 Tim. 2:4-7).

The "flee/pursue" pair (v. 11), a convention of the moral literature of antiquity, outlines what kind of character proffers a persuasive witness to God. The catalog of six virtues is headed by "moral rectitude" and "piety," which, taken together, form a generic whole, a correct spiritual affection (piety) and correct moral character (rectitude), that is then foundational of all other good habits.[3] The familiar pairing of faith and love, already mentioned as the byproduct of saving grace (see 1:14), combine with the final pair, patience and gentleness, to define the qualities of a working relationship with God in the world.

Paul uses a metaphor from athletic contests to underscore the seriousness of Timothy's pursuit of this manner of life. Already Paul has warned him that his future with God depends on faithful attention to his vocation (4:16); and here again, the reward of "eternal life" is based on "fighting the good fight of faith" (v. 12). The exhortation to "lay hold" suggests the effort of an athlete who trains hard for victory. Eternal life is not the entitlement of those whom God elects but God's gift to those who obey.

The pairing of the verbs "call" (i.e., called by God) and "confess" (i.e., Timothy confesses) recalls Timothy's prior ordination when the elders commissioned him to charismatic ministry in response to prophecy (4:14; cf. Acts 13:1-3). Here Paul emphasizes a past event when Timothy responded to public confirmations — in prophecy and liturgy — of his sacred call to ministry. He "confessed the good confession" (6:12) before a panel of witnesses that includes God, who called him, and Christ Jesus, who exemplifies the faithful response to God's bidding (6:13). The repetition of "good" in phrases that combine verbs with their cognate nouns frames a résumé of faithful witness that results in a verdict of eternal life. Moreover, the exhortation to "lay hold of eternal life," sandwiched between these two phrases in verse 12, aims at the eternal God, who alone can give such life (v. 13). The point scored by this grammar is that the hard evidence demanded by God at the eschatological trial, which confirms the waging of a "good fight of faith," consists of work that embodies "the good confession" of faith.

What Timothy had earlier confessed at his ordination, which has become the criterion of his present ministry and future status with God (see 4:14-16), coheres with the confession the Messiah made before Pilate (v. 13). "Confession" literally means "same saying" *(homo-logia)*, which invites the reader to recall the gospel tradition of Christ's Roman trial before Pilate as roughly analogous to the situation now fac-

---

3. Raymond Collins, *1 and 2 Timothy and Titus: A Commentary* (Louisville: Westminster John Knox, 2002), contends that moral rectitude and piety form an inseparable pair in designating a way of life that exhibits a right relationship with God and neighbor (pp. 123-24).

ing Timothy in Roman Ephesus. Initially, one realizes that this tradition is part of the body of "teachings about our Lord Jesus Christ" (6:3), which forms the continuing criterion that measures the content and character of a teacher's faithfulness to the sacred tradition. For Timothy, then, to "confess the good confession" is to give public expression to the same kind of response Jesus made when he was interrogated by Pilate.

In this regard, perhaps Paul has in mind the expanded gospel tradition of the church's memory of the Lord's responses to Pilate received in John's Gospel (see John 18:28-38). The addition of the Lord's "testifying before Pontius Pilate" uses an important catchword of John's Gospel, one that concentrates particularly on Jesus' trial before Pilate, to whom he says that "to testify to the truth" of his kingdom, which is not of this world, is the very purpose of his messianic vocation (John 18:36-37).

John's Gospel's "teaching about the Lord Jesus Christ" is cued to trigger Timothy's memory of the pledge he made at his ordination (4:14). His personal struggle over its obligations, a central thematic of 2 Timothy — and hinted at throughout this letter — may well envision the same kind of conflict instantiated in Jesus that led him to the cross. Timothy's opposition to false teachers, whose confession is "deprived of the truth" (6:5), reflects such a conflict. The deeply ironic question Pilate puts to Jesus — "What is truth?" — is the implied question now put to Timothy, especially since a "knowledge of the truth" is God's chief desire (1 Tim. 2:4) and thus the central motive of Christian ministry and worship. To pledge one's allegiance to a sacred calling is to commit oneself to a costly ministry of the truth that encounters the same enemy and perhaps the same destiny as Jesus did. Paul strikingly calls Timothy's ordination "the command" (v. 14), and his absolute obedience to it — "without fault or failure" — intensifies the importance of compliance, since his salvation and that of others depend on it (see 4:16).

The image of giving testimony "before many witnesses" evokes a courtroom scene. The identity of these "witnesses" is unclear, but they are probably the elders who presided over Timothy's ordination (4:14; cf. 2 Tim. 1:6) and now assume the role as the jury that reviews evidence of his obedience. More important to this judicial trope is the mention of "the appearing of our Lord Jesus Christ" to complete his messianic mission. In the Pastoral Epistles (2 Tim. 2:10; 4:1, 8; Titus 2:11, 13; 3:4; cf.

1 Thess. 3:13; 5:23; 2 Thess. 2:8), the idiom of Jesus' appearance is about his future work: if he came into the world initially to bring sinners salvation from their sin (1 Tim. 1:15), his future "appearance" will bring an impartial judgment of works (see Rom. 2:5-11) that will include a judgment of whether Timothy is obedient to his sacred call.

The related terms used in the Pastoral Epistles for Jesus' return are *epiphaneia/epiphainō*, from which the word "epiphany" derives. In antiquity, this word was sometimes used religiously to express the pagan belief that the gods would show up at their shrines in response to vigorous worship. Such a belief extended to the deified emperor of the state cult, which justified the elaborate celebration that often accompanied his arrival, similar to media attention surrounding our own political leaders, to convey a sense of their power and importance to the public. In 2 Maccabees, a Jewish text probably known to Paul's Diaspora community, this verbal idea is repeatedly used with dramatic irony to narrate God's "appearances" *(epiphainō)* to defend Israel during its revolt against the Syrian despot Antiochus Epiphanes. While Paul's christological claim linking God's coming triumph with Jesus' return may well be echoed in the doxological refrain "King of kings, Lord of lords" (Rev. 19:16), the point of this exhortation regards, not the cosmos, but whether Timothy will measure up to the Lord's standard when the latter returns to assess Timothy's faithfulness. The surety and effect of this eschatological tribunal may already be in view by the startling mention of the Roman judge Pilate, who presided over the execution of Jesus: on that future day, the judged will become the judge. The jarring subtext illuminated by the assumed tension between Rome (and its emperor cult) and Timothy's public confession of allegiance to the one and only King of kings and Lord of lords underscores the cost that must be paid for his favorable verdict.

The grammar of the concluding doxology (vv. 15-16) is awkward, and its referent is unclear: that is, whether it refers to the majesty that accompanies Jesus' arrival as "Lord of lords, King of kings" (see Rev. 19:16) or to the sovereignty of the God, who alone knows its date (cf. Acts 1:6-7). Most commentators agree that its subject is God and parallels 1 Timothy 1:17 in summarizing the core beliefs about Israel's God. While one might allow that the Lord's appearance will witness to the truth of these claims, even as it is this God to whom he testifies before Pilate, the primary focus of this passage is the contrast between Timothy and false teachers, their character and their respective destinies.

The significance of Paul's laudation is to emphasize the eventual triumph of those whose values and activities side with God's redemptive purpose. The unhappy future of those teachers who spread falsehoods rather than Jesus, and who seek money rather than piety, is made certain by the kind of God who awaits them. The transcendent authority of the one and only God will guarantee a just verdict of what people have done with their lives that accords with who God is. The catalog of divine attributes in verse 16 reverses what is essential to human nature but is unessential to divine nature: God is not mortal, not approachable, not visible (1:17). In the same way, God's judgments are unlike those of human culture: they are certain and eternal. In a world that deified its rulers — Caesar was routinely confessed as "lord of lords" — and whose gods were paraded in public as "the most powerful, the mightiest of the gods, the far-seeing master who fulfills everything," as Homer would say of Zeus (*Ode to Zeus* 1-2), Paul's implied claim is that sovereignty belongs only to the Creator and lordship only to Jesus Christ. This doxology registers a community's unwavering confidence in the ultimate triumph of God's way of ordering reality precisely because of the nature of God, who does the ordering.

Finally, the juxtaposition of the Lord's confession before Pilate, a symbol of Rome's unholy reign in Palestine, and the doxology of the incomparable "Lord of lords, King of kings" is politically pregnant. Similar to Paul's earlier instruction for the community to pray for civil rulers (2:2) while believing in the singularity of God's redemption through Christ Jesus (2:3-6), the community's God-centered faith allows no wiggle room for the prerogatives of Rome's manifest destiny. The idiom of faithful suffering that we find in 2 Timothy, which is the consequence of following the pattern of Pauline teaching in a public square policed by Rome, makes it impossible for us to accept the modern critical verdict of the church's wholesale domestication. In the end, the conflict between the church and empire is never a seditious one: the church is a household of good citizens. Yet, no matter how compliant the church is with Roman rule or how virtuous its leadership is, its core belief in one God, who alone is King over all other kings, including Caesar, must be (and was) assessed as a challenge to Roman sovereignty.

Most recent commentators have recognized the close connection between this passage and the opening of this letter, even suggesting that they form a bracketing within which the entire letter is read. Both passages sound an alert against false teachers, and both support Paul's instruction as normative for Christian faith. Within the immediate context, however, this passage resumes Paul's instruction regarding wealth (see 6:3-10), in this case targeting rich Christians: those who place their hope in God rather than in their riches are most able "to be rich in good deeds" (6:18), thereby preparing for themselves a future reward (6:19).[4] Timothy's "good confession" (6:12) is particularly exemplary of his congregation's "self-sufficient" piety, according to which greed is exchanged for generosity.

If the Letter of James addresses the problem of poor believers' lack of wealth (James 4:1-5:6), this letter addresses the opposite problem for wealthy believers: their Christian confession must include their use of their resources "to do good" (v. 18). This instruction continues from the prior affirmation of a sovereign and transcendent God, whose eschatological judgment at the appearance of the church's returning Lord either "gives life to all things" (6:13) or assigns those who substitute senseless desires for love of God to "ruin and destruction" (6:9). This haunting sense of a future judgment is reflected by the location of the rich "in the present age," the idiom of Jewish apocalypticism that Paul uses to contrast the symbols of present and coming "ages." Moreover, the storage of good works awaits a future whose prospect is "what is truly life" (v. 19). Though Paul's belief in the consummation of God's salvation is not cast here with customary urgency or in the idiom of its imminent arrival, the future reward of faithfulness remains an important motive for a community's obedience to God.

The uncertainty of wealth is a theological and not an economic judgment. Christianity does not demonize money or possessions — only the preoccupation with and privatization of them. But within apocalypticism, money (and doubtless the class system that money sponsors in human culture) belongs to "the present age" that God indicts, which is passing away and will be replaced by a new creation in the coming age. In this letter, perhaps in response to the asceticism of

4. In a recent study, A. J. Malherbe shows how 1 Timothy 6:17-19 fits within a longer discussion about the congregation's right uses of wealth that begins with 5:1. Moreover, he contends that the passage immediately prior to this one, 6:11-16, typically thought intrusive, is of a piece with the thinking of 6:17-19 and 6:3-10: Timothy's "good confession" includes a moral mandate that includes a kind of contentment that rejects greed. He (rather than Paul) becomes in turn the exemplar-on-the-ground for the wealthy of his congregation to imitate ("Godliness, Self-Sufficiency, Greed, and the Enjoyment of Wealth: 1 Timothy 6:3-19," *Novum Testamentum* 52 [2010]: 376-405).

false teachers (4:1-4), the generosity of the rich embodies the material generosity of God, who "richly offers us all things for our enjoyment" (v. 17). The rapid repetition of the *ploutos-* words does not demand the forfeiture of wealth, which other biblical witnesses may imply (e.g., Revelation; Luke 6:20-26); rather, it is a reciprocal action according to which the congregation's wealthy members follow the example of God, who richly gives good things for people to enjoy (vv. 17-18).

Unlike previous instructions that were aimed at middle-class women who put their wealth to use in public ways to demonstrate their virtue for evangelical ends (see 2:10), the purpose of the redistribution of personal wealth is oddly to "store up for themselves a good foundation [*themelios*]" for eschatological ends. While the repeated use of *kalos* in this concluding exhortation (vv. 12, 13, 18, 19) may connect a "good confession" with "good deeds" in securing a favorable verdict from God, the use of "foundation" — when a more appropriate metaphor would do — may be an intentional allusion to the word's strategic use in the Gospel tradition to refer to the "good person," whose fruitful production of good works is compliant with the teaching of Jesus (cf. 6:3), which is then illustrated by the parable of the builder whose house is constructed on a solid foundation that enables him to be secure against the coming storm (Luke 6:45-49; cf. Matt. 7:24-27).

Paul's earlier definition of the philanthropy of Christian women of influence (2:10) is a public practice of worship that is especially directed toward outsiders. In this case, however, the use of wealth benefits the congregation: it is the practice of a community of goods, which is the social hallmark of the church in Acts. We have tried to sound this echo with our use of the word "communicant." The sense of shared partnership implied in this word family suggests a generosity expressed within the bounds of the congregation.

The phrase we have translated "what is truly life" *(tēs ontōs zōēs)* concludes this letter's foreshadowing of the Christian concept of real living. The prior doxology fills out the persona of "the living God" (3:15), who gives life to all things (6:13) — but particularly "eternal life" (1:16; 4:8; 6:12) to those who obey God. The ultimate proof of what is "truly life" is a life with God that endures forever.

This exhortation is a window into the diversity of social classes within the urban congregations that Paul founded in his mission. While clearly there are poor people who belong to the congregation (e.g., those who are "widows indeed" and household servants), there are also wealthy members from the middle class who have both time and money to engage in philanthropic works (see 2:9-10; 6:18). The measure of their religious commitment is how they use their time and money, whether on themselves or to improve society (cf. 2:9-10). This is why Augustine says in *The City of God:* "Those who have given liberally of their riches have had great gains to compensate them for light losses. Their joy at what they assured for themselves more securely by readiness to give outweighed their sadness at the surrender of possessions they more easily lost because they clung to them fearfully" (1.10.2).

Engaging 1 Timothy 6 for Congregational Leaders

It was the first time that David, a thoughtful middle-aged man, had ever made an appointment to see me, his pastor. I was curious. What did David have on his mind? Money, it turned out, and more specifically the offering in worship. I believe we were in the midst of the annual stewardship campaign, and perhaps David was, like some of the rest of us, growing weary of it.

David was not the kind of guy to complain. Nor was he given to those broad-swath accusations on the order of "All the church cares about is money," which are often a cover for "pocketbook protection" — or for strong habits of weak giving. A talented and successful architect, David was in many ways the very definition of a refined person. He asked me why the church insisted on making a to-do about money and giving, and particularly why it was necessary to have an offering in worship, something he found, well, crass and unseemly.

"Wouldn't it be better," he suggested, "and really more spiritual not to deal with money in worship? Couldn't people simply mail in their contribution, or drop it off at the door as they leave the service? Why do we have to have this passing of plates right in the middle of the service? It seems to me," he said in conclusion, "that it distracts from what we're really here for."

David is hardly alone in finding the actual presence of money, appeals to congregants to give generously, and frank talk about money in the church to be uncomfortable and off-putting. I run into clergy who have pretty much the same take on the whole business of money. Some clergy, for example, indicate — often with thinly veiled pride — that they have nothing whatsoever to do with the church's annual stewardship campaign, with fundraising or budgets, because that is really the concern and responsibility of "the laity." It is apparently beneath them; they are concerned with more important, more spiritual, matters.

A variation on this is the minister who claims — again, often with evident pride — that he or she has no knowledge at all of what people in the congregation pledge or give to the church.

"No, I don't want to know," sniffed one such minister. "If I did it might affect how I treat people." Certainly the desire to treat members of the church fairly, equitably, and without discrimination based on their giving or their income is a laudable one. But something about such protests of sanctified ignorance raises red flags. If a minister is likely to treat people differently because of their wealth or their giving to the church, perhaps she or he is inclined to prejudicial treatment of people on other grounds as well. Moreover, as a pastor, I have found it important to know something of people's patterns of giving and generosity, or lack of same, as an indicator of what is going on with them spiritually. A significant decline in giving may signal problems or needs to which pastors and congregations should be attentive. Likewise, a jump or growth in giving (it does happen!) may also indicate something important.

As a pastor, I have tried to work toward a culture of respectful openness about money and giving — preferring that to a culture of secrecy. In my experience, a strong culture of secrecy about money tends to protect and encourage attitudes of fear and tightfistedness about money. Perhaps it is paradoxical, but where there is secrecy about money in a church, money acquires undue power. In my experience, a church culture that is more open about money and giving tends to encourage a generosity that mirrors God's own graciousness and generosity (1 Tim. 6:17). Of course, this doesn't mean boasting about one's giving, pledges, or tithes. Nor does it mean using information about giving to manipulate or embarrass. Such information is to be treated with care and respect. But honesty and openness about money does tend to help people avoid either extreme, of taking money either too seriously or not seriously enough. In speaking about secrecy with regard to money stewardship, consultant Michael Durall reports, "I have found that the higher the level of secrecy, the lower the level of giving."[5]

---

5. Michael Durall, *Creating Congregations of Generous People* (Herndon, VA: Alban, 1999), p. 15.

As I engaged in conversation with my parishioner David, I expressed my appreciation for his concern and my gratitude that he had spoken directly with me about it. I also expressed my belief that the way we, as Christians, deal with money is an important matter, one where "the rubber meets the road," so to speak. Elton Trueblood, a prominent writer from an earlier generation, said, "If a man's faith doesn't affect his pocketbook, it is phony." One of my own mentors frequently observed, "If you want to know what you really believe, look at your checkbook register. It will tell you." By receiving an offering as an act of worship, the church builds a bridge between Sunday and Monday, between worship and work. These are not separate worlds, and God is not limited to Sunday (or one hour on Sunday). Our God has to do with all of life.

I summarized my own view to David, saying that by passing the plate and inviting people to give money as an offering to God, we are indicating that we understand that money and our use of it matter, but also that money is not an ultimate value nor finally of ultimate importance. We give it away, offering it to God. By offering money to God, we indicate that money is not God, in somewhat the same way that prayers for kings and those in authority (1 Tim. 2:2) indicates that kings are important but are not God. Only God is God. All of these affirmations and values make the inclusion of money and offering in worship both important and appropriate.

When I was a young pastor, my attitudes about money, church fundraising, and the annual stewardship campaign were closer to David's and those of pastoral colleagues who seemed to take pride in having as little as possible to do with that aspect of the congregation's life. In my first year or two as a pastor, I approached stewardship season as pretty much a necessary evil. It had to be done, but there were certainly other things that were far more important and, frankly, better uses of my own valuable time and energy. Or so I thought.

Only later did I realize that this reluctance on my part was because I had not myself come to terms with money's role in my life, or with my own giving and generosity. I was in danger of participating in a common cover-up: pretending money wasn't all that important precisely because it was so very important. It was so important — so charged, you might say — that I hadn't faced it directly or spoken of it openly. I hadn't brought it before God, which is, of course, precisely what we do in the offering. We bring this potent matter of money before God, just as in worship we seek to bring our whole selves before the one true God, who is "acquainted with all [our] ways" (Ps. 139:3).

This is true of so much of my experience as a pastor. Ministry has led me to places, people, and experiences that I would not have chosen if left to my own devices. But God has, I believe, patiently led me to the sick rooms of the suffering, the open AA meetings of the addicted, to jails and detention centers, to fancy public events of the socially prominent, and to the corporate boardrooms of the financially powerful. I don't think that I would have made it to any of these places or people without God, without Jesus saying, "Follow me." Likewise, God has led me to pay attention to how I use money and to talk with others about the role money plays in our lives. And I am grateful for that.

In my second year as a pastor, in a small but growing church located in a little town in the foothills of Washington's Cascade mountain range, the church members began to talk about a long-delayed and overdue capital-fund drive. The idea was to build a fellowship hall, expand space for classes and community ministry, and bring the existing church buildings up to date. I thought to myself: *Lord, what have you got me into? I've never been involved in a capital-fund drive. I've never been involved in any fund drive. Asking people for money is the last thing I want to do. I don't know a thing about this.* All of that was true. It was also true that the congregation was moving ahead on this — and with good reason.

So I went to visit an older minister in a nearby larger city, a man who had a reputation for knowing something about stewardship and fundraising. He became my mentor on these matters, and he became my congregation's consultant for its capital-fund drive. An experience I was, at best, ambivalent about and, at worst, anticipated with dread, turned out to be a very good one — even a transformative one — for me, for my family, and for that congregation. I learned that there is an integral relationship between our faith and how we use money. Moreover, I learned that, for many people, the challenge to give generously was an opportunity for significant growth in faith. And, honestly, that started with me and my family. Our consultant challenged us to adopt what he called "the modern tithe": giving 5 percent of our income to God's work through the church and 5 percent to God's work through other agencies, institutions, and causes. We accepted that challenge. In doing so, I learned something life-changing: the only way to ever have enough money is to learn to give money away.

So perhaps it should not come as a surprise that Paul, in his instructions here to Timothy about pastoral leadership, addresses the challenges and opportunities of money head-on. As the preceding exegesis notes, this text forms a kind of parallel bracket with the opening text (1 Tim. 1:3-17), in which false teachers and the pernicious consequences of false teaching are also a concern. The two texts and their mention of false teachers are the bookends of 1 Timothy, and that indicates their importance.

It is true that Paul does not go into any great detail about particular false teachers or the content of their teaching. But he does point to the consequences of unsound or unhealthy teaching. It results in controversy, dissension, slander, and wrangling (6:4-5). Unhealthy teaching results in an unhealthy congregation. Without spelling out the details, there are points in the Pastoral Epistles where Paul suggests that at least some of the false teaching posits a spiritual/material dualism. Thus, in 1 Timothy 4:3-4, he indicts false teachers for forbidding marriage and demanding abstinence from certain foods, "which God created to be received with thanksgiving. . . . For everything created by God is good, and nothing is to be rejected, provided it is received with thanksgiving." Moreover, there is among the false teachers a preoccupation with "myths," "genealogies," and "speculations" (1:4). It appears, then, that a false teaching is one that proposes a sharp duality between the spiritual and the material, looking on the material world with suspicion rather than holding that "everything created by God is good." To put it another way, there is in the false teachings an antipathy toward incarnation and embodiment.

Thomas G. Long describes such a spiritual sensibility as one holding that "human bodies and coarse emotions belong to 'this world,' to the lower material world, but minds and spirits are part of the transcendent God, from which they came and to which they return." Long terms this a "Gnostic impulse" and notes that whenever "early Christian preachers began to speak about material reality, bodies and flesh — about creation, incarnation, and resurrection of the body — the early Gnostics recoiled."[6] It is not difficult to imagine that such a dualistic bent, with its suspicion of earthly and earthy reality, would also result in a view that money has no place in worship and that a concern with the use of money has no place in Christian discipleship.

---

6. Thomas G. Long, *Preaching from Memory to Hope* (Louisville: Westminster John Knox, 2009), p. 95.

Thus, what is at stake here — theologically — is our affirmation that our God is the Creator, that creation is good, and that God's presence is known and faith is embodied here in this world. "The Word has been made flesh" here (John 1:14). It is precisely because of such sound and healthy teaching that Jesus leads Christians, not out of this world, but more deeply into it. And it is because of such convictions that we do not turn away from money as "crass, dirty, or unspiritual," but see it as part of God's good creation. As such, money is also — like food and sex — good and yet not God.

The Gnostic impulse is persistent and appears today both within the Christian church and perhaps especially in the frequent distinction expressed by those who speak of themselves as "spiritual but not religious." There are certainly important messages for the church to hear in this refrain, but it also seems obvious that it allows its adherents to keep their distance from such earthy realities as institutions, budgets, buildings, and involvement with suffering people and others in the body of Christ whom we have not chosen ourselves and might not consider preferred company. The temptation of those who are "spiritual but not religious" is to float above life rather than enter into it. This posture involves an implicit devaluing of actual historical existence, of our participation in community, and of the choices we make. If the real action is in some other spiritual realm, none of this really matters much.

As a budding seminarian, I arrived in New York City a week before classes began at Union Seminary. One bright autumn day I stood on the corner of Broadway and 110th amid the bustle of that great city. Cabbies honked, fruit vendors hawked their wares, and buskers sang, as people of all sizes, shapes, and hues busily thronged the sidewalks. As a young man from the Pacific Northwest, I was dazzled — and probably looked bedazzled.

Suddenly I heard a question whispered into my ear: "Where is God? Where is God in all this?" The clear implication in those words was that God was nowhere to be found in all this noise, color, and confusion. I could have pretended not to notice, not to hear. But since I was soon to be in seminary, I thought it appropriate to respond and do so boldly. So I lifted my arms as if to embrace the crowded urban scene and said in a loud and cheerful voice, "Why, God is here, God is in all of this!" With that my whisperer vanished back into the throng. Only later did I learn that she was a representative of the Reverend Moon and his Unification Church and was out on the streets trolling for people to take to one of the church's enclaves for indoctrination. My theological affirmation was broad and unsophisticated, but in the face of an implication that the true spiritual realm is elsewhere and would have nothing to do with such a tawdry world and creation, it was not far off the mark. Ours is an incarnate faith.

But here's the odd thing: as we read on in 1 Timothy, it seems that the very teachers who were, on one hand, propounding the unsound teaching of sharp spiritual and material dualism were simultaneously motivated by acquiring material wealth. Paul cautions Timothy about "those who are determined to be wealthy" (6:9) and those who imagine that "piety is profitable" (6:5), culminating in his famous warning: "The love of money is the root of all kinds of evil" (6:10). Note that this is more nuanced than the way it is often expressed by those alleging to quote Scripture, that is, "Money is the root of all evil." That's not what Paul says.

Still, there is a clear recognition of the dangers of a craving for money and of the temptation and trap of acquisitiveness. If, as we have argued, money is not to be demonized or despised but is a part of God's good creation, it can nevertheless be misused and abused, like all other created goods. Moreover, like food, drink, sex, work, or power, it can become an idol — a false god. Devotion to this false god, or any other, leads to ruin (6:10).

But how is it that teachers who may have been teaching (falsely) a material and spiritual dualism would then come to be pursuing money and wealth as their goal, and seeing spiritual or religious teaching as a way of gaining wealth? While a conclusive answer cannot be given based on the text, it seems possible that the very doctrine that dismisses money and the material world might paradoxically also make it attractive and compelling. What is demonized by the conscious mind and by a misdirected morality may nonetheless exercise a deep fascination and power. This is what I had in mind above when commenting on the tendency in some churches to veil all discussion or consideration of money in secrecy. In such congregations, only one person has any information about pledges. In such congregations no members would dare to openly discuss their own pledge to the church and how they arrived at it. One simply does not talk about such things! And yet, it is my observation that when those cultural norms prevail, it is hardly the case that money is unimportant or deprived of its power. On the contrary, money protected by secrecy and fear grows in power. Perhaps, then, it is not entirely surprising to find the juxtaposition of a false material/ spiritual dualism, on one hand, with a venal preoccupation with money and gain, on the other. Indeed, both churches and individuals that practice secrecy about money on one hand often hoard it up on the other.

If the Gnostic impulse and its avoidance — even demonization — of money is evident in some Christian circles, a different doctrine is taught in other churches and Christian settings today — the so-called "prosperity gospel." Preachers of this gospel indicate that faith leads to wealth, and that wealth is a sign of right faith and of divine approval. There is nothing particularly new about this. There is a strain in the Old Testament that regards prosperity as a sign of God's blessing, and in one sense it is. The problems come when this is changed from a metaphorical to a literal interpretation. It becomes problematic when joy in the goodness of God's creation is supplanted by a teaching that sees a strict correlation between the value of a person and his or her income or possessions. If dualism and denigration of money are a threat, perhaps a far greater threat in our society today is the idea that money and wealth are the real indication of a person's value and worth.

A related dimension of this phenomenon is that the preachers of the prosperity gospel often seem to feel entitled to a materially lavish lifestyle, not to mention huge fees for speaking engagements. Paul calls Timothy, as a pastoral leader, to be cognizant of the temptation and trap of making money and wealth, rather than the living God, the center of one's life. These are false gods, idols that will come to own and destroy him. As elsewhere in the Epistle (1 Tim. 2:9), Paul says that Christians are to practice a material modesty: money is neither to be despised nor worshiped. Money is part of God's good creation. It is a gift of God, but it is not God, and is not to be confused with ultimate value.

Thus does Paul's teaching about money chart a course between two extremes, both of which are operative in society today as they were in his time. Paul guides Timothy and us between the Scylla of a spiritual/material dualism and the Charybdis of avarice or material ostentation. The "man of God" (6:11) and the people of God are to seek other ends. They are to "pursue moral rectitude, piety, faith, love, endurance and gentleness," and thus "lay hold of eternal life for which you were called."

In the concluding verses the focus on money continues, but with an important shift, apart from which Christian teaching about money remains incomplete. Here Paul addresses those with financial resources, "the rich of the present age." In the current world order, it is perhaps true that all of us living in the First World are, by global standards, "the rich of the present age." Paul does encourage Timothy to remind those with means that their relative wealth is not a basis for either a sense of superiority or security. But he doesn't stop there. He encourages Timothy to invite those who have the means to participate in the spiritual practice of generosity — as a response to "God, who richly offers us all things for our enjoyment" (6:17).

This points us toward at least part of the focus of the church's teaching about money and the deep agenda of stewardship efforts and campaigns. The point is not simply to raise funds or even to meet the budget. In addition to supporting the missional church in its witness to the world, what churches and their pastoral leaders are up to here is to help individuals and communities grow in the spiritual practice of generosity. Paul instructs Timothy to encourage members of the congregation to be "rich in good deeds and to be generous communicants" in order that they may "store up for themselves a good foundation for the future in order to lay hold of what is truly life" (6:18-19). While this may sound as if it means only the promise of an eternal reward, it may also be the recognition that being a generous person changes a person's life right now. It builds a person's character.

The stewardship consultant Michael Durrall makes this observation:

> A great deal of difference exists between asking people for money and creating a congregation of generous people. Asking people for money eventually becomes routine. But creating congregations of generous people is an engaging, rewarding endeavor that takes on ever more meaning with passing time.[7]

Such is the work to which Paul calls Timothy: the shaping of healthy, faithful lives characterized by, among other things, generosity.

---

7. Durrall, *Creating Congregations,* p. ix.

DISCUSSION QUESTIONS

1. "The love of money is the root of all kinds of evil." This famous biblical aphorism comes with a biblical context, which concerns the importance of cultivating the leader's inward affections. Why does Paul argue that a preoccupation with material things undermines the effectiveness of one's Christian ministry?

2. How does what one thinks about the future, particularly one's future status before God, shape one's present practices — especially regarding one's wealth?

3. The author advocates creating, in the congregation, a culture of respectful openness with respect to money, in contrast to a culture of secrecy. What do you think about this?

4. Is there a difference between making an offering and making a donation? How would you describe the difference?

A Crisis of Courage

2 Timothy 1:3-14

3 *I give thanks to God whom I serve, as did my ancestors, with a clear conscience. I remember you in my prayers day and night.* 4 *I long to see you, remembering your tears, so that I may be filled with joy.* 5 *I take hold of your earnest faith as a reminder — the kind that first found a home in your grandmother Lois and mother Eunice and am certain is in you.*

6 *For this reason, I remind you to reignite God's gift that is in you through the laying on of my hands.* 7 *For God did not give us a cowardly spirit but a Spirit of power, love and discernment.*

8 *Therefore, do not be ashamed of the Lord's testimony or of mine, his prisoner. Rather, share the suffering for the gospel by the power of God:* 9 *God saved and called us with a holy calling, not according to our works but according to God's own purpose and grace. God gave grace to us in Christ Jesus before time began and* 10 *now it has been revealed through the appearing of our savior, Christ Jesus, who abolished death and illumined life and immortality. For this gospel* 11 *I was appointed herald, apostle and teacher;* 12 *for this reason I suffer as I do. But I am not ashamed; for I know the one in whom I have placed my trust and am convinced that God is strong enough to protect my tradition until that day.*

13 *Hold to a pattern of healthy teaching you have heard from me with the fidelity and loyalty that are in Christ Jesus.* 14 *Protect the good tradition through the Holy Spirit, who dwells in you.*

Part 1: Engaging 2 Timothy 1:3-14 as Scripture

Paul's thanksgiving rehearses a set of powerful memories that define Timothy's call to ministry: his religious education, supervised by his mother and grandmother, cultivated an "earnest faith" (1:5), which the apostle personally confirmed at his ordination (1:6). Paul also reminds Timothy that his call is accompanied by the Spirit of power (1:14), whose spiritual gift animates his ministry (1:6-7). Thanksgiving prepares for an initial exhortation that challenges Timothy to accept the costs of his "holy calling" (1:8-9a) and succeed Paul in a ministry of the gospel revealed by Christ Jesus (1:9b-10), which he was appointed to publish and because of which he now suffers (1:11). In commending this apostolic legacy to Timothy for safekeeping, Paul instructs him to uphold faithfully the "pattern of healthy teaching" of the "good tradition" learned from the apostle (1:13-14).

Typical of Paul's canonical letters, the personal greetings are followed by a note of thanksgiving to God, which often includes prayer for the recipients of his letter. This petition often signals, as here, the letter's occasion and thus anticipates the instruction that follows. Paul's thanksgiving for Timothy is personal and emphatic and reflects a deeply personal contour of the apostle's relationship with his protégé and successor. Significantly, the phrase *charin echō* ("I give thanks") is found only here and in 1 Timothy 1:12, where Paul thanks Christ for his conversion and calling as a minister of the gospel. The resulting intertext forges an integral whole: Paul is grateful for his own ministry as an apostle (1 Tim.) and grateful for a well-prepared successor who is fit to take the apostolate over from him as his death approaches (2 Tim.).

Paul's passing mention of his Jewish faith (1:3) may also be cued by his story in the book of Acts, where his mission engages rather than rejects his Jewish legacy. Strikingly, the import of Timothy's circumcision in Acts (16:1-5) assures "the Jews who were in those places" that Paul's mission will bring the Jewish past forward into the Christian present. This implicit antisupersessionism is a central feature of the Pauline apostolate, which corrects not only the exclusive use of those passages within the Pauline canon that might justify the church's "gentilization" of Paul's gospel (e.g., Gal. 2:15-21), but which Paul's successor is appointed to continue into the future.

Thanksgiving always occasions a remembrance of the past. Paul expresses gratitude to God for gifts already received, and Paul's repeated invocation of his memories in this letter seems more urgent because his death is imminent (see 2 Tim. 4:6). Raymond Collins is among the letter's recent interpreters who have recognized these extensive personal reminiscences as a literary convention of the testamentary genre. He concludes, as do other interpreters, that 2 Timothy is an epistolary example of farewell discourse: Paul's "last will and testament," which he wrote for his spiritual heir.[1] But Luke Timothy Johnson correctly points out that in antiquity memory was also used to frame personal models of imitation.[2] That is, Paul's personal reminiscence, whether of himself or others, is a form of instruction that prepares Timothy for ministry by imitating his. The exhortation is not to *be* Paul, whose calling and charisma are uniquely given (cf. Titus 1:3; 1 Tim. 1:10-11); rather, it is to *imitate* Paul, to make his personal virtue and practices of ministry a guide.

The phrase "for this reason" (1:6) reclaims the confidence Paul has just expressed in Timothy's "earnest faith" (1:5) in order to frame an exhortation for Timothy to act on what they both remember is true. The verbal idea *anazōpyreō*, which we have translated "reignite," plays off the verb used to cue the memory of this shared experience *(anamimnēskō)*, the one *ana-* word triggering the other. The ongoing operation of "God's gift that is in (Timothy)" is confirmed by recollection of his "earnest faith."

Our task is to define more carefully the nature of Timothy's charisma and investigate why Paul should say that it needs reigniting. Some commentators find a mirror image of Timothy's self-doubt here. For example, Jouette Bassler takes Paul's exhortation of a "reignited" charism without irony as a pastor's exhortation to someone lacking inner fortitude to get on with the business at hand.[3] St. Hilary did as well, wondering why Paul would need to otherwise remind Timothy of his

---

1. Raymond Collins, *1 and 2 Timothy and Titus: A Commentary* (NTL) (Louisville: Westminster John Knox, 2002), pp. 181-85.

2. Luke Timothy Johnson, *The First and Second Letters to Timothy: A New Translation with Introduction and Commentary* (New York: Doubleday, 2001), pp. 340-41.

3. Jouette M. Bassler, *1 Timothy, 2 Timothy, Titus* (ANTC) (Nashville: Abingdon, 1996), p. 129.

ordination, an event he surely would have remembered (*De trinitate* 11.23). Although I do not think the real issue at stake is self-doubt, at the very least the history of the interpretation of this text would seem to suggest that the letter's occasion is its recipient's vocational crisis, which is no doubt made worse by the apostle's absence!

The mention of Timothy's spiritual gift cues the preceding discussions of *charismata* in Paul's Epistles (Rom. 12; 1 Cor. 12-14). God's Spirit allocates gifts to individuals to empower their loving ministry within the body of Christ, with an aim of bringing every believer to spiritual maturity (1 Cor. 12:4-11). The spiritual maturity and unity of Christian fellowship depend on the community's capacity to discern the work of the Spirit in its midst and to distinguish it from the range of religious practices that flood the marketplace. Clearly, from this correspondence, the agent of charisma is the Holy Spirit, who not only enables the church to confess that "Jesus is Lord" (1 Cor. 12:3; cf. Rom. 10:9) but allocates a variety of *charismata* according to God's will in fashioning what benefits the whole church, crucial for a ministry of reconciliation within a community that is in conflict over rival claims (cf. 1 Cor. 1:10-12).[4] Perhaps for this reason, the central metaphor of the church in the Corinthian correspondence is the human body, which Paul upgrades to the "body of Christ" (1 Cor. 12:27; Rom. 12:4-5), in which each gifted member works in solidarity with other gifted members and their risen Lord to form a cohesive working whole. Paul's exhortation to "reignite" a divine charisma, when it is read with these Pauline texts, confirms Timothy's call to bring other believers to spiritual maturity. Moreover, Timothy's charisma comes with the Spirit whose "power" (rather than Timothy's talents) animates his gift and makes it effective for the public ministry to which he is called (cf. 1 Tim. 1:3; 3:15-16; 4:14-16; 6:20).

The final word that characterizes the indwelling Spirit's performance is *sōphronismos*, which we translate as "discernment." Its more precise definition is contested, but most agree that discernment is an intellectual competence that enables the moral agent to weigh competing goods and to decide rightly between them. If love and power are readily understood from its co-text (1 Corinthians) as necessary con-

---

4. Margaret M. Mitchell, *Paul and the Rhetoric of Reconciliation: An Exegetical Investigation of the Language and Composition of 1 Corinthians* (Louisville: Westminster John Knox, 1991), esp. pp. 266-83.

trols in the effective performance of a spiritual gift, discernment is not, especially if perceived as a secular virtue. While this word is used only here in the New Testament, it belongs to the *sōphron* word family that Paul often uses. Most uses are in the virtue lists that he uses to characterize competent persons capable of good works appropriate to their position or task. For example, the woman who is saved according to 1 Timothy 2:15 maintains both *sōphrosynē* (prudence) and *agapē* as the public mark of the faithful life (see the commentary on 1 Tim. 2:9-15). Elsewhere in Paul's writings, the use of *sōphroneō* frames a discussion of *charismata*, for example in Romans 12:3, where he admonishes each believer to discern *(sōphroneō)* the particular portion of divine grace that he or she has received to more effectively use it within the body of Christ, in whom each "belongs to one another" (Rom. 12:5). When we read it within this canonical context, then, the mention of this virtue recalls a much broader valence of spiritual gifts that thickens a belief that the indwelling Spirit is not only agent of the community's spiritual formation but the one whose presence gives gifted individuals the capacity to discern how best to use their extraordinary ability in ministry toward others within the household of God.

The practice of the "laying on of hands" (1 Tim. 4:14) was borrowed from Judaism, where it was used as a liturgical gesture in the ordination of rabbis. The gesture not only symbolized the transference of spiritual authority to those who were qualified to lead, but was also a public recognition that the authority of individuals was something for an entire congregation to observe. In this case, the Spirit's gift is confirmed by Paul's apostolic authority, since the gesture is personal ("my hands") rather than congregational. Paul's personification of a congregational practice suggests that he has handpicked Timothy as his successor and that Paul's apostolic authority has in some sense been transferred to him.

Simply put, this is a gesture of apostolic succession rather than simply a congregational laying on of hands, such as in Acts 8:17, where Peter and John "handed off" the Spirit to repentant Samaritans. Nonetheless, this connection with Acts 8:17 may supply an added layer of meaning to this text. Not only there, but also in Acts 9:17-18 and 19:6, the gesture of the laying on of hands signals the baptism of the Spirit as a confirmation of salvation from sin (Acts 8:17-18; 19:6; cf. 2:38) — but then to empower Christian ministry (9:17-18). Paul's laying on of hands assumes that Timothy's succession comes with the Spirit's power and gift for ministry to imitate Paul in his absence. It is a succession of the Spirit of apostleship.

In this regard, the following exhortation presents the details of Timothy's Spirit-empowered imitation of Paul. The repetition of "shame" language — "do not be ashamed" (2 Tim. 1:8) . . . "for I am not ashamed" (1:12) — forms a literary bracketing, which we can understand if we examine the backdrop of Paul's Greco-Roman world. The codes of conduct in antiquity were typically fashioned to stipulate what behaviors or situations to avoid because they would bring shame to individuals and disrepute to their household and their public associations. Most people understand intuitively what to avoid in order to escape public ridicule. The social shaping of intuition, especially during one's early education (1:5), remains to this day an effective means of maintaining social order. The virtuous person — the one who is "above reproach" — is capable of detecting and avoiding shameful behaviors in order to maintain good relationships with those who count.

Typically, only those who influence us or are important to us can say or do something that evokes feelings of shame. In this case, Paul's mention of himself and the Lord as potential players who incite Timothy's shame is ironic: while imitating Paul's scandalous testimony of Christ (cf. 1 Cor. 11:1) may provoke the ridicule of outsiders, it is precisely being like Paul that counts. Paul's offense is what Timothy should embrace rather than avoid!

The repetition of *parathēkē* ("tradition," 1:12, 14) clarifies the nature of an apostolic succession, which turns on the ultimate importance of Paul's "pattern of healthy teaching" (1:13) for the future of the church (cf. Acts 20:29-35). Paul's appointment as "herald, apostle and teacher" (1:11; cf. 1 Tim. 2:7) carries with it a sacred trust that has been protected by God (1:12b) but is now passed on to Timothy for safekeeping with the Spirit's help (1:14). Rather than reading the book of 2 Timothy as Paul's "last will and testament," as many do, we see this as a letter of succession that sets out a pattern of instruction received from Paul (1:13) that will be used to catechize the future church into the apostolic faith (2:2).

Especially if Timothy's firm grasp on the tradition is predicated on the "fidelity and loyalty that are in Christ Jesus," then his task is not conditioned on raw talent but on God's faithfulness to deliver the necessary goods. As Paul puts it, "not according to our works but according to God's own purpose and grace" (1:9; cf. Eph. 2:8-9): that is, Timothy's confidence in the apostolic tradition, especially in the face of potential shame, is predicated on God's purpose already achieved at "the appearing of our savior, Christ Jesus" (1:10) and now protected by the Spirit (1:14). This proto-Trinitarian formulation in the Second Epistle to Timothy of a purposeful God, a saving Christ Jesus, and an empowering Spirit supplies the theological soil in which the movement of the apostolic tradition is rooted.

Paul's passing reference to his imprisonment (1:8) evokes a sense of the personal costs involved. If shame avoidance prompts the wise of this world to remove themselves from any situation that will land them in prison or make them an object of public ridicule for Christ's sake, then a rethinking of the source of shame is called for as a crisis of discipleship (cf. 1 Cor. 1:18–2:5). Paul's jarring juxtaposition of shame and gospel in Romans 1:16-17 — and now here — does just that. Even though Paul focuses on Timothy's imitation of him throughout this entire correspondence, the addition of "the Lord's testimony" is a reminder that Paul himself is the imitator of the Lord, and that his faithfulness proved costly. The reader may recall from the First Letter to Timothy that the gospel traditions of Jesus (1 Tim. 6:3) establish the normative pattern of the teacher's piety and more directly of Timothy's compliance with his sacred calling (6:12). Even though "the Lord's testimony" in Paul's idiom would include an account of his costly faithfulness to God (cf. Rom. 3:21-26; Phil. 2:5-8), the following summary regards only "the appearing of our savior, Christ Jesus, who abolished death and illumined life and immortality" (1:10). While perhaps alluding to Christ's share of suffering, the focus of this formula is Christ's triumph as "our savior."[5] That is, the transformation of the concept of shame that follows the lead of the faithful Messiah and his apostle requires refocus from suffering per se to its redemptive effect. And if it is God's "own purpose and grace" that plot "the appearing" of the cruciform and risen one as the climax of the gospel narrative, which is instantiated in the costs of Paul's mission and the content of his message, then this same plot line should continue to shape the narrative of apostolic succession.

The kerygmatic claim that Christ Jesus is "our savior" who "appeared" to defeat death is exceptional apart from the Pauline Epistles and demands comment. There were many saviors in antiquity, both political and religious; and Paul uses "savior" in reference to Jesus in

---

5. Cf. Bassler, *1 Timothy, 2 Timothy, Titus*, p. 131.

Philippians 3:20 with evident political meaning. Moreover, Greeks loved and told tales of the grand appearances of legendary heroes (e.g., Alexander). Even today we populate our symbolic worlds with esteemed political leaders and sometimes even present them as our "saviors," whether from economic disaster or terrorist threat. Their public "appearances" occasion considerable pomp and circumstance, so Christians are bound to be confused over which allegiance to pledge. Implicit in the politics of Paul's confession of faith in Philippians 3:20 is that true believers must *never* negotiate a dual "citizenship" *(to politeuma)* that splits loyalties between the powers of the present age and the triune God, who providentially guides the world toward the coming age. To reject the one, which is earthbound and whose political leaders are "enemies of the cruciform Christ, whose end is destruction" (Phil. 3:18-19), for the other, whose heavenly body politic is led by "a savior from there, the Lord Jesus Christ" (Phil. 3:20), is the mark of Christian maturity. As Stephen Fowl sharply expresses it, "This is a politics governed by a practical reason shaped by Christ's own person and work as exemplified in the life and practice of Paul and those who live according to that Christ-focused pattern."[6] Christ's epiphany from heaven brings with him a messiah's tools and heaven's final powers of salvation, which are not of this world or in the possession of its messianic pretenders. This is an appearance of real power — God's power — which promises to replace that which kills with "life and immortality."

The summary of the gospel Paul heralds is spread across a long and complex sentence, a sentence that secures its truth as definitive (1:9-10). The gospel is the means by which this truth comes "to light" *(phōtizō).* The repetition of "gospel" brings two ideas together. If suffering (and shame) results from a ministry of the gospel, then suffering is justified by the gospel's critical role: its proclamation discloses the truth about God's salvation, without which people would die without "life and immortality." Because the gospel's proclamation brings about the redemptive purpose and transforming grace of God, Paul repeats (for Timothy's benefit) the fact that he is not ashamed to do so. Of course, the opposite would be equally true: if the gospel did not have a salutary effect, the glad acceptance of public shame or personal suffering would not be rational.

The experience of suffering and the prospect of shame signal an

6. Stephen E. Fowl, *Philippians* (THNTC) (Grand Rapids: Eerdmans, 2005), p. 176.

important subtext of this letter: the preaching of the gospel will provoke a political disturbance. This is true not because Paul's mission is directly opposed to Roman rule, which the book of Acts makes clear. Rather, it is because the embrace of the gospel forges a vision of life and daily practices that threaten the empire's way of doing business. The juxtaposition of the "power of God" and the believer's "suffering for the gospel" is a political declaration (1:8): it implies that a life molded by a Pauline "pattern of healthy teaching" under the aegis of the indwelling Spirit constitutes a real problem for those holders of secular power. Of course, Paul makes clear that his gospel does not summon the congregation to political revolution; rather, it announces the epiphany of a savior, Jesus, not one of Rome's pretenders to his messianic throne (1:10).

The idiom of time in this exhortation is important to note. Because it concerns a succession, the past interplays with the present and the present interplays with the tradition's forward movement into the future to form a continuum of the sacred. Therefore, Paul speaks not only of his past appointment to proclaim the gospel about what has "now been revealed" in the coming of Christ Jesus (1:10); he also speaks of God's pattern of grace as something planned "before time began" (1:9; cf. Rom. 8:28-30; 1 Cor. 2:7; Eph. 1:4) — a "promise of life" that God has already brought to realization for those who are "in Christ Jesus."

The memory of his apostolic appointment and the gospel Paul has proclaimed, and for which he is now imprisoned, fashions a sacred tradition that he passes on to Timothy — until Jesus returns (1:12). The apocalyptic catch phrase "until that day," which Paul uses often and strategically (see 1:18; 4:8; cf. Rom. 2:16; 13:12; 1 Cor. 1:8; 1 Thess. 5:4; 2 Thess. 1:10), refers to a future, finite, and final date of reckoning when God the judge will demand a rigorous accounting of everyone's faithfulness. The repetition of this phrase in the positive example of Onesiphorus's household that follows (1:16-18) suggests that its sense here is to emphasize Timothy's faithful succession, for which he will be rewarded by God "on that day."

The phrase "pattern of healthy teaching" has added importance in a concluding exhortation about apostolic succession. While Timothy's reception of what he has heard from Paul is made inherently important because it reveals God's redemptive purpose and because its faithful reception has a powerful effect on the believer, the pair of imperatives "to hold" and "to protect" this apostolic word invite a more practical question: What is Paul's kind of Christian to do now that he is in possession of it? Commentators are mostly interested in identifying the body of Paul's teachings in succession here, and they are right to see "healthy teaching" and "good tradition" as synonymous. The relationship between the message and the messenger whose competence stands firmly within Paul's apostolic legacy is characterized by his earnest faith in God (2 Tim. 1:5) and loving relationships with others (cf. 1 Tim 1:5), which are formed "in Christ," where believers dwell with the Lord's Spirit (2 Tim. 1:14). Especially in light of the later reference to Paul's imminent death (2 Tim. 4:6), the present exhortation for a faithful and loving Timothy to pass on this teaching to others (2:2) has real purchase.

However, what is less often considered is the performance of this good tradition implicit in the noun *hypotypōsis* ("pattern"). Although exceptional in the New Testament, the word had broad currency in the Greco-Roman world as referring to a summary or outline of someone's teaching. Rather than understanding Paul's use as a type of imitation, I take the word in a curricular sense, much like the role performed by the Torah for the Moses of Deuteronomy: to prepare Israel for entering into the promised land. David Trobisch has argued that it was Paul himself who collected, edited, and put into circulation a canonical edition of his standard letters (Romans, 1-2 Corinthians, Galatians) for the teaching of his catechumens — a kind of theological curriculum. This theory is not without problems, but such an activity of canon-building certainly coheres with the portrait of Paul found in his Epistles: the instruction to Timothy is to preserve and transmit his memory and message to others.[7] It seems to us that Paul's use of *hypotypōsis* within an exhortation about Timothy's succession may have such a collection of "healthy teachings" in mind. Timothy can use this collection of Paul's letters to teach those who will be teaching the tradition in order to preserve it for the next generation of the church (cf. 2:2).

---

7. David Trobisch, *Paul's Letter Collection: Tracing the Origins* (Minneapolis: Fortress, 1994), pp. 113-24. Although I am favorable toward his argument, see Stanley E. Porter's measured criticisms of Trobisch's proposal in "When and How was the Pauline Canon Compiled? An Assessment of Theories," in Stanley E. Porter, ed., *The Pauline Canon*, vol. 1 (Leiden: Brill, 2004), pp. 113-24.

Part 2: Engaging 2 Timothy 1:3-14 for Congregational Leaders

If there are several texts in the Timothy correspondence that are perhaps notorious — we have noted above the misuse of 1 Timothy 2:12 on women and 1 Timothy 6:1 on slaves — there are also other texts in these pastoral epistles that are especially beloved. One thinks of 2 Timothy 4:7, "I have fought the good fight . . . I have kept the faith," which is frequently heard at funerals and memorial services. Another is this one, 2 Timothy 1:6: "Rekindle [or, in our even more robust translation, 're-ignite'] the gift of God that is in you," and the following verse: "For God did not give us a cowardly spirit but a Spirit of power, love and discernment." Not only is this text one of the relatively few from the Pastoral Epistles that makes it into the Common Ecumenical Lectionary; it is often turned to at ordinations and installations of pastors.

When I was a young and energetic pastor, an older minister named Roger smiled at me knowingly and said, "The problem in pastoral ministry is to keep the beast alive." An odd remark in some ways, but provocative — maybe even true. Ministry wears you down. Congregations press pastors to adjust to their known ways, customs, and limits. The gospel is reduced to a comfortable size and scope, and the church is domesticated to the culture's requirements. Most of all, members of the clergy are expected to be "nice." The prophet Jeremiah, for whom the Word of God was as a fire burning in his bones, morphs into Mr. Rogers presiding over the friendly neighborhood. Paul, who went toe to toe with the philosophers at the Areopagus in Athens and precipitated riots in Ephesus, becomes the president of the local Kiwanis chapter and an empathic Rogerian therapist. The fires are banked, the beast is tamed, and the instrusive Word of God is lost somewhere between the seemingly endless litany of parish announcements and the latest appeal to "make the budget."

That this is all completely understandable doesn't make it less of a problem. Whether the metaphor is fire and "reigniting the gift of God that is within you" or the beast and keeping some wild thing alive and undomesticated, this text addresses a vocational crisis as familiar as it is challenging. Ministry and pastoral leadership require great and sustained courage.

Timothy faced a vocational crisis — a crisis of courage — that both pastoral leaders and really all Christians have continued to face in subsequent eras, including our own. In exploring this "crisis of courage," I want to focus on three dimensions of this text that may have particular resonance for pastoral leaders today: (1) trusting one's call, (2) not being ashamed of the gospel, and (3) the challenges of pastoral and leadership succession. Each of these three calls on pastoral leaders to exhibit courage, the cardinal virtue, even as courage is held in relationship — at times in tension — with the other cardinal virtues of the professions: practical wisdom, justice, and temperance.[8]

Trust Your Calling

Not long ago a minister named Meredith, a woman in her midthirties, told me the following story. Meredith had been invited to preach at the ordination of a close friend from seminary. As it happened, this friend's husband was a professor of homiletics at a seminary. "That," said Meredith, "was a little intimidating, but it got worse, much worse." Arriving on Saturday evening for the Sunday afternoon service, Meredith learned that a host of leading preachers and teachers of preaching, friends of her friend's husband, would be in the congregation for the ordination and for her sermon. Late Saturday night Meredith panicked. She threw out the sermon she had prepared and started over. Sometime in the wee hours of the morning, with her sermonic efforts floundering on the rocks of fatigue and anxiety, Meredith heard a word: "Yes, this great preacher and that great preacher will be there, but you, Meredith, were the one invited to bring the message. Trust your calling. You don't have to be Fred Craddock or Barbara Brown Taylor or Tom Long. You have to be Meredith, servant of God, preacher of the Word. Trust your calling." With that, Meredith tumbled into bed and slept peacefully. The next day she preached boldly, without fear, and with power, love, and discernment on 2 Timothy 1:7.

Most — perhaps all — preachers can readily think of someone more able, more gifted, more eloquent than they, preachers who should be preaching the sermon and leading the congregation. Most of us, given a little time and anxiety, can talk ourselves into a failure of confidence and courage. And yet, like Meredith, we are the ones who, in

---

8. Jeffrey Stout, *Ethics After Babel: The Languages of Morals and Their Discontents* (Boston: Beacon Press, 1988), p. 269.

the strange wisdom of God, have been called to this ministry, to lead and to preach in this place and at this time. Who knows why God thought that was a good idea, but there it is. Perhaps someone else could do it better. But God has called us — or you — to this task, to this ministry, to this moment. And while nervousness is natural (public speaking ranks at the top of every list of people's phobias), courage lies in trusting and obeying God's calling.

Thus Paul reminds Timothy of his own calling and does so from several angles. First, Paul reminds Timothy of those who have nurtured his life and faith: these include Paul himself, but also Timothy's grandmother, Lois, and his mother, Eunice. Most of us can call on the memory of teachers, mentors, parents, and friends who have contributed to our formation. I once began a first sermon at a new congregation by saying, "As you look up here at me now, you see one person, one man. But that's not exactly the case. Actually, it's crowded up here. I'm surrounded. There's my last congregation, grieving the loss of me as I grieve the loss of them. There are seminary teachers and college professors. There are ministers who have touched my life and guided me. There are public heroes like Martin Luther King Jr. and Dietrich Bonhoeffer, and there are personal ones, like my grandmother, Victoria Moon Robinson. In truth, I am surrounded by an invisible cloud of witnesses, just as you the congregation are also surrounded by a great cloud of witnesses, the saints who have gone before us in this church. So today, church is really packed, isn't it?" My point was — as Paul's was to Timothy — to remember and draw strength and courage, as well as humility, from those who have touched us and in many ways made us who we are. That's a part of trusting our calling.

Paul also calls on Timothy to "reignite God's gift that is in you through the laying on of my hands." Those words point to two dimensions of a pastoral leader's call. There is the inward call, accompanied by "God's gift that is in you," and there is the outward sign and confirmation of that call, "the laying on of my hands." It is important that the inward, and perhaps more subjective, call and associated gift for ministry be confirmed by the outward and more objective act. Some who feel a strong inward call do not find that call confirmed by the church or stewards of its tradition, which should be cause for hesitation. Both dimensions are important.

Moreover, the outward act, "the laying on of hands," has an objectivity that is important. It happened whether our feelings, at any given moment, attest to it or not. As Luther found spiritual comfort in the objective knowledge of his baptism — repeating in times of spiritual crisis, "I have been baptized," meaning "I belong to Christ, so get your hands off me, devil" — Timothy was also reminded of the outward confirmation of his calling. Still, the outward act also requires the inward sense of call; otherwise, it risks becoming mere formality, an office but not a vocation. Inward and outward calls are the two sides of one coin. And Paul's description of the call attests that it comes with a gift, the particular gift that God granted Timothy for ministry. Paul seeks to re-ignite Timothy's trust in his calling and appropriation of God's gift. Paul reminds Timothy of both calls: the inward call with its gift that must be claimed, and the outward confirmation that can be trusted.

Finally, in verse 9, Paul speaks explicitly of God's calling, in Christ, of himself and of Timothy: "God saved and called us with a holy calling not according to our works, but according to God's own purpose and grace." It's God's call — trust it and live. It doesn't mean you're perfect; it is about grace, not your works (achievements or abilities).

After ten years as a pastor, which included some seasons of vocational crisis and questioning, I gave myself three "rules," and I would remind myself of them before going into the pulpit: (1) trust your calling; (2) trust the words you have been given; and (3) enjoy yourself! Not rocket science, but getting up before a congregation to preach the Word of God is no small thing. Good preaching requires such courage because it means, in the end, loving God more than you love your congregation. And that means — at least sometimes — telling them not what the congregation (as well as yourself!) wants to hear, but what they need to hear.

In what may be a time of vocational crisis, a crisis of courage, Paul reminds Timothy to trust his own calling and take his bearing from its several dimensions: those people who have formed him (vv. 3-5), the inward and outward experience of his call to pastoral ministry and leadership (v. 6), and the grace and initiative of God in Christ operative in his call (v. 9).

Not Ashamed of the Gospel

Twice in this text Paul sounds a note that calls to mind, as the exegesis points out, the opening notes of Romans. Twice Paul urges Timothy not to be ashamed: in verse 8, "Therefore, do not be ashamed of the Lord's testimony or of mine, his prisoner," and again in verse 12, "But I am not ashamed, for I know the one in whom I have placed my trust." Likewise, in Romans 1:16, Paul writes, "For I am not ashamed of the gospel; it is the power of God for salvation to everyone who has faith. . . ." Why does Paul say this? Why does Paul urge Timothy not to be ashamed? What was shameful about the gospel or about the ministry? Are pastoral leaders and Christians today tempted to be ashamed of the gospel?

For a number of years I wrote a column on faith and culture for one of Seattle's daily newspapers. My take on religion in general, Christianity in particular, was usually — though not exclusively — positive, and it received varied responses depending on the particular topic. But one litany of response proved so predictable that I dubbed it "Crusades yada, yada." Such a respondent would invariably find religion, and Christianity specifically, to be the source of all the problems and evil in the world. The person would substantiate this by way of a predictable, almost script-like recitation of Christianity's failures. It would begin with the Crusades, move on to the Inquisition, throw in a few burnings at the stake, cite the alleged destruction of native peoples, and wrap up with references to anti-Semitism or to more recent religiously inspired homophobic violence. The fact that this litany was predictable as well as selective did not lessen my discomfort or embarrassment. The truth is that the Christian record is a very mixed one. Christians, as well as people of other faiths, have at times done shameful things, and have sometimes done them in the name of God. Today, church leaders and Christians may be cowed and ashamed by this record and by contemporary acts of Christians that are embarrassing and shameful. One thinks of threatened burnings of the Qur'an or the picketing of military funerals when the dead soldier is a homosexual. But if Christianity can — and must — repent, it must not whimper.[9]

While there is important truth in these accusations, and while the alliance of some Christians with a right-wing political agenda in recent years has had, according to a recent study by Harvard sociologist Robert Putnam (*Amazing Grace*, 2010), a chilling effect on young people in their relationships to the church, it is also true that Paul would not have had these things in mind when he cautioned Timothy not to be

---

9. Leander Keck, *The Church Confident* (Nashville: Abingdon, 1993), p. 2.

ashamed of the gospel. They may be a source of shame to us, but they were not the issue then. The church was too young and powerless to have accumulated such a record. So what did Paul have in mind when he urged Timothy, "Do not be ashamed of the Lord's testimony or mine"?

Paul enlarges on these themes in both Romans and 1 Corinthians; it is particularly clear in the latter epistle that the source of shame is the cross. "For Jews demand signs and Greeks desire wisdom, but we proclaim Christ crucified, a stumbling block to Jews and foolishness to Gentiles, but to those who are called, both Jews and Greeks, Christ the power of God and the wisdom of God. For God's foolishness is wiser than human wisdom, and God's weakness is stronger than human strength" (1 Cor. 1:22-25).

At that time, as in our own time, some people insisted on verification, proof, and evidence — or, as Paul puts it, "signs." Others insisted that the gospel must confirm existing human wisdom and accepted forms of knowledge: that is, the gospel must be credible according to the world's and culture's standards of evidence and even fashion. In both instances, faith is something that makes sense to the standards of the conventional world. There is proof to which one can point, or there is the confirmation of attendant success. These have their parallels in our time. The gospel "works," or "it makes sense." Faith is confirmed by material blessing and worldly success. Or faith is a form of personal enlightenment and of our becoming more "spiritual." In the face of both, the cross seems at best odd — and quite possibly embarrassing.

At the conclusion of my first year of seminary I went to visit a small rural church with the idea that I might be a student-pastor there the following year. During my initial seminary year I had done fieldwork at an exciting multiracial urban church, where the music was contemporary and the life and ministries of the congregation were viewed and described as "cutting-edge." But there wasn't a thing "cutting-edge" about this small rural church of farmers, truck drivers, hair dressers, old women, and a couple of awkward, not particularly attractive, teenagers. Moreover, the hymns were jarring to me. We struggled through "Rock of Ages," "The Old Rugged Cross," and wrapped up with "Abide with Me." The contrast with the upbeat music of the congregation in the city was telling and somehow, to me, embarrassing.

For some time I pondered the response I had — my uneasiness, even embarrassment. Some of it may have been my own class bias. But it was something more. I had been raised to think of myself as a helper, leader, giver, and doer. Church and Scouts, college and seminary had formed and confirmed such a self-understanding. The hymns of that small church told me I was something else, something different: a sinner in need of the Savior. I wasn't so sure. Moreover, the hymns and prayers implicitly said that our world was not "day by day getting better in every way." Instead, it was a broken and a fallen world, a world captive to the twin alien powers of sin and death. But in Christ and his cross those powers had been disarmed and broken. All of this was a challenge. It was a challenge to my view of myself as a giver but not a receiver, as a helper but not a person in need of help. It was a challenge to the modern, progress-shaped construal of the world that told us we were improving steadily — with enlightenment and worldly salvation just around the corner. The claim that we are sinners in need of salvation was troubling and embarrassing. It was also, I came to believe, true.

The gospel's story of who we are and what the world is, is neither easy nor conventional. It doesn't flatter the sensibilities of a culture bent on self-esteem. Often in modern America we prefer a different story, one that tells us we are basically good people in need of education and not sinners in need of the Savior. Moreover, there is the difficult, even scandalous, particularity of the gospel: the claim that, in a particular life at a particular point in history, God acted decisively to redeem all. In the face of human claims of ascent through wisdom, progress, and scientific miracles, the gospel speaks of the descent of the Savior, who comes among us, while we are yet sinners (Rom. 5:8). Perhaps there is something embarrassing, even shameful, about such a story, particularly for high achievers, for the successful, and for Americans given to ideas of self-sufficiency. But it is also, as Paul puts it, "for those who are called . . . the power of God and the wisdom of God." "For this gospel," Paul tells Timothy, "I was appointed herald, apostle, and teacher; for this reason I suffer as I do. But I am not ashamed . . ." (2 Tim. 1:11-12).

The Challenges of Pastoral Leadership Succession

If 1 Timothy is occasioned by Paul's absence and desire to provide Timothy with instructions for the care and leadership of the household of God, 2 Timothy takes this a step further. Not just Paul's absence but his impending death is now in view, making this a letter of succession. It is interesting, if you have this theme in mind, how many parts of Scripture pay attention to the idea of leadership succession. A good bit of Deuteronomy has the end of Moses' leadership and Joshua's succession in view. The passing of the mantle from Elijah to Elisha is famously related in 2 Kings. The book of Acts begins with the risen Lord preparing his disciples for his departure and for their new job description as apostles (Acts 1). In Acts 20, Paul speaks to the elders in Ephesus (probably including Timothy) of his departure and their subsequent roles and responsibilities. And now, here in 2 Timothy 1, Paul encourages Timothy to be a faithful steward of the tradition that Paul himself has received and passed on.

Leadership transitions are perilous moments in the life of the church, but not only the church. Whether the transition is in a family business or in a nation, changing leadership — letting go of the old and establishing the new — is full of risk and danger, as well as opportunity. There is ample evidence that we in the church today don't always do such changes well. Different congregations and denominations have different approaches to leadership succession and transition. Some clergy select and groom their own successors. In other churches, an outgoing pastor has no role in choosing or overlapping with a successor. For many denominations and congregations today, it is common practice to turn to a specially trained interim or transition minister, who then leads a congregation for a period of time (one to two years) between settled pastors. Acknowledging the many differences between the first century and the twenty-first century, what insight does 2 Timothy 1 offer to pastoral leaders and to the church today?

In some sense, all of 1 and 2 Timothy is concerned with these issues. At various points Paul highlights core and foundational teachings. At other points he addresses specific issues, as in the care of the vulnerable, the role of church elders, and deportment in worship. What is perhaps notable is that Paul does not lay out, as contemporary practice does, a well-defined process of transition and selection. However, he does address the substance of his successor's message, the character of his successor, and the intended effects of his successor's ministry and teaching. In some respects, our contemporary preoccupation with processes of transition may miss these arguably more substantive concerns.

First, it is clear that Timothy is the recipient, inheritor, steward, and guardian of a particular tradition or body of teaching. That is, there is a defined content to the Christian revelation and faith that transcends and even constrains various pastors and teachers. Too often, it would appear, different pastors have completely different messages, emphases, and enthusiasms. In fact, our cultural preoccupation with the newest and latest may encourage clergy in such a direction. Of course, there may be value in the emphasis on the new and different; but there is also danger. A church member may be forgiven for getting the impression that every time the minister changes, so does the message. This may prove to be not only exhausting but deeply misleading for a congregation. Time and again Paul emphasizes Timothy's responsibility to "hold to a pattern of healthy teaching you heard from me with the fidelity and loyalty that are in Christ Jesus." Different clergy don't create or re-create the gospel; they receive it, steward it, and interpret it in the ongoing life of a congregation. There is a body of teaching, a "rule of faith," to which the church and its leaders are accountable. At times of leadership succession it seems wise to emphasize both what continues and what changes. In other words, during times of leadership transition it is important to attend to the core message, the pattern of healthy teaching that is a constant in the church's life and faith, even as that teaching is brought to bear on new issues and challenges occasioned by cultural and historical change. In addition, wise pastoral successors need to be aware of a particular congregation's story, identity, and mission. While these can be recalibrated, it is usually best to build on a congregation's past strengths rather than ignoring them or proposing a completely new identity and mission.

Paul also emphasizes the idea that, while the gospel has a defined and definite content and is thus a tradition to be stewarded, the life and character of the pastoral leader is itself a message. Time and again — as we shall see in the next chapter in particular — Paul urges his successor to embody holiness. While salvation is not earned by behavior, God's grace requires and sustains a holy life as its fitting response. The destructive effects of bad behavior on the part of pastoral leaders has been amply documented in recent years. Still, the problems of sexual abuse, financial malfeasance, grandiosity, and hypocrisy persist, and when they occur in the life of a pastoral leader, they have far-reaching, ripple effects. It is not simply or only a personal failure; it is in some sense a church failure, one that belies the church's witness in its missional context and one that all too often utterly destroys trust within the household of God.

Finally, Paul repeatedly emphasizes the intended effect of healthy teaching, which is a hallmark of a healthy church and lives marked by loving relationships. Where there is disorder, illness, or simply lack of health in the life of a congregation, Paul would have his successor attend to his teaching and to his example. Sound teaching of the Christian tradition, which Timothy is called to "protect" and "hold to" (1:13-14), matters. That is not to say that there is something magical about this, as if repeating the Apostles' Creed often enough will automatically result in a healthy church. The teaching forms a way of life together that is sound and healthy. Good theology matters. Whatever a church's particular mode of leadership transition, Paul's words mark out crucial qualities and responsibilities of a successor in pastoral leadership: "Hold to a pattern of healthy teaching you have heard from me . . ." (2 Tim. 1:13). If you are a pastoral leader, you might try writing a letter to your successor, real or imagined. You may be surprised by that successor's gratitude for your advice and support!

DISCUSSION QUESTIONS

1. The language of memory is important for reading and applying this letter to the Christian life. What is remembered/reminded, and why is this crucial for the success of Timothy's ministry?

2. Paul mentions the Spirit twice in this passage (2 Tim. 1:7, 14). How does this strategic repetition define the terms — perhaps even the crisis — of Timothy's ministry?

Claiming the Power, Sharing the Suffering: A Pastoral Work Ethic

2 Timothy 2:1-7

1 You then, my child, be empowered by the grace that is in Christ Jesus. 2 And pass on the things you and many other witnesses heard from me to faithful people, competent to teach still others. 3 Share the suffering. Like a good soldier of Christ Jesus, 4 none who soldiers gets entangled in daily affairs so that he might please the enlisting officer. 5 Likewise, if anyone competes and does not follow the rules, he will not be crowned. 6 The hardworking farmer must receive the first share of the crop. 7 Think about what I say; for the Lord will give to you clarity in everything.

Part 1: Engaging 2 Timothy 2:1-7 as Scripture

This pivotal exhortation reprises and extends the letter's central theme: Timothy's succession of Paul involves the catechesis of other converts into Pauline Christianity. The grace that saves them from sin also empowers Timothy to carry on the legacy of the Pauline apostolate so that he might enable "faithful people" who are competent to teach still others (2 Tim. 2:1-2). The final exhortation to "share suffering" sounds a cautionary note that a succession such as this is hard work. To emphasize this point, Paul appeals to a triad of familiar exemplars: the good soldier (2:3b-4), the disciplined athlete (2:5), and the hardworking farmer

(2:6). Each illustrates the kind of faithful, competent, and self-sacrificial character necessary to move Paul's legacy into the next generation of believers. Paul's concluding note to "my child" (2:1), that Timothy should "think about what I say" (2:7), rounds out this exhortation.

The opening "you, then" is emphatic and indicates that the following triad of related imperatives — be strong, pass on, share the suffering — aims the preceding example of Onesiphorus at Timothy. Even as the former served an imprisoned Paul (1:15-18) and thus shared in his suffering, so too should Timothy, in his case by passing on the goods of the Pauline apostolate to others. Moreover, by recalling the letter's opening address, "my child" (2 Tim. 1:2; cf. 1 Tim. 1:18), Paul reminds Timothy that the basis of his responsibility in protecting and passing on Paul's legacy is their close personal relationship: their mission is a family business.

The first imperative, which we have translated as "be empowered," suggests that Timothy must take possession of the power made available to him "in Christ Jesus" through the indwelling Spirit (2 Tim. 1:14). Earlier, Paul had reminded Timothy that the Spirit of "power" dwelled in him, not only to supply him with the "charisma of God" (1:6-7) but to cooperate with him in protecting the apostolic tradition (1:14) and thus the Pauline pattern of faith (1:13) that he was to pass on to others (2:2). This exhortation elaborates the same idea in different words. For this reason we prefer to translate the prepositional phrase "by the grace" instrumentally rather than as a location or source of Timothy's strength. If it is read with this sense in mind, "grace" is less a theological concept and refers instead to the experience of divine charisma that enables Timothy to perform those tasks delegated to him in the apostle's absence. The source of this empowering charisma is found "in Christ Jesus"; therefore, it will not quit on Timothy (2:13) but will be there for him to appropriate whenever necessary.

The second imperative puts this matter plainly: Timothy's central obligation to Paul is to "pass on" to others what he and other "witnesses" have heard the apostle say. For the church fathers, this exhortation — along with 1 Timothy 6:20 and 2 Timothy 1:13-14 — form the biblical imperative for an ecclesiastical episcopacy whose responsibility was to maintain and manage an unbroken and indissoluble connection with the Lord's apostles and their witness of the incarnate "Word of life" (cf. 1 John 1:1-3). This doctrine of apostolic succession provided a principal theological warrant for the church's use of the Rule of Faith as the *norma normans* (a "rule that rules") by which the episcopacy could measure publicly and consistently any claim for theological orthodoxy. This apostolic rule proved invaluable not only in developing the range of materials useful in Christian catechesis and proclamation, but also to control the influence of nonapostolic forms of Christianity, especially during the second and third centuries.

The form of this apostolic legacy is expressed differently in this letter than it is in the collection of Catholic Epistles in one important respect: the preservation of the Pauline witness within the church is not secured by its unbroken episcopate but by competent congregational leaders, who, like Timothy, are able to teach others to pass on their memory of Paul to still others (2:2). This more democratic kind of expansion may be reflected by Paul's use of the generic "people" for those spiritually competent recipients of Timothy's ministry. Paul does not yet think of them as composing an episcopate but as a community of believers whose teachers remain faithful to his "pattern of healthy teachings" (1:13-14). Nor, finally, does he view the principal threat to their succession as heretical teaching but as a failure of nerve in face of shared suffering (2:3a; cf. 1:8-12a).

If the words of a Greek sentence are ordered by their importance in meaning-making rather than locution, the witness to what Paul himself taught is the most valuable qualification for participating in a succession of his apostolate. What we and his readers hear from Paul in 2 Timothy 1:13 is a "pattern of healthy teaching." This is the content, then, of what a spiritual leader must "pass on" to other believers. Raymond Collins argues that the implicit sense of this verbal idea (to pass something along) is to explain the tradition as you pass it along — to "hear" it afresh.[1]

The phrase "many other witnesses" could be understood instrumentally, so that Timothy's religious formation as a Pauline leader is facilitated by "many witnesses." However, this makes little sense of the images that portray Timothy's relationship with Paul in this letter, which are based on an intimate and immediate access to each other. Thus the question remains: What role do these other ear-witnesses perform in the unwritten narrative of apostolic succession? It is likely that this cloud of witnesses is a tacit reference to those who could still recall

---

1. Raymond Collins, *1 and 2 Timothy and Titus: A Commentary* (NTL) (Louisville: Westminster John Knox, 2002), p. 220.

what Paul taught and are able to confirm Timothy's imitation of the apostle as reliable. This would be especially important for a community whose accurate "hearing" of Paul's gospel is a condition of its future salvation (cf. 1 Tim. 4:16). The shape of succession is catechetical and forward-moving. The exhortation to teach others is, of course, central to the Pastorals' vision of organizing a Christian congregation. Who has the authority to teach and what they teach are the truck-and-trade concerns of church ministry.

The reader would be surprised to learn that the concept of Pauline succession in the letters to Timothy was something other than a succession of instruction and instructors. The contribution of this text to the overall scheme regards the recipients of right doctrine. Paul uses two adjectives to define the community of reception: faithful and competent. The quality of "faithful" in the Pastoral Epistles is measured by Paul's example (cf. 1 Tim. 1:12) and his canonical (or "faithful") teaching (cf. 1 Tim 1:15), that is, by the Pauline tradition. The faithful community of reception is a community of faithful believers (cf. 1 Tim. 4:10, 12; 5:16). A second adjective, "competent," is a more practical quality that concerns the effectiveness in not only learning what is taught but also in teaching others, which is thematic of the Pastorals.

The final imperative, sharply issued in a single verb, which we translate as "share the suffering," repeats Paul's earlier charge to Timothy to "share the suffering for the gospel" — imitating both Paul and "our Lord" (1:8). This exhortation and the following three illustrations make clear the personal expense of an apostolic succession. What is provocative is the gospel's claims, not Paul's persona and surely not Timothy's, because the latter evidently needs reminding that he already possesses both the charisma and indwelling Spirit to conjure the power necessary to suffer (1:8) and to cooperate with the Spirit of power to safeguard the tradition (1:14). If this succession guarantees the trajectory of the Pauline tradition into the future, then suffering is the expected cost that must be paid by Paul's successors in Ephesus. Conflict is the inevitable consequence of imitating the testimony of our Lord and his apostle. But the question remains: What manner of suffering does Paul envision? Will it be martyrdom, shame, or yet another species?

The diverse and abrupt character of paraenetic literature such as the Timothy correspondence sometimes makes it difficult for the reader to follow the flow. There is no plot line, no clear rhetorical design that enables the reader to easily track the argument made. But there is an overarching flow chart that the passage follows to link together the discrete bits of *paraenesis* via repeated words that help readers cobble together a vision for life and work. Paul uses familiar materials to help craft such a vision that will be easily accessible to the reader. In this case he uses familiar motifs, much as he does when cataloging cardinal virtues to inhabit or commonsense vices to avoid. Stories of the good soldier, the disciplined athlete, and the hardworking farmer are used even today to illustrate our moral instruction. Their use in canonical texts is routine because their ambiguity allows for more flex when applying the gospel truth to faithful practice. But this same literary characteristic sometimes makes it difficult for the reader to understand the particular motive and plain sense of what is written. In the case of this passage, the themes of hard workers shape an impression of why the faithful successors of Paul must share in the suffering of the Lord's apostle. The importance of hard work is characteristic of faithfulness and a familiar feature of Pauline exhortation (cf. Col. 4:13).

Timothy surely understands the task at hand in general terms: he is a custodian of memories that map a Pauline pattern of instruction, which he has been delegated to pass on to others in Paul's absence. The idiom of suffering cues the personal and political expense of this body of work, which, even though conducted in the company of the indwelling Spirit, is vulnerable to acts of unfaithfulness and the treachery of others. Pairs of opponents are repeated in this letter to emphasize the sense that there are insiders who, unlike Onesiphorus, have abandoned Paul or rejected his instruction. Of course, in his references to imprisonment and abuse, Paul also implies those political elites for whom the preaching of the Christian gospel and its sponsorship of an alternative way of life constitute a threat to Rome's prerogatives. But what initially surprises the reader is that Timothy's imitation of Paul's suffering does not seem to follow from its initial mention in 2 Timothy 1:8, where a share of suffering is implicit in his imprisonment, expanded later to include the physical abuse he suffered during his mission to the nations (cf. 3:11). Curiously, these profiles of courage do not suggest a way of suffering that results from the trials of difficult circumstance, whether social rejection or financial hardship; there is certainly no hint in these illustrations of prison time or martyrdom. These examples are of competent professionals whose personal sacrifice and hard work pay dividends of excellence: it is a kind of "no pain, no gain" approach required for a successful succession.

The first motif of the disciplined soldier (2:3-4) does not intend to baptize professional soldiering as a Christian profession; rather, this vignette of the "good" soldier typifies a species of suffering that the faithful successor should anticipate.[2] The analogy is plain: "Christ Jesus" is likened to the soldier's enlisting officer, and the single-minded attentiveness to the task of soldiering that pleases him is likened to the Lord's pleasure in Timothy's single-minded attentiveness to the tasks of succession. The use of the adjective "good" to describe this single-minded soldier repeats its earlier use in the "good tradition" (1:14), which Paul has entrusted to Timothy to pass on to others. That is, Paul likens the good soldier to the good successor: they are both professional protectors.

Although unwritten, a working knowledge of how the Roman soldier was used — as well as the virtuous person in Hellenistic moral discourse — makes us more aware of the impression Paul is making. If soldiering represented dedicated service and a willingness to suffer for a noble cause, the kind of suffering used here implies the rigors of a soldier's training that puts aside personal pleasure to become battle-ready, the sacrificing of personal prerogatives, whatever they might be, in obeying a chain of command. The "good soldier of Christ Jesus" is single-minded in his obedience to a sacred calling (1:6-7).

The second figure, the competitor, follows a game plan similar to that of the soldier. In antiquity, as in today's culture, the successful athlete was sometimes put forward as an example of someone whose hard work pays off in competitive excellence (cf. Phil. 3:12-14; 1 Cor. 9:24-25). Paul's use of the type in this case, however, features the athlete's faithful attention to the rules of the game, or perhaps a precise regimen of training as decisive for victory (cf. 2:10-13; 4:8). The relevant issue for the purpose at hand is not one's personal struggle and self-sacrifice in becoming successful; rather, it is obeying the rules. Paul wants Timothy to be a faithful son.

---

2. The history of interpreting this typology of the "good soldier of Christ Jesus" is remarkable; see Jay Twomey, *The Pastoral Epistles through the Centuries* (Chichester, UK: Wiley-Blackwell, 2009), pp. 132-38. Very little of this history — into the modern period — reflects an effort to settle the plain sense of the text but rather more clearly to adapt Christian faith to its political setting. Moreover, the reception of this text routinely divided it, so that the first part pertained to Christian soldiering, literally and figuratively assessed, while the second part pertained to a believer's preoccupation with the mundane matters of everyday life, whether a necessary evil or a distraction from Christian discipleship, which is avoided by becoming a monk or nun!

The exegetical question remains: What kind of suffering does the compliant athlete embody that is analogous to the faithful successor? Perhaps the key is hidden in a subtext of *nomimōs,* which we translate as "follow the rules."[3] Towner points out that these rules may refer either to rules of the game itself, which the athlete must follow so as not to be disqualified, or to the standard protocol of preparation that an athlete submits to in preparation for a contest.[4] We suspect that the latter is in play here, so that Paul's implied exhortation to Timothy is to continue or make use of the rigorous preparation that has prepared him for the work at hand (2 Tim. 3:14). It is interesting that Paul uses this same word in 1 Timothy 1:8, where he speaks of a "lawful" use of the rule of law to criticize Torah teachers who make claims without understanding. Without pressing this intertext beyond its breaking point, perhaps the antecedent text glosses this one to suggest that the suffering experienced in the successor's training results from the hard work in preparing to teach the word of truth rightly (see 2:15).

The third motif is also used frequently of someone worthy of imitation: the hard-working farmer (2:6; cf. 1 Cor. 9:7, 10; James 5:7). The word order of this text favors the farmer's toil *(kopiōnta)* over his reward, even though the two are integrally linked: good work begets a bumper crop. Again, Paul links the exhortation to "share the suffering" to hard work. In this case, however, there is a future benefit or reward stipulated as its motive. Bassler suggests reading these three types as parables whose primary point is finally made: Timothy's suffering, the result of doing the work instructed, is conditional of his future reward (cf. 4:8; 1 Tim. 4:13-16).[5]

The phrase that concludes this triad of examples is puzzling (2:7). Kelly calls it a "parenthesis" without a clear role to perform.[6] Perhaps it is best understood as a tagline similar to liturgical formulae (e.g., "Amen" or "Praise the Lord") placed within poetic or proverbial passages as literary prompts to denote transitions or pauses to readers and

3. Luke Timothy Johnson, *The First and Second Letters to Timothy: A New Translation with Introduction and Commentary* (New York: Doubleday, 2001), p. 365.

4. Philip H. Towner, *The Letters to Timothy and Titus* (NICNT) (Grand Rapids: Eerdmans, 2006), p. 494.

5. Jouette M. Bassler, *1 Timothy, 2 Timothy, Titus* (ANTC) (Nashville: Abingdon, 1996), p. 141.

6. J. N. D. Kelly, *A Commentary on the Pastoral Epistles* (BNTC) (London: A. & C. Black, 1963), p. 176.

listeners. Towner finds here a possible allusion to Proverbs 2:6 (Septuagint) and its mention of the way of wisdom: that is, wisdom based on careful observation and practical experience clarifies the pathway that one should travel into the future. If this allusion holds, the intertext that is created links together suffering and the way of wisdom in which the cost of discipleship is the price of spiritual understanding.[7]

Part 2: Engaging 2 Timothy 2:1-7 for Congregational Leaders

Power is a mixed bag and a tough issue these days, and nowhere more so than in the church. It is surely true that simply possessing or wielding power does not make someone a leader, much less an effective leader. And it is also true, sadly, that power has often been misused, sometimes abused, by pastors and church officials with grievous consequences for congregations, their members, and for the missional vocation of the church in the world. Moreover, we have learned, particularly in the postmodern era, to be suspicious of power and to exercise a "hermeneutic of suspicion." Often, in our postmodern period, it seems that texts are studied not with an eye toward the truth they may convey but for the power interests that are being served. This is a challenge for those who would teach and interpret sacred texts, as well as for those communities grounded in such texts.

And yet, effective leaders, including pastoral leaders, do manifest power, power they have claimed and exercise responsibly in service of their vocation and for the health, vitality, and mission of the church. So Paul, as this text opens, reprises a theme from the previous chapter (2 Tim. 1:7) and urges Timothy to "own" the power made available to him: "You then, my child, be empowered by the grace that is in Christ Jesus." You *are* empowered; so then, *be* empowered. This "be empowered" is the first of three imperatives that structure 2:1-7 and its description of a pastoral leader's work and work ethic.

It would appear that, given Paul's insistence on this theme, Timothy has been reluctant or hesitant to claim the power that has been entrusted to him. He needs to be reminded that "God did not give us a cowardly spirit but a Spirit of power, love and discernment" (2 Tim. 1:7). Moreover, he needs to "be empowered" (2 Tim. 2:1), and as we have ex-

---

7. Towner, *The Letters to Timothy and Titus*, pp. 496-98.

pressed it in the above exegetical section, to "own the power made available to him." It seems that power needs to be claimed.

Several years ago I taught a seminary summer school class for pastors, forty of them, on pastoral leadership. As we began our week together, I had them complete a questionnaire that was designed to reveal and help us understand what motivated us as pastors and leaders. What excites us and moves us? What gets us out of bed in the morning and gets our engines going?

The way the questionnaire worked, people would be identified in one of three categories with respect to motivation. Those in the first category were motivated by *affiliation:* this group focused mostly on relationships and caring interactions with others. "Affiliators" were concerned that everyone be included, and they noticed whether people participated or not. Those in the second group were motivated by *achievement:* the "achievers" sought results, accomplishment, and products. They wanted to do something, and they wanted a visible outcome. The third group in this diagnostic tool's menu was made up of those motivated by power and *influence:* the "influencers" wanted to change hearts and minds and influence the thinking and actions of people and organizations. All three, I hastened to point out, are important and necessary to the mix, and most effective pastoral leaders will demonstrate aspects of each one. If one were to imagine a dinner party, the affiliators would be concerned that all the guests felt welcome and comfortable; the achievers would be planning the menu and making sure dinner itself was wonderful; the influencers would be focused on the dinner-table conversation, the topics discussed, the connections made, and where those discussions and connections might lead.

The questionnaire had a self-scoring mechanism. We discovered that, among our forty pastors, we had twenty-three motivated by affiliation, fifteen by achievement, and two by power and influence. I asked the class what they made of these results. Initially, the students — all of them pastors — were somewhat self-congratulatory. Noting the strong bias toward a concern for people and individuals and an apparent lack of interest in power and influence, their comments suggested that this was a desirable and laudable shift from pastors of an earlier time. But after the discussion had gone on in this direction for a while, a young pastor raised her hand and said, "Our denomination [United Church of Canada] has been telling us for so long now that all power is suspect, even bad, that I'm surprised that even two people would own up to being motivated by power or influence." This was followed by short, somewhat stunned, silence. Then another pastor, also a younger woman as it happened, added: "Yes, and the fact that we have described power as 'inherently bad' doesn't mean that power realities and issues in the church simply go away, because they don't. They go underground and come out in weird, often destructive ways."

I noted to the class that two of the vocations that tend to attract those motivated by power and influence, teachers and politicians, were arguably vocations in crisis in our society these days. I then said that I would worry about a denomination where only five percent of its clergy (the sample in our class) wanted to change hearts and minds.

This exercise and the subsequent discussion suggested, at least to me, that in the church — and among its leaders — we have become, at best, deeply ambivalent about power and, at worst, completely suspicious or negative concerning power and the exercise of it. This is worrisome. For while willfulness (autocratic use of power) is one form and expression of sin, another expression of sin these days — though it is sometimes overlooked — is will-lessness, or the failure to claim and take responsibility for the power that has been entrusted to us to fulfill our calling. If leadership failure owes to willful abuse of power in some quarters, in others it may be traceable to the failure to exercise power responsibly and for the health of the household of God.

Fleming Rutledge, a onetime colleague of mine at the Toronto School of Theology, offered the following assessment in an unpublished lecture:

> The problem as I see it is that mainline preachers of the gospel have become frightened of their own power, and afraid to exercise it. I have listened to more sermons by more different preachers in more parts of the English-speaking world than any other ordained person that I know, and what I see more often than not is preachers pulling their punches, especially when it comes to sermon endings. I think we have been sold a bill of goods, this idea that we are afraid of oppressing other people. Sometimes this concern arises out of the preacher's own personal insecurity, the fear of being rejected — which, God knows, we can all understand. Sometimes, though, a conscious decision has been made: a strong presentation of the Christian story is going to oppress someone else, so we have to present it in a tentative way, lest anyone be hurt. One reason, I think,

for the popularity of telling one's own story today is that it can't be seen as oppressive. You have your story and I have mine. That way we can avoid metanarratives. That way no one will be offended.[8]

If Rutledge is correct — and I believe she is — Timothy is not the only one who needs to be reminded and encouraged to "be empowered" and to own the power made available to him. Moreover — and crucially — preachers and teachers of the gospel need to be reminded that the gospel itself has power, as Paul indicates elsewhere and as both he and Jesus demonstrate. For example, in 1 Thessalonians 1:5: "Our message came to you not in word only, but also in power and in the Holy Spirit and with full conviction." The gospel is not simply a series of concepts to be entertained or some helpful suggestions that may make your life a little better. The gospel is an event of power — life-changing power (1 Tim. 1:12-14). Preaching and teaching that are biblical and authentic, as we suggested in the first chapter, constitute an event that is transforming. Such proclamation is an event of the living word that has the power to bring forth a new creation. But again, as Rutledge says, "[o]ur faith in the power of the Word of God has become tremendously weakened. The sermons I am hearing today are not, for the most part, events of the living word."[9]

Related to this discussion of power, Paul's use and understanding of "grace" here in 2 Timothy is noteworthy: "You then, my child, be empowered by the grace that is in Christ Jesus" (2:1). As we have noted in the exegesis, the way Paul uses *en tē chariti* here is as "the source of Timothy's strength." If we read it with this sense, then, grace is less a theological concept and more the experience of charisma that enables Timothy to perform those delegated tasks made necessary by the apostle's absence.

Often when we use the term "grace," it lacks this element or accent. It is either a theological concept or it is something that happens to us; but it is not a power active in and for us. Here Paul offers a different — and much needed — corrective. The reception of grace is not merely a passive experience. Grace is a gift to be claimed and used toward the faithful exercise of ministry and the transformation of life.

---

8. Fleming Rutledge, "The Hammer of the Word," unpublished lecture presented at Wycliffe College, Toronto, October 16, 2008.

9. Rutledge, "Hammer of the Word."

An adequate pastoral work ethic will entail the claiming and owning of the power entrusted to a pastor by virtue of God's gift and confirmed in ecclesiastical ritual and sign. Moreover, grace is not simply the one-time experience of justification or forgiveness; it is the power that God grants to those resolved toward new life in Christ and vocational faithfulness. If and when we fall into the trap of demonizing all power, we are in peril. As that perceptive student in my class noted, one result is that power realities and issues don't go away but rather go "underground" and find expression in destructive ways. Equally seriously, the church loses the power of the gospel to change lives and communities and to allow God to raise the dead to life and bring forth a new creation. As an African-American pastor friend put it to me, "If my people don't leave church with more power than they had when they came in, they ain't coming back."

As I noted initially in the "engaging" part of this chapter, there are three imperatives that structure the text before us. Thus far we have focused on the first of those three: "be empowered" (2:1). But this empowerment cannot be separated from its end or goal, which is indicated by the second key imperative: "And pass it on" (2:2). Timothy is reminded of the core task of his pastoral ministry and leadership, to "pass on the things you and many other witnesses heard from me to faithful people, competent to teach others." Timothy is the steward of a living tradition, one that has a particular content, and one that serves as a set of norms guiding the household of God, ensuring its health and its capacity to form loving relationships, and inspiring it toward faithful witness.

The tasks of a leader are several, including direction, protection, orientation, dealing with conflict, and especially, establishing and conveying norms. It is noteworthy here that Paul does not define leadership as the holding of an office, but as "norming" and equipping others to "norm" the life of the household of God. To put this slightly differently, leadership isn't simply holding an office or position; it is a function in the life of a community, congregation, or organization. Some hold what might be thought of as a leadership office or position but fail to lead because they do not perform the function. And in a corollary fashion, sometimes people who have not been designated or officially chosen to lead actually perform the function. Such "leadership from below" was manifested by, among others, Martin Luther King Jr. and Lech Walesa. Neither had been elected to national office or leadership, and yet both fulfilled the leadership function.[10] In the end, leadership is less a matter of status, office, or even power, and more a matter of function.

So Paul makes it clear that Timothy's leadership is not about an inherited office but about an assigned function, that of passing on a body of teaching, a living tradition, that norms the household of God by reminding it who it is and whose it is.

This is important for contemporary clergy and pastoral leaders. Our task is to be teachers of the faith and, in doing so, to provide a center of theological integrity for the church. We, too, are to "pass on the things" we have received. Doing this involves both skill and courage, which chart a course between twin dangers. One danger, or temptation, is relativism: we might describe this for our purposes as the idea that the Christian faith is whatever a person or group wants it to be, that it has no core content, no enduring norms. On the other hand, the tradition cannot be passed on woodenly, without sound interpretation. If relativism is one danger, perhaps legalism (or literalism) is another. On the one hand, pastoral leaders are stewards of a tradition that has a particular and discernible content as revealed truth. We aren't free to disregard this content. And at the same time, interpretation in the light of changing contexts and conditions is required, or, as the famous hymn puts it, "New Occasions Teach New Duties."

Being this kind of pastoral leader, one who guards the tradition against both relativism and legalism, means, among other things, that leadership is dangerous. Ron Heifetz notes that "exercising leadership can get you into a lot of trouble."

> You appear dangerous to people when you question their values, beliefs, or habits of a lifetime. You place yourself in the line of fire when you tell people what they need to hear rather than what they want to hear. Although you may see with clarity and passion a promising future of progress and gain, people will see with equal passion the losses you are asking them to sustain.[11]

This contention — that leadership is dangerous — one that is confirmed by both experience and observation, links the three imperatives

---

10. Ronald Heifetz, "The Work of Leadership," *Harvard Business Review* reprint.

11. Ronald Heifetz and Marty Linsky, *Leadership on the Line* (Boston: Harvard Business School Press, 2002), pp. 2, 12.

of 2 Timothy 2:1-7, "be empowered," "pass it on," and "share the suffering." Faithfully protecting, stewarding, and passing on the living tradition of the gospel requires power, and it will entail suffering. Some of that suffering is occasioned by the provocative nature of the gospel, a power that calls other powers into question, a truth that challenges other claimants to truth, a way of life in the way of Jesus.

While Paul certainly is aware of that kind of suffering for the gospel and of faithful leaders, the primary kind of suffering he speaks of in 2:1-7 is somewhat different. As the exegesis notes, what is in view here is less "social rejection or financial hardship," "prison time or martyrdom." Rather, these examples (soldier, athlete, farmer) are of competent professionals whose personal sacrifice and hard work pay dividends of excellence — a kind of "no pain, no gain" approach. What is in view is the suffering of a solid pastoral work ethic, one that is entailed by excellence in the practice of ministry. The famed business consultant Peter Drucker once responded to those who imagined that leadership was largely a matter of personality or personal charisma by saying it is neither of those. "What leadership is," concludes Drucker, "is mostly hard work." So Paul conveys this to Timothy with three classic examples of hard workers who are prepared to sacrifice and suffer and to do their work excellently.

These three examples are the good soldier, the disciplined athlete, and the hard-working farmer. Each of the three is willing, in order to do her or his work well, to make sacrifices. The soldier doesn't get to head home when he feels like it. The athlete has to stay in training not only when it is easy or convenient but when it is not. The farmer puts in long hours in preparation for a harvest that is as yet invisible and down the road. None of this is to say that a pastor's winsome personality and gifts for ministry are unimportant. They are important, but they are not in themselves sufficient. Too often clergy do try — perhaps because of the public nature of much of the work — to get by on charisma or personality. Sometimes clergy even try to get by on good looks or short-lived doses of "rah-rah" enthusiasm. It may work for a time, but it will not sustain a long-term faithful ministry in what is certainly one of life's most complex and demanding yet rewarding vocations.

I have known some who have come to ministry attracted by the spotlight, the prominence, or the attention. Perhaps most clergy, if we are honest, have some of those desires, some ego needs we are trying to meet. Seldom are human motivations wholly pure. But it is my observation that even if there is something of such factors — or fantasies — in one's initial motivation, excellent ministers soon grow beyond such self-interested motivations. They learn that while ministry does require a strong ego, an inflated ego is a liability. They come to understand that excellence in pastoral leadership does require a good deal of honest self-awareness, but it has no place for self-absorption. Truly, it isn't about you; it is about the work. As another example, a minister's work, like the work of being a good parent, is a sacrificial vocation and is so in a time and culture that is not particularly big on sacrifice.

Those, like the good soldier, the disciplined athlete, the hard-working farmer, and the good parent, who understand that it is about the work and not about them, will be a blessing to the household of God and through it to God's world. Those who do not, who are casual in their discipline, who fail to continue in learning, who do not welcome correction, and who do not put in the time, prove to be, sadly, a curse on the household of God. Pastoral leaders have a core task: to "pass on" a living tradition, the gospel, providing healthy teaching in and for the household of God. For this challenging work, we must "be empowered," claiming the power that is ours by God's grace. And as we "share the suffering" entailed in vocational excellence, we will then also share in the many and unique rewards of the vocation of pastoral leadership.

Discussion Questions

1. 1 and 2 Timothy are letters that are full of instructions that guide ministry in the absence of the great apostle. Such is true for today's Christian congregation, which may confess itself to be "apostolic" without ever having met the apostles of Christ. How might 2 Timothy 2:1-2 help Christians define what they mean when they confess their faith in "one, holy, catholic, and apostolic" church?

2. The language of suffering is also important in this letter. How does Paul's use of well-known examples of the hard worker in 2:3-6 define suffering, and how does this notion of suffering compare and contrast with other biblical definitions of suffering?

3. Paul urges Timothy to claim the power of the gospel. Is power, in your view, a good thing or a bad thing? How would you say power is understood and used in your congregation?

Remember Resurrection

2 Timothy 2:8-26

8 *Remember Jesus Christ: raised from the dead, from the family of David. This is my good news* 9 *for which I suffer bad news — bound like a common criminal; but the word of God cannot be bound.* 10 *Because of this I endure all this for the Elect, so that they may also experience salvation in Christ Jesus with eternal glory.* 11 *This saying is a core belief: "For if we shared in death, we will share also in life;* 12 *if we persevere, we will also share in rule; if we deny, he will also deny us;* 13 *if we are faithless, he remains faithful (for he cannot be other than what he is)."*

14 *Remind them of these things and warn them before the Lord to avoid disputed teachings. There is no benefit and it only destroys the hearers.* 15 *Make every effort to prove yourself in the presence of God as a worker who is unashamed to interpret the word of truth.* 16 *Avoid profane chatter, for it will lead many into godlessness,* 17 *and their word will have the effect of spreading gangrene. Among them are Hymenaeus and Philetus,* 18 *who have missed truth's target, claiming that the resurrection has already occurred and subverting the faith of some.*

19 *Even so, God's firm foundation stands, displaying this marker: "The Lord knows those belonging to him," and, "Let all those calling upon the Lord's name turn away from unrighteousness."* 20 *That is, in an impressive house there are not only gold and silver utensils but also some made with wood and clay; some are for*

special uses, some for ordinary uses. 21 Therefore, if someone thoroughly cleanses himself of these [teachings], he will be sanctified as a "special utensil," useful to the master for every good work.

22 Stay away from the passions of youth and instead pursue righteousness, faithfulness, love, peace with those who call upon the Lord from a pure heart. 23 Avoid foolish and thoughtless discussions, since you know they produce conflicts. 24 The Lord's slave must not quarrel but should be kind toward all, able to teach, patient, 25 schooling opponents with gentleness. Perhaps God might permit them a change of mind, then knowledge of the truth, 26 and so they will come to their senses, escaping the devil's trap that holds them captive to do his will.

Part 1: Engaging 2 Timothy 2 as Scripture

This passage begins with a reminder of a core belief of Paul's gospel: "Jesus Christ [is] raised from the dead" (2 Tim. 2:8). On this basis, suffering is endured (2:9-10), and Christian existence is formed by participating with the risen Christ in ministry (2:11-13). The injunction "remind them" introduces a range of related practices undertaken by the congregation's leader: "Remind . . . warn . . . avoid" (2:14). In particular, Paul warns the congregation to avoid false teachers whose pedagogy and instruction do not follow the pattern of Pauline instruction (cf. 2 Tim. 1:13-14) and thus subvert the community's life with Christ in salvation (2:15-18). By contrast, Timothy is a "special [time] utensil" whose personal and pastoral practices (2:19-25) make it possible for the spiritual restoration of those false teachers (2:26).

John Chrysostom rightly wonders why Paul would encourage Timothy to "remember Jesus Christ" (2:8a), but then answers his own question: "[I]t is directed chiefly against the heretics, at the same time to encourage Timothy by underscoring the divine blessings accompanying sufferings, since Christ, our Master, himself overcame death by suffering" (Chrysostom, *Homilies on 2 Timothy* 4). In this letter, the exhortation "to remember" rarely introduces apologetics but rather the core beliefs of Paul's gospel, including Jesus' "resurrection from the dead" and his messianic credentials as a "descendent of David" (cf.

Rom. 1:3-4). Chrysostom may be right, however, that Paul anticipates a subsequent correction of his opponents (2:18), even if his immediate concern is Timothy's reluctance to share his and the risen Lord's suffering. In this light, then, remembering Christ's resurrection recalls the deep logic of Paul's gospel by which Jesus triumphs over sin and death by "becoming obedient to the point of death, even death on a cross" (Phil. 2:8). It is further logical that this same obedience-suffering-triumph pattern is reflected by his own missionary experience (2:10), which he entrusts to Timothy and others.

But the formulation of Paul's exhortation strikes us as odd. The reordering of the name "Jesus Christ" is unprecedented in this letter and may suggest that it is borrowed from an early Christian creed or lyric already known to Timothy. But within the bounds of Paul's writings the reader expects the antecedent note sounded by Romans 1:3-4, where the historical Jesus' Davidic pedigree is followed by his resurrection (and exaltation) as God's Son. In this new sequence Paul prioritizes the Lord's bodily resurrection — perhaps because Hymenaeus and Philetus are arguing against it (2:18) — to emphasize suffering as a resurrection practice. His mention of Jesus' Davidic lineage, which seems unnecessary, may refer to the church's claim of Jesus' royalty and may be especially provocative to imperial Rome; that could explain why Paul is being made to suffer "like a common criminal" (2:10).

The interplay of three powerful contrasts conveys the extent of Paul's suffering for Christ's sake. First is the contrast between Paul's proclamation of "good news" *(euangelion)* and his personal experience of "bad news," *kakopatheō* (literally, "bad suffering"). Second, he elaborates this experience of "bad news" as his treatment like a "common criminal," which is our translation of a second *kakos* ("bad") word, *kakourgos* (literally "bad-doer"). But these two contrasts frame a third: the dramatic irony between a "bound" Paul and the unbound word of God. Paul recognizes that he (and, by implication, Timothy) is but a human agent who serves a divine purpose (cf. 1 Tim. 2:3-7). Paul makes the relationship between his suffering and his gospel ministry clear in 2:10. In fact, those ushered into God's salvation during his evangelistic crusades are the fruit of his suffering! That is, the power of God's salvation mediated by Paul's gospel is not in spite of his suffering and imprisonment but because of it.

The passing mention of "the elect" retrieves an important Old Testament trope of the covenant community. The modern discussion of a

Protestant conception of election is hopelessly muddled in the offense of its particularity: if only certain people are the "elect" of God and, on this basis, are saved from sin, then most are not saved — through no fault of their own. But Scripture's theology of election, especially witnessed in the ancestral narratives of Genesis, is not interested in this theodicy; rather, it is interested in how people respond to God's plan to save the world (cf. 1 Tim. 2:3-7). The problem is not God, to whom salvation belongs; the problem is for those of us who freely choose whether or not to participate in the salvation-creating benefit. Of course, the crucial choice God has freely made is not of a particular apostle, Paul, or even of a particular people, but of a particular Christ, Jesus, whom God has sent into the world to reconcile all things to God (cf. Col. 1:20). It is the resurrection of Christ Jesus that makes this choice perfectly clear, and it is "in Christ Jesus" that those who identify with him by faith "may also experience salvation with eternal glory" (v. 10).

The saying added in 2:11-13 is as complex as it is gapped. It consists of four conditional statements expressed by verbs without subjects or objects. To fill in these gaps and add the substantive markers to this saying, the reader must "remember Jesus Christ" cued by the opening confession: he "is raised from the dead, from the family of David" (2:8a). In fact, the very purpose of the surprising "for" that introduces this saying (v. 11) is to point back to this confession as its antecedent. In this sense, then, the saying expounds the Christian confession of the living Christ. Paul adds a final footnote, presumably to explain the theological difficulty that the saying itself raises.

The opening line, "for if we shared in death, we share also in life" (2:11b), is programmatic. Again, assuming this canonical saying recalls interpretations of the risen Christ in the Pauline canon, a clear allusion to a participatory Christology that is found especially in Romans 6:1-14, and we should note it. Both uses of the verb "share" express the present effect that logically follows from the believer's prior baptism into the dying and rising of Christ. The importance of the confession that "Jesus Christ is raised from the dead" is more fully expressed in this sentence: "For if we shared in the death of the risen Christ, we now share life with him" (Rom. 6:8; cf. 2 Cor. 7:3; 1 Thess. 4:17). According to Romans 6, the prior initiation of the believer into the death of Christ redefines Christian existence in terms of moral rectitude and freedom from sin. In 2 Timothy, this same core belief emphasizes the faithful imitation of Christ's faithfulness in suffering for the gospel (cf. 1:8).

The second and third lines form a parallelism based on verb tenses to expand on Paul's participatory Christology. According to this parallelism, the present experience of Christian fidelity *(protasis)* yields a realistic hope for future blessing *(apodosis).* If we gloss each line by the opening remembrance of the risen Christ, the second line would read, "If we persevere [present indicative] with Christ, we also will share in his rule [future indicative]" — and would thus express a thoroughly Pauline thought. Further, the combination of a trio of *syn-* verbs, spread across these first two lines, fashions the sacred chronology of Paul's participatory Christology: to die (past), to live (present), to rule with Christ (future). This idea lies at the center of Paul's "epistolary and theological vocabulary" of Christian existence expressed in "his baptismal catechesis."[1] Perseverance is a hallmark of the justified, whose inward dispositions are transformed by divine grace (Rom. 5:3; 8:24; 12:12; 1 Cor. 13:7).

The third line — "if we deny (Christ), he will also deny us" (2:12b) — retains this same dynamic between present existence and future blessing, but restates its truth in negative terms, perhaps as a warning against disaffection. If we take this as a warning and not merely as a dogmatic assertion, Paul would have in mind those who have rejected his interpretation of the risen Christ, such as Hymenaeus and Philetus (2:16-18). Paul would consider them apostate, outside the "elect," and their "eternal glory" would thereby be imperiled (2:10, 19). If, however, an apostolic succession is the implied referent of the saying, the denial by Hymenaeus and Philetus of Paul's teaching about the risen Jesus Christ warns Timothy to continue in his work as an interpreter of the word of truth (2:15). The idea that Timothy's salvation is conditioned on his performance of ministerial practices is already found in 1 Timothy 4:14-16 and may be implicit here. The Lord's faithfulness to a promise made is undeniable on evidence of the resurrection, and so the warning implicit in this line should be read in a qualified way: God's preferential option is always for the remediation and repentance of the faithless. The prospect of God's denial of a believer's "eternal glory" must be seen as a last resort when every effort of correction, whether mediated by the apostle or by Satan (see 1 Tim. 1:19-20), is refused.

---

1. Raymond Collins, *1 and 2 Timothy and Titus: A Commentary* (NTL) (Louisville: Westminster John Knox, 2002), pp. 226-27.

Paul departs from this negative pattern in the main clause of the fourth line — "if we are faithless, he remains faithful" (2:13a) — to conclude on a positive note: Christ's resurrection vindicates the faithfulness of God to promises made to the elect community of a Davidic messiah. The rhetorical effect of ending the canonical saying in this way underscores the surety of divine promise in resolution of any theodicy, which while dependent on human agency for its fulfillment, is nonetheless independent of human influence. To express it in sharp relief: whether Timothy ultimately decides to succeed Paul in the gospel ministry or not, his choice will not affect God's decision to grant eternal life to those who trust in Christ Jesus. The presumption, of course, is that if Timothy fails God, another gifted disciple will be called to succeed Paul. While human faithlessness grieves the Lord, it does not subvert God's mission in the world to save everyone from sin and everything from death.

The explanatory footnote that Paul adds at the end of the saying, introduced by a second "for," teases out an original and stunning implication of the Lord's resurrection: Messiah's fidelity in performing his tasks according to God's redemptive plan coheres with who he is, which makes faithlessness a real impossibility (and thus comes our salvation). While Paul routinely declares that God raised Jesus from the dead to confirm his messianic triumph, his obedience is not predetermined by his nature but rather by the free exercise of a real choice that we now must imitate (e.g., Phil. 2:5-11). Paul suggests that what believers are capable of doing — denying the truth of Paul's proclamation of Christ — is something that Christ does not do. It is on this christological basis that the Pauline tradition must be carried forward by faithful believers in the apostle's absence.

Positively, Timothy is advised to be a hard "worker" who "proves" himself in a juridical review before God, presumably in the future, when God will measure workers by their faithfulness, competence, and self-sacrifice (2:2-3a) in their teaching of the "word of truth" to others (2:15). On this basis one might anticipate a positive result. But the plain emphasis here is on the character of the worker, forged during a costly discipleship, and on the content of her instruction, both of which must pass God's test for excellence.

Images of the daily laborer occur throughout the New Testament (e.g., Gospel parables, 1 Tim. 5:18; James 5:4; Acts 19:25), and the previous triad of popular types — soldier-athlete-farmer (2:3-6) — illustrates the laborer whose craft is forged by discipline and diligence. The crucial predicate linked to the competent worker of 2:15 — he is unashamed when interpreting the word of truth — is glossed by the Epistle's overarching theme of succession. The worker who passes God's muster is one who is faithful to Paul's gospel and unashamed to suffer when teaching it to others (2:2-7; cf. 1:8). The use of "interpret" (literally, to "make a right path") probably echoes its only other uses in the biblical canon, Proverbs 3:6 and 11:5 of the Septuagint, where it characterizes the wisdom of obeying God: the wise pave a "right path" in God's direction (3:6) that leads to deliverance (11:5). Perhaps the diction of this echo helps the reader sense the force of the following warning against "profane chatter" (or "worldly chitchat," 2:16), which repeats 1 Timothy 6:20 and recalls that letter's concluding exhortation that Timothy mind the apostolic tradition rather than impious practices that miss the target. An on-target word safeguards the tradition and leads one to salvation (2 Tim. 3:15).

Characteristically, Paul notes the contrasting content and pedagogy of a pair of false teachers, though it is rare for him to spell out what his opponents teach, and he rarely names them. He is generally more interested in using them as rhetorical foils to clarify what he teaches (see 1 Tim. 4:1-4). However, in 2:17b-18a, he names Hymenaeus (see also 1 Tim. 1:20) and Philetus as having departed from Paul's interpretation of the Lord's resurrection (see 1 Cor. 15:12). He uses medical images to make this point, which was commonplace in the philosophical discourse of antiquity. The implicit contrast between "healthy teaching" (1 Tim. 1:10; 6:3; cf. 1:13) and the spread of gangrene casts a vivid and familiar reminder of the awful effects on the human spirit of any departure from Paul's orthodoxy: it putrefies spiritual health. And the mention of this pair of troublemakers, whose reputation is no doubt familiar to Timothy and other readers of this letter, may well be a rhetorical ploy to indicate their potential for wreaking havoc, which only intensifies the urgency of Paul's exhortation that Timothy warn members to avoid their influence (2:14) and instead listen keenly to the word of truth (2:15).

A few manuscripts of 2 Timothy substitute the indefinite "a resurrection" (cf. 2:18), which indicates that an unspecified resurrection of some kind is being taught. By choosing to retain the definite article in "the resurrection," even though the manuscript support for doing so is mixed, we take it that Hymenaeus and Philetus have misinterpreted

Paul's teaching about the resurrection of Christ, and especially its theological implication for Christian existence set out by the prior canonical saying. Although the text does not discuss the teaching of Hymenaeus and Philetus, most interpreters infer from the prior saying that their teaching promoted some version of an overly realized eschatology that promises an escape from present suffering (cf. 2:10), a kind of "prosperity gospel."[2] Paul clearly anticipates suffering for those who follow in his footsteps (2:9), and participation in the coming victory of the risen Christ is conditioned on faithful perseverance through that suffering (2:12a; cf. 4:7-8). While Paul nowhere denies the existential benefits of one's ongoing participation with the risen Christ, the immediate problem is how this experience squares with the prospect of participating in his suffering as well.

His response here is clipped and uncertain, but it seems similar to the responses he gives in Romans 6 and 1 Corinthians 15 to Christians who are struggling with similar crises of faith. While the believer's participation in Christ's resurrection comes with a new capacity for good works, it does not deny the body's "mortality" (Rom. 6:12) nor "the sufferings of the present moment" (Rom. 8:18). There simply is no spirit-body duality — or an "already" that has absorbed salvation's "not yet" — that might allow for a doctrine of salvation that avoids "bodily" suffering (2 Tim. 3:12). This idea fits Paul's use of medical (or "body") terminology, which also counters a body-denying resurrection that seeks to privatize salvation or to avoid suffering, ironically similar to the creation-denying asceticism that Paul rejects in the first letter (1 Tim. 4:3-4).

Christ's second epiphany, "to judge the living and the dead" (2 Tim. 4:1), especially when glossed by Paul's teaching about a future resurrection of the body (1 Cor. 15), resolves this theodicy when believers suffer because they are faithful to the Lord. That haunting line in the canonical saying about the reciprocity of denying God (2:12b) only underscores the plot line of an experienced salvation that follows those who persevere into the future, when they will share in the future reign of Christ (2:12a; cf. 4:1b). Paul is a central character in this story, too, in that his faithfulness to the Lord, served at great personal cost, is justly rewarded "on that day" (4:8).

The emphatic "even so" (2:19) draws a necessary conclusion from

---

2. For a summary of the history of interpretation, see I. Howard Marshall, *The Pastoral Epistles* (ICC) (Edinburgh: T. & T. Clark, 1999), pp. 771-74.

2:13: God's faithfulness to the truth of Paul's gospel remains secure. In the face of the threat posed by the rival gospel of Hymenaeus and others, then, the rock-solid referent of "God's firm foundation" remains the apostolic tradition (cf. 1 Tim. 6:19-20; 1 Cor. 3:10-12; Eph. 2:20; see also Rom. 15:20), on which the congregation's faith is made secure (1 Tim. 3:15). The first citation from Numbers 16:5 (Septuagint) cues the story of the rebellion of Korah (= Hymenaeus) against the sacred leadership of Moses (= Paul) and Aaron (= Timothy), forming an intertext that adds an important layer of meaning to the reader's understanding of what is at stake in this current conflict. Korah's rebellion is a democratic one: on the premise that the presence of God has made every member of the community equally holy (Num. 16:3), Korah and his Levitical colleagues demanded equal authority to exercise the priestly dispositions and duties granted exclusively to the Aaronic priesthood. But Israel is not a democracy; rather, it is ruled by God alone and is sanctified by God's choices of leaders, namely, Moses and Aaron (Num. 16:8-11). Korah's rebellion was ultimately not against Moses and Aaron but against God. Paul draws on this intertext to make a similar point: God has appointed Paul as apostle of Christ Jesus (1 Tim. 1:1), has entrusted him with God's glorious gospel (1:11), and has sanctified his teaching as the means of salvation. In this same sense, Hymenaeus and Philetus are not progenitors of an apostolic tradition since they have no portfolio from God to define the word of truth that saves.

The second citation is more difficult to pin down, but it probably is composed of bits and pieces of different Old Testament texts (e.g., Sir. 17:26; 35:3; Job 36:10; Isa. 26:13) to re-create a biblical prohibition against duplicity: there should be consistency between a congregation's profession of the Lord's name and its holy conduct (cf. James 3:6, 9-12). In this case, rivals of Paul's apostolic tradition are engaged in twin evils: they do not interpret the "word of truth" rightly, and their false teaching "spreads like gangrene" through the congregation, provoking spiritual defection and contaminating its life with God.

Paul adds the analogy of the "impressive house" (2 Tim. 2:20-21) to illustrate the truth of these two biblical markers. The expansive use of the "house" metaphor in the Timothy correspondence alerts the reader that this house targets Timothy's congregation (esp. 1 Tim. 3:15). For this reason, the motive of the analogy is clear, if also imprecise: if upon entering an "impressive house" one expects to find utensils made of precious materials for use on special occasions, so also, upon entering

God's household, should one expect to find members who serve "special uses." One also expects to find utensils made of ordinary materials, such as "clay and wood," which serve more mundane matters. But the conclusion Paul draws from this analogy in verse 21 has no interest in that part of the analogy; his interest is to define those members, such as Timothy, who have special duties to perform. Appropriately, Timothy's Greek name, Timotheos, creates a purposeful wordplay with *timē* ("special"): Timothy's calling and charism have assigned him a special role to perform (cf. 1:6-7).

Paul's reference to "someone" is purposefully vague and would seem to include any member of the household who "thoroughly cleanses himself of these [teachings]." In light of a congregation unsettled by a misinterpretation of Easter, we have added "teachings" in brackets to complete the thought of the phrase "of these teachings": that is, each member of the congregation must take the responsibility to purge false teaching from the congregation. The congregation's decision to "cleanse" itself of false teaching effects God's sanctifying grace, and this divine cleansing produces the raw material of a "special utensil." Paul's practical sense of "sanctified" is that the convert's participation in Christ's death and resurrection transforms him from "ordinary," as it were, to "special" (cf. 1 Cor. 6:11).

The hard evidence of sanctification is the polar opposite of gangrene's self-destructive spread, that is, the production of "every good work," characteristic within the Pastoral Epistles of the Christian life that coheres to God's redemptive purpose (2 Tim. 3:17; cf. 1 Tim. 2:10; 5:10; Titus 1:16; 3:1). The word "useful" underscores the collaborative activity of one whose choices allow another to prepare him for the good work of a "special utensil."

We have translated the Greek phrase *eis atimian* as "for ordinary use," which seems appropriate for utensils made with wood and clay. The common mistranslation of this phrase in moral terms — "dishonor" (KJV, NASV) or "ignoble" (NIV) — tries to press the analogy too far as a moral contrast between Paul and his unrighteous opponents, or even between God's and the devil's intentions (2:25b-26). Nor is there any indication here of the destiny of those opponents, though most commentators think they are likely damned. The response of Moses to Korah is precisely the point Paul wants to make for Timothy: any contrast between Paul's "word of truth" and the teaching of his rivals regarding the Lord's resurrection — extended to any member of God's household who stands with Paul — is rooted in a prior choice God has made regarding the Pauline apostolate. To cleanse oneself of teaching that disagrees with his gospel is not ultimately to agree with Paul but with God (cf. Rom. 9:20-23).

The final unit of this passage (2 Tim. 2:22-26) continues the theme of the prior passage (cf. 2:14-21), which sets out the hard work of Paul's apostolic succession in remembrance of Christ's resurrection by concentrating on its most essential practice: to rightly interpret Paul's gospel, or the "word of truth" (2:15). Here Paul catalogs the practices and characteristics of the congregation's ideal leader, a "special utensil" in God's service (see 2:20-21). The initial exhortation to "pursue righteousness," with its complement of virtues, repeats these same attributes of Christian existence found elsewhere in the Pastoral Epistles: "peace" is found only in the opening salutation (1 Tim. 1:2; 2 Tim. 1:2), so its use here may highlight a particular kind of peacekeeping that avoids those "foolish and thoughtless discussions" that produce interpersonal conflict rather than knowledge of the truth (2:23-25). The word translated "thoughtless" is the antonym of *paideuō*, a kind of "schooling" that brings even Paul's opponents to repentance and to a knowledge of the truth (see 1 Tim. 2:4). Towner comments that the irony of Paul's criticism is that the effect of the opponents' pedagogy is precisely the opposite of what they intend: they seek to educate by debating the merits of Paul's gospel, but they only produce thoughtless Christians who are prone to spiritual defection.[3]

The address of the final exhortation is to "the Lord's slave," which recalls the ironic use of "slave" in Romans 6:16-20, where the new believer, baptized by faith into the resurrection of Christ for "newness of life" (Rom. 6:4), is no longer a "slave to sin" but a "slave to righteousness leading to sanctification" (Rom. 6:19, 22). This material relocates Paul's powerful vision of Christian existence to a passage that may well have in mind the misreading of Romans 6 by opponents who suppose that Christian existence — indeed, the believer's liberation from sin — is the assumed state of those baptized into Christ by God's grace alone. Clearly, the imperatives befitting the Lord's slave commend a pattern of moral resolve characteristic of the "special utensil's" self-cleansing and purposeful pursuit of righteousness (2:21).

---

3. Philip H. Towner, *The Letters to Timothy and Titus* (NICNT) (Grand Rapids: Eerdmans, 2006), p. 545.

Moreover, the description of the prospective repentance of the opponents indicates the conditional nature of the believers' covenant-keeping. The precise meaning of this more optimistic approach on Paul's part to his opponents is contested among scholars; but Paul's confidence in the capacity of God's truth to change the minds of his opponents is a theme in these Epistles (2:25; cf. 1 Tim. 1:19-20; 2:4; 3:6-7; Titus 1:1). Timothy's pattern of life, especially his pastoral kindness "toward all" and his ability to teach the truth to others, suggests that the repentance of opponents is the principal motive of his moral rigor. That is, truth must be embodied in personal virtue to have its fullest influence on others.

Although the repentance of opponents is clearly the purpose for Timothy's gentle and deliberative approach to a group that includes Philetus and Hymenaeus, the meaning of God's granting them permission to flip-flop is less clear. Why should God's permission be so equivocal ("perhaps God might permit"), especially if "the Lord knows those belonging to him" (2:19)? Perhaps the issue at stake is less about divine foreknowledge and instead concerns the mechanics of a repentance-from-below and the powerful role of the "word of truth" that prompts people to turn from their error back to God.

The distinctive use of "knowledge of the truth" in these two letters to Timothy (1 Tim. 2:4; 2 Tim. 2:25; 3:7; cf. Titus 1:1) gives formulaic expression to an element central to Pauline thought: criteria of knowing God are used whenever the Christian missionary combats misinformation and ignorance. Even though God's role in conversion is unconditional and clear, the gospel's accessibility to all depends on its rational presentation. Paul's earlier exhortation regarding the right interpretation of the word of truth (2:15) makes plain this final exhortation: God's permission of restoration is granted only to those who respond to the "word of truth," kindly but rationally presented, and "come to their senses."

This point helps discern the nature of the relationship between the devil and God indicated by this text, which remains difficult to assess with any exegetical precision. The First Letter to Timothy mentions delivering Hymenaeus to Satan for church discipline, with the prospective loss of covenant blessings promised to members of the community (see the commentary on 1 Tim. 1:18-20 above). Some have complained about the ambiguity of the final phrase, which literally means "for that one's will." The syntactical problem concerns the pronoun: whether its antecedent is the previous pronoun, which refers to the devil, or to God, since God's intention to grant repentance is the principal verb of the sentence. Our translation of verse 26 reflects an exegetical decision: it is the devil who holds opponents "captive to do his will" (cf. 1 Tim. 4:1-2). But if so, in what sense is the devil an agent of God's redemptive purpose, which is that all come to a "knowledge of the truth" and be saved (1 Tim. 2:4)?

The earlier use of the devil's entrapment of the congregation's administrator in 1 Timothy 3:6-7 may be instructive here. While Paul demonizes false teaching elsewhere (e.g., 1 Tim. 4:1-2; 5:15), the point here is closer in sense to a spiritual test aptly used when distinguishing the mature from the immature leader. The ancillary benefit of mature leadership is that it also cultivates a good reputation with outsiders (cf. 1 Tim. 3:7). The "devil's trap," then, symbolizes the manner of the opponents' spiritual immaturity, which disqualifies them from leadership, but also the deleterious consequence of rendering the gospel ineffective in converting the outsider. The "good work" of the mature believer cuts both ways, not only in sustaining a life with God but also as evidence to the outsider of the penetrating clarity of the word of truth.

Although the profile of Paul's opponents in 2 Timothy is an important historical construction, the most important element of this passage is the profile of the ideal disciple. Again, drafting both the persona and tasks of a competent successor, into whose hands the community can entrust its future, is central to this kind of testamental literature. The moral purpose of one's life — to "pursue righteousness" (2:22) — is a decisive ingredient of Timothy's success as Paul's successor and custodian of the Pauline apostolate. According to the Dead Sea Scrolls (CD 1.11; 20.32; 1QHab 2.2), the individual who had the most important role in shaping the life of the community was called "the Teacher of Righteousness" *(moreh hatsedeq),* a sobriquet that reflects his spiritual authority to interpret Torah and to exemplify the manner of holy life that might "direct (Israel) in the path of God's heart" (CD 1.11) and thus the terms of eternal life (cf. 1QpHab 7.1-5). Significantly, the Dead Sea Scrolls also speak of the Teacher's opponent within Israel — a so-called "Wicked Priest" (cf. 1QpHab xi.4-8; 4Q171 4.8-10) who is sometimes called the "Liar" because he teaches falsehoods (cf. 1QpHab x.9) — as one who might lead Israel into Belial's traps (CD 4.15; cf. 2:26). While the idiom used in the Scrolls to describe their unfriendly competition over Israel's future with God reflects the ascetic values of the

Qumran community, it does emphasize the importance of purity in a way that rings true to the polemic Paul uses in 2 Timothy 2 — both to castigate his opposition (2:16-18) and to encourage Timothy to live a holy life (2:20-21).

Part 2: Engaging 2 Timothy 2 for Congregational Leaders

The constants in 1 and 2 Timothy are three: Paul's focus on the critical role of the pastoral leader; the importance of that person "tending to your teaching" (1 Tim. 4:16); and the axiomatic relationship between healthy and sound theological teaching and the health and vitality of the household of God, the church. These are the steady and repeated refrains: Remember the core teachings and focus there. Don't stray off into arcane matters, into "myths and endless genealogies that promote speculations" (1 Tim. 1:4). "Give attention to the public reading of Scripture, to exhorting, to teaching" (1 Tim. 4:13). And, first and last, the health of the congregation is dependent on sound teaching and preaching. If you get this wrong, everything else is a mess. These various qualities and emphases may be summed up, as we suggested in the first chapter, by describing a faithful pastor as a "center of theological integrity" in the life of the congregation.

Some may respond to these interrelated themes and priorities by saying, "Isn't that obvious? Isn't it clear that pastoral leaders are responsible for sound teaching? Isn't it apparent that there is an integral relationship between healthy and faithful teaching of the gospel and the health of the church?" If these themes are obvious, it is not evident in the life and practice of clergy and congregations. Pastors attend to many other things, often with far greater energy and enthusiasm. In some quarters, market research and analysis is a key driver. Or the "production values" and pacing of a worship service, which itself begins to feel more like entertainment for an audience than worship of a holy God. Music type and style is a frequent preoccupation and sometimes a battleground. In some other settings, emphasis falls on the latest social or political issue or crisis, while in others you wouldn't know there is world out there, so thoroughly does the congregation focus on its own history and customs — "the way we do things here." In still others, the most recent techniques for church growth or profiling generational preferences are all the rage.

As I've noted above, pastors are properly cautioned against "majoring in the minors." That's an easy thing to do in a church and society that isn't all that clear what the majors are. Majoring in the minors remains a constant temptation for the church and its leaders, and the minor and extracurricular options are truly endless. Though the centrality of faithful Christian preaching and teaching and its importance to the health of a congregation may be viewed as conceptually obvious, in practice it often is anything but. In reality, Paul's steady drumbeat on such themes throughout 1 and 2 Timothy is very much needed today, in the church and by its pastoral leaders. The opening words of this chapter's text are consistent with these themes: "Remember Jesus Christ, raised from the dead, from the family of David. This is my good news" (2 Tim. 2:8). It seems so obvious: "Remember Jesus Christ." But as the storied man of letters Dr. Johnson said, "Never be afraid to remind people of the obvious; it is what they have most forgot."

An image that makes this point comes from Australia. Following her graduation from college, my daughter worked on a huge cattle station in the Australian outback. She discovered that there the land is so vast and arid that ranchers don't always bother with fences. If they were to rely on fences to keep their cattle in, they would be fencing forever. What keeps their livestock around in the outback is the well, a deep well with ample pure water.

Two Aussies, Michael Frost and Alan Hirsch, apply this bucolic image to their discussion of the "centered-set" congregation — in contrast to either the "open-set" or the "bounded-set" congregation:

> In some farming communities, the farmers might build fences around their properties to keep their livestock in and the livestock of neighboring farms out. This is a bounded set. But in rural communities where farms or ranches cover an enormous geographic area, fencing the property is out of the question. In our home of Australia, ranches (called stations) are so vast that fences are superfluous. Under these conditions a farmer has to sink a bore and create a well, a precious water supply in the Outback. It is assumed that livestock, though they will stray, will never roam too far from the well, lest they die. That is the centered set. As long as there is a supply of clean water, the livestock will remain close by.[4]

4. Quoted in Jim Belcher, *Deep Church* (Downers Grove, IL: IVP, 2009), p. 86.

In many churches the emphasis does fall on the boundaries, on who's in and who's out. Both theological liberals and theological conservatives can be found focusing on the boundaries. The Aussies offer a different image and focus: a deep well and a centered-set congregation that focuses on what is central. Paul's insistent focus in 1 and 2 Timothy on sound core teaching is a call to keep to core truths, to keep the water deep and pure, to attend to the essentials. "Remember Jesus Christ, raised from the dead. . . ." To some, that core resurrection teaching may not even seem to be the place to either focus or to start. "Wouldn't it make more sense," many might ask, "to focus on the moral teachings of Jesus?"

That is the question Martin Copenhaver addresses in his book *To Begin at the Beginning,* which is aimed at those new to the Christian faith.

> In some respects . . . Easter seems the least likely place to begin any quest for Christian faith. The faith claims made at Easter are perhaps the most difficult of all to accept. It can seem as if Easter is the advanced course for Christians, to be approached only after completing the introductory courses that deal with Jesus' life and teachings. Begin with the Sermon on the Mount. Marvel at Jesus' wisdom. Learn from him. Become fascinated by his life. If one begins there, perhaps then one will be better prepared to hear this mysterious tale about Jesus rising from the dead. It is interesting to note, however, that the disciples in the early church customarily started their sermons with the proclamations about Easter, as if it were the only place to begin.[5]

Furthermore, Copenhaver continues, this is clearly the focus for Paul:

> Paul, writing in the generation after Jesus, makes only passing reference to the teachings of Jesus. . . . Instead, Paul proclaimed that God fulfilled ancient promises by sending Jesus, God incarnate, that this Jesus was willing to suffer and die on our behalf so that we might be reconciled to God, and that God's gifts of everlasting love and eter-

5. Martin Copenhaver, *To Begin at the Beginning* (Cleveland: Pilgrim, 1994), pp. 58-59.

nal life were ultimately triumphant in the resurrection. This was enough for Paul to know. It is enough for us to know as well.[6]

But why is it "enough"? How can knowledge of the resurrection be both central and in a sense sufficient? Of course, this is not to say that the teachings and acts of Jesus are unimportant; but it is to say that we probably wouldn't know of them today were it not for the resurrection. So Paul instructs Timothy: "Remember Jesus Christ, raised from the dead. . . ." Here in 2 Timothy, Paul doesn't develop a *theology* of the resurrection. The reader will have to turn elsewhere — perhaps 1 Corinthians, Galatians, or Romans — for that. Here he reminds Timothy, a pastor of a church, of the centrality of Jesus Christ and his resurrection.

It is a reminder that I have needed myself. Because I grew up in the so-called mainline church and was formed by theological liberalism, the Easter faith, however personally compelling, was not the first hand to be played nor the easiest to expound. As a young pastor, serving a congregation peopled by liberal intellectuals who had drunk deeply at the wells of Enlightenment rationalism, I would often have someone come to me around Easter and say, "I just can't buy it."

"Buy what?" I might respond naively.

"Easter, the resurrection, bodies flying out of tombs, the whole fantastic thing. I'm a scientific person. I just can't buy it."

As a young pastor, my first impulse was to try to make the resurrection easier for my parishioners who were not so much worried as offended. I would try a kind of Bultmannian "de-mythologizing" move. "Well, don't you think it's a metaphor, a symbol really? Isn't life a succession of deaths and resurrections, letting go and starting over?" My interlocutors weren't buying it. They wanted me to declare myself as having fully "come of age," à la the Jesus Seminar, and to reject this "superstitious claptrap." I couldn't do that, but neither did I offer much that was convincing to them or, frankly, to me.

But at some point that changed. I remember the year — the Easter — that an attorney took me aside with what he may have imagined to be something original.

"I can't buy Easter, the resurrection," he said. "It's just too much. I'm a rational man, a modern person."

I pondered his lament, then smiled and said:

6. Copenhaver, *To Begin*, p. 58.

"You have trouble with Easter? Well, yes, I'd think you would. I mean, what would you want with a God who shatters the world as we know it, who breaks our closed, cause-and-effect, explained world — the world of modernity — wide open?"

The attorney looked at me as if I were nuts. Undaunted, I continued:

"But listen, stick around, I think we can help you with this. With God all things are possible." The attorney staggered away from me as if fleeing someone who was suffering from psychosis.

While this is probably not the correct response to someone experiencing a genuine crisis of faith, it may be a worthy challenge to those who presume the finality of modernity, of the Enlightenment project, of rationalism *über alles,* and who consider themselves too modern or too enlightened to be bothered with the resurrection. What this particular person and many like him really object to, I believe, is the notion that they are not in charge, not in control, but that God was and is. The resurrection asserts that God is God, and that God, not we, has the last word. For human beings bent on control, which includes all of us sinners, the conviction that God, not we, has the final word, is both bad news ("you're not in charge here") and good news ("the very last word is always God's, always God's word of hope, of victory over sin and death, of reconciliation, of life"). Truly, *this* is the deep well, the living water, the fount of mercy. "Remember Jesus Christ, raised from the dead. . . . If we are faithless, he remains faithful" (2 Tim. 2:8, 13).

In my work as a teacher and speaker in a host of congregations, I have encountered — at least in the mainline Protestant world — what I have come to think of as "a strange absence." At a congregation in California, where I was directing a leadership retreat, a young woman, a newer member of the church, suddenly went off the agenda.

"What I want to know," she said with no little passion, "is what we believe. I don't think we're at all clear about that."

Stunned silence. Then another person, also young, added:

"Yes, I have wondered about that, too." But an older man, a long-time member, huffed and said:

"Discussions about what we believe make me nervous." What he left unspoken seemed to be: "Believe what you will, but kindly keep it to yourself." After an uncomfortable bit of back and forth, the pastor did what we pastors often do to quell the conflict. I said, "This is an important discussion, but this probably isn't the time or place."

When I was working with a cluster of congregations near Toronto, the planning team explained the four priorities of their common work to renew their churches: leadership development, greening our buildings, community ministry, and renewing our faith. "It's that last one, renewing our faith, that we haven't really made any headway on," they said, "that we don't seem to know how to get a handle on." How interesting and how telling!

When I was working with another congregation, in Massachusetts, the discussion was interrupted by an attractive middle-aged woman, who said, "I'm not sure I know quite how to say this, but what I think we're longing for, but what we're missing, is the experience of God's presence." And in yet another congregation, this one near Seattle, a man rose to "report out" on his small group's discussion. "We're not sure," he said, "that our church is still God-centered." I have heard these and similar laments time and again: indications of something missing, of a strange absence.

Notice Paul's appeal. "Remember Jesus Christ, raised from the dead, from the family of David. This is my good news." And a few verses later: "For if we shared in death, we will share also in life; if we persevere, we will also rule; if we deny, he will deny us; if we are faithless, he remains faithful, for he cannot be other than he is" (vv. 11-13). And in verse 15: "Make every effort to prove yourself in the presence of God as a worker who is unashamed to interpret the word of truth." That word of truth is first of all a word about God and about what God has done in Jesus Christ. The message is theological. Moreover, it is first and foremost about God's action in the history of Jesus Christ. In him, God has made the decisive, the apocalyptic intervention, initiating a new age.

My observation is that we have lost this theological center in many congregations today, the focus on God's action and decisive initiative, signed and sealed in the cross and resurrection. It is not that Paul is indifferent to the teachings of Jesus, nor to moral imperatives (there are plenty of those in 1 and 2 Timothy, as in all of Paul's writings). Rather, it is the resurrection upon which all else is founded. But often in contemporary congregations the emphasis falls, not on God's action in Jesus Christ, but on what we are to do, that is, on *our* action, *our* human response. This takes different forms, depending on the kind of church we are talking about. In many evangelical churches the emphasis falls on our faith. We must accept Jesus as Lord and Savior. It is our faith that justifies us. If our faith is wobbly (and whose isn't sometimes?), if we are faithless, then it's all over. But note what Paul says here: "If we are faithless, he remains faithful, for he cannot be other than what he is." Moreover, by so emphasizing our faith and positioning it over against our works, we create a false dichotomy — faith versus works — that is actually foreign to Paul's teaching.

If in evangelical circles the emphasis shifts from God's action to our faith, in mainline churches the move to our human response takes a somewhat different form. There it typically moves to justification by ethical acts or moral behavior. Thus one may hear countless sermons in mainline churches urging people to be, for example, inclusive or welcoming. But this is seldom grounded in God's action in welcoming sinners, in dying for the ungodly (Rom. 5:6), which turns out to be the most inclusive category of them all! If it sometimes seems that it's all about our decision for Christ (rather than God's decision for us in Christ) in evangelical churches, in mainline churches it seems that Christianity is really (and only) about being and doing good. Both have failed to heed Paul's admonition to Timothy: "Remember Jesus Christ, raised from the dead."

Huston Smith sums up the dilemma of churches that have lost theological focus and conviction this way:

> Conservative churches, commonly tagged as fundamentalists, incline toward a biblical literalism that is unworkable because it ignores the contexts that give words meaning . . . and they are in constant danger of slipping into disastrous political agendas. Worse yet, they are untrue to Jesus. Jesus was inevitably generous, whereas fundamentalists tend to be narrowly dogmatic and chauvinistic.
>
> Liberal churches, for their part, are digging their own graves, for without a robust, emphatically theistic world-view to work within, they have nothing to offer their members except rallying cries to be good. . . . The chickens are coming home to roost; we are seeing the culmination of a two-century transformation of liberal theology into ethical philosophy, and piety into morality.[7]

Thomas G. Long makes a somewhat similar point under the title "No News Is Bad News." He speaks of what he calls

> the one language entrusted to us, the language of the gospel, the language of what the God we know in Jesus Christ through the

---

7. Huston Smith, *The Soul of Christianity* (San Francisco: Harper, 2005), pp. xx-xxi.

Holy Spirit has done, is doing, and will do among us. Oddly, though, this is the one language that seems most missing from much current preaching. Yes, there is plenty of God-talk and religious chatter in the pulpit today, but what seems absent is the vibrant sense of the living divine reality, the holy presence.[8]

Not long ago I was invited to lecture at Plymouth Church of the Pilgrims in Brooklyn, New York, a church that had risen to prominence in the middle decades of the nineteenth century under the leadership of a minister who was America's most famous preacher in that era, Henry Ward Beecher. Beecher was a leader, perhaps *the* leader, of the abolitionist movement. For nearly forty years his voice rang forth from the Plymouth Church of the Pilgrims pulpit and across the nation. During those years that church gained a reputation as the "Grand Central Station of the underground railway," which conveyed escaped slaves to freedom in Canada.

But in the twentieth century Plymouth Church of the Pilgrims struggled to maintain its prominence. Minister after minister failed to emerge from Beecher's long shadow. In the second half of the twentieth century the congregation dwindled steadily. When I arrived to give my talk, I was met by the congregation's chief lay officer, its moderator, who was an older African-American man. Since I was early, he asked me if I would like a tour of the church buildings. We set off, and he told me the story of his beloved church as we walked. "Yes," he said, "a few years back I really didn't know if we'd still be here today. I feared that by now we might have closed our doors. We were down, you see, to a congregation of about fifty elderly people in this grand sanctuary," he said with a sweep of his hand toward seating that would accommodate more than a thousand. "But," he said, "we've experienced renewal. We're in the midst of a kind of revival. New people are coming. We've got new ministries in the community. Our congregation is over four hundred now, most Sundays."

I asked him what he attributed this change to.

"Well," he mused, smiling, "our new minister didn't do it all by himself, but he's been important."

"And what," I persisted, "did he do?"

8. Thomas G. Long, *Preaching: From Memory to Hope* (Louisville: Westminster John Knox, 2009), p. 34.

"Well, he got us to studying the Bible. Yes, he gives a wonderful Bible study. In fact, our minister can give you the entire message of the Bible in just six words."

That got my attention — and skepticism. I wondered if a minister who claimed to distill the entire message of the Bible into just six words could be anything but a charlatan. I had to ask.

"And what might those six words be?"

My host smiled broadly and said, "The six words that summarize the entire message of the Bible? 'I am God and you're not.'" We laughed together. I suppose these six words might be considered a gross over-simplification, or they might invite misuse. Still, there seemed to me something important in this lapidary phrase, reminiscent in some respects of the "core truths" that Paul highlights throughout 1 and 2 Timothy. That once prominent congregation had been so caught up in its glorious past, its prestige and power, that it had lost sight, according to my host, of something crucial.

"We lost sight," he said, "of Jesus Christ and what God has done in him for us and for the world." Their pastor had reminded them of what they had lost sight of, and the church found its health and vitality renewed. Sound teaching — in this case, that there is a living God who is active and doing something in the world and in the church — proved crucial to the congregation's life and health.

Toward the conclusion of this passage, Paul returns to the image of the house and household as a way of reminding Timothy, yet again, of the importance of his work and his teaching. "That is, in an impressive house there are not only gold and silver utensils but also some made of wood and clay; some are for special uses, some for ordinary uses" (2 Tim. 2:20). While Paul's intention in offering this image is not entirely easy to discern, it seems that he is reminding Timothy that, like a special utensil or vessel, he has been set aside for a special use or task in the household of God. Other people in God's household have other tasks, some of which are, though important, more ordinary. Timothy's task, the exercise of his pastoral leadership as teacher of the faith and a center of theological integrity for the household of God, is special — as special as the fine china, as the special silver. That doesn't mean that Timothy is only to appear on special occasions; nor does it mean that Timothy is a special person. It means that his is a special — and an especially important — task, function, and calling.

Clergy members sometimes have trouble with this — and in one of two ways. One way is to think themselves special, not because of the work to which they are appointed but because of who they are. Such members of the clergy may consider themselves entitled to large salaries, big homes, and fancy cars. They may expect prominence and deference, and they may get irritated when it is not shown to them in the way they expect. Paul did not have this kind of specialness in mind. It was not "You are a special person," but "You have a special task or function" — as a utensil might. If this is one distortion, the other one I sometimes note is when clergy have no clear sense of their special vocation and importance and even demean themselves and their office by becoming "need-fillers." "Whatever you need me for, that's what I'm here for" might be their motto. "I'll run grandma to the doctor's, set up tables for the bazaar, or fix the copier." Each of these tasks is important in its way, but there are other instruments and utensils and gifts in the church to use for these tasks. Timothy's task, and the task of pastoral teachers and leaders, is a special one. "Remind them of these things and warn them before the Lord to avoid disputed teachings. . . . Make every effort to prove yourself in the presence of God as a worker who is unashamed to interpret the word of truth" (2:14-15). It is his task and calling to convey the word of the gospel, the word of truth on which the integrity of the church depends.

DISCUSSION QUESTIONS

1. The theological importance of the church's profession of Jesus' resurrection is of non-negotiable importance. How might this passage be used in responding to today's questions and skepticism about Jesus' resurrection?

2. What connection does this passage make between a congregational leader's "special" calling and her moral and spiritual character?

3. A number of times in this book, and again in this chapter, we have described the pastoral vocation as that of being "a center of theological integrity" for the congregation. How do you respond to this theme?

The Final Charge

2 Timothy 3:10–4:8

10 *You, however, have closely observed me — my teaching, way of life, purpose, faith, loyalty, love, patience,* 11 *physical abuse, and my suffering in places like Antioch, Iconium, and Lystra. What abuse I put up with, and the Lord rescued me from it all.* 12 *In fact, anyone who desires to live a godly life with Christ Jesus will be persecuted,* 13 *while evil people — swindlers! — become ever worse, deceiving and being deceived.*

14 *You, however, stay steady in what you have learned and found convincing, knowing from whom you learned:* 15 *from infancy you have known the holy writings, which enable you to be wise for salvation through faith in Christ Jesus.* 16 *Every scripture is God-inspired and is useful for teaching, for showing mistakes, for correcting, for training rectitude,* 17 *so that the man of God is mature, made mature for every good work.*

4:1 *In the presence of God and Christ Jesus, who is coming to judge the living and the dead, by his appearing and by his kingdom, I firmly command:* 2 *Proclaim the word! Stand ready at all times! Refute! Rebuke! Always encourage with patient instruction!* 3 *For a time will come when people will not tolerate healthy teaching. Because they are self-centered, they will accumulate teachers who say what they want to hear.* 4 *They will turn from hearing the truth toward conspiracies.*

5 *You, however, remain sober-minded whenever suffering bad news. Do the work of a preacher of the good news. Carry out your*

service fully. 6 As for me, I've already had my fill, and the time of my death is at hand. 7 I have fought the fight, finished the race, kept the faith. 8 At long last there remains for me the champion's wreath for rectitude that the Lord will give me on that day. He is the just judge, not only of me but of all those who have loved his appearance.

Part 1: Engaging 2 Timothy 3:10–4:8 as Scripture

This passage forms an expansive exhortation that begins at 2 Timothy 3:10, concludes at 4:5, and is centered (3:14) by Paul's use of the rhetorical formula *sy de* ("you, however"). Paul's usage aims this instruction more directly at his young apprentice, "the man of God" (3:17), to set out the core practices of pastoral leadership. The first practice (3:10-13) is to recall the apostle's missionary career, which is worthy of imitation. The second and pivotal practice (3:14-4:4) concerns the use of the community's Scripture in a ministry of the word (cf. 4:2). The concluding exhortation (4:5) calls Timothy to the practice of sober-minded attentiveness to his service as Paul's successor.

If the use of personal example is an important convention in a speech of succession (e.g., Acts 20:18b-21), we would expect to find its use in a letter of succession as well: the imitation of the apostle's past practices and core beliefs is the imperative of a future succession. Paul encourages Timothy to recall his close observations of his mentor's "teaching, way of life . . . and my suffering." There is a sense in which a witless rejection of God's truth, characteristic of the opponents envisioned in the prior polemic (3:1-9), has already prepared the reader for the apostle's résumé, its polar opposite. Each of the nine virtues listed — which embody appropriate behaviors (moral), missionary tasks (vocational), teaching (theological), suffering (experiential), and his anticipated destiny (eschatological), and which define the ideal mixture of personal characteristics, experiences, and practices — was exemplified by Paul and mark out a competent and faithful succession (cf. 2:2).

Not surprisingly, the first characteristic of Paul's ministry cataloged is *didaskalia* ("teaching"). The repetition of this catchword in this canonical correspondence integrates a range of interests, including the orthodoxy of what is taught (cf. 2 Tim. 1:13; 1 Tim. 1:10; 4:6; 6:3), its religious purpose (cf. 1 Tim. 1:5; 4:16; 2 Tim. 4:3) and social manner (cf. 2 Tim. 3:16; 4:13). To "closely observe" Paul's instruction is to "pass on the things you have heard from me to faithful people, competent to teach still others" (2 Tim. 2:2). In sharp contrast to subversive teachers who take their cue from the likes of Jannes and Jambres (3:6-9), the succession of the Pauline apostolate depends on a faithful transmission of his instruction (cf. 2:8-13), its aim and manner (cf. 2:14-26), to still others.

Two other comprehensive terms are added to form this first trio of practices: "way of life" and "purpose." Although used only here in the New Testament, the currency of "way of life" *(agōgē)* in Paul's Greek Bible, the Septuagint (Esth. 2:20; 10:3; [LXX] 2 Macc. 4:16; 6:8; 11:24; [LXX] 3 Macc. 4:10), implies not just a lifestyle but an involvement with the surrounding culture or world where such a life is lived and shaped. We would argue that this is the sense of Paul's use here: to "observe" Paul is a form of catechesis into a way of life, an idea that stands behind the concept of mimesis in antiquity.[1] The final overarching ministerial practice, "purpose" *(prothesei),* recalls its earlier use in 2 Timothy 1:9 of God's purpose that shapes how Paul understands his apostolate. The impression of this threesome, then, is of a comprehensive purview of the person whose tradition Timothy is charged to safeguard and transmit, and they are extended by a second trio that gathers together qualities of Christ (cf. 1 Tim. 1:14-16; 6:11-15; 2 Tim. 1:13) to characterize self-sacrificial service to others.

The final triad reprises themes mentioned earlier with his imprisonment and anticipated death as its backstory. Reading Paul's recollection in the canonical setting provided by the book of Acts provides stories that help elucidate the "physical abuse and my sufferings . . . in places like Antioch, Iconium and Lystra" (2 Tim. 3:11; cf. Acts 13–14) and missionary practices (cf. 4:2). In many ways, the rule of life implied by this passage is anticipated by a prior reading of his Miletus speech (Acts 20:18-35) in both purpose and content. In both texts Paul distills his experiences into a general mark of Christian discipleship: "[A]nyone who desires to live a godly life with Christ Jesus will be persecuted" (3:12; cf. Acts 14:22; 20:23-24, 29-30).

But such a sentiment is really quite extraordinary, since the nature of a godly life is drawn by the conventional virtues of exemplary citizen-

---

1. S. Critchley, "The Catechism of the Citizen," *Continental Philosophical Review* 42 (2009): 5-34.

ship. Why, then, are Christians subjected to such abuse? Why should Paul's "teaching, way of life, purpose, faith, loyalty, love, patience, physical abuse, and suffering" (vv. 10-11) pose such a threat to those who hear the gospel? Paul's pessimistic assertion that "evil people . . . become ever worse" (3:13) comes from apocalypticism's playbook and reminds the reader that the timing of this difficult succession of the Pauline apostolate will occur during "the last days" (3:1), when evil will proliferate because of the insidious progress of bad theology (3:2-9).

The abrupt insertion of "swindlers" injects a pejorative of ancient rhetoric that was familiar when one was dismissing an opponent; however, in wider Hellenistic use, it refers to a snake charmer or con artist skilled at deception. This usage not only explains why Paul would add the comment "deceiving and being deceived," but in this compositional setting it may also recall those swindlers just mentioned, Jannes and Jambres, who, according to tradition, are the nameless "enchanters" of the Exodus story ([LXX] Exod. 8:18-19). This potential intertext supplies an important subtext to this catalog: even as those earlier "enchanters" deceived the Pharaoh, whose hardened heart prevented him from turning to God, so also the religious "swindlers" deceive a public whose heart has been hardened against the gospel. This description of religious culture during "the last days" anticipates the difficulty of Timothy's task.

The second *sy de* ("you, however") located in 3:14, cues a related but different theme of imitation. As an observant Jew, Paul practices Israel's Scripture. Following Jesus, whose own interpretations of Scripture led him into conflict with other biblical interpreters (cf. Matt. 5:17-20), Paul's testimony of personal suffering is in large part due to his messianic interpretation of Scripture (cf. Acts 17:1-9). The issue is not about divergent Bible practices or a battle for the Bible's authority, since on these issues Paul's use of Scripture is of a piece with his Jewish tradition. The issue is Jesus, whose messianic mission grinds the hermeneutical lens for his reading of Israel's Scripture, but also occasions his suffering.

Imitation of Paul's Bible practices requires more than careful observation; it requires Timothy's catechesis into the core beliefs of his teacher. While the clause "knowing from whom you learned" (3:14b) is pivotal, it is variously understood. In part this is because the textual witness to the pronoun "whom" was corrupted by copyists during transmission. Although the earliest manuscripts support a plural number, the majority use the singular — "from the certain one" *(para tinos)* — to refer only to Paul. We prefer this reading because it better fits the letter's canonical intent, according to which only the instruction of the apostle is counted as normative. The more relevant issue of Timothy's catechesis, however, is not that it is guided by *sola Scriptura* or Jewish tradition, but that he learned to interpret God's gospel directly from Paul.

The repetition of "learning" *(manthanō)* makes clear the penultimate aim of Timothy's schooling: to "stay steady" (literally, "to remain") in the things learned from Paul. The motive to do so derives from trusting Paul's interpretation of the gospel, without which a succession would not occur. In part, Timothy's trust is earned by Paul's virtue, for in his cultural setting the reliability of what is taught was based on the virtue of the one who teaches it; the use of "found convincing" (literally, "believable") roots the reliability of what is taught in the hard evidence of its effectiveness (cf. [LXX] 2 Sam. 7:25; 1 Kings 1:36; 8:26; 2 Macc. 7:24; 12:25; Ps. 92:5; Sir. 27:27; 29:3). Timothy's confidence in Paul's instruction expects this more functional idea: that is, Paul's christological reading of Israel's Scripture, however idiosyncratic it may have been within his community of Jewish interpreters, imparts a special wisdom that gets people saved. In some sense, religious authority is granted on evidence of what actually works where the rubber meets the road!

The catch phrase "the holy writings" *(ta hiera grammata)* has occasioned considerable discussion about its precise meaning and its subsequent use as typological of Christian Scripture. Most now agree that the use of the phrase here is "technical" of Israel's Scripture in Greek translation, that is, the Septuagint.[2] But the use of *grammata* (literally, "letters") in antiquity includes the more colloquial connotation of a

---

2. See G. Schrenk's word studies in *TDNT,* 1:763-65; 3:221-30. Ross Wagner raises important questions about whether the modern interpreter's interest in finding a *particular* text of Scripture to study (text criticism) should include a preference for the Septuagint Old Testament, since the Septuagint was used by most if not all of the New Testament writers when citing or alluding to Hebrew Scripture. Moreover, according to 2 Timothy 3:14-17, God inspires a *particular* text, the Septuagint, for teaching and training, for showing mistakes and correcting those in the household of God. On this basis, Wagner defends using the Septuagint for Christian translations and explorations of the Old Testament. Wagner, "The Septuagint and the 'Search for the Christian Bible,'" in Markus N. A. Bockmuehl and Alan J. Torrance, eds., *Scripture's Doctrine and Theology's Bible* (Grand Rapids: Baker, 2008), pp. 17-28.

child's curriculum, more like learning the letters of an alphabet. In this case, the addition of the adjective *hiera* (literally, "holy letters") would suggest a theological curriculum in which Scripture is the student's principal course text.

The technical referent of this phrase, the Septuagint (LXX), indicates that Paul does not yet include a collection of his letters in the same way that 2 Peter implies (cf. 2 Pet. 3:15-16). Rather, Paul considers normative what is heard and observed from him as "the pattern of healthy teaching you have heard from me" (1:13; cf. 2:2; 3:10-11). Nonetheless, the depiction of Paul's relationship with Timothy in this chapter makes the collection and circulation of Paul's letters a logical next move.[3] When the Pastoral Epistles collection was received and included in the Pauline canon at the end of the second century, 2 Peter's verdict about Paul's letters reflects a Christian consensus and would have interpreted this passage: not only Paul's Bible but also a collection of his inspired letters formed the church's canon of holy writings.

The effect of learning Scripture "enables [Timothy] to be wise for salvation through faith in Christ Jesus" (3:15b). Raymond Collins observes that this more functional reason for Scripture's importance is made clearer by a literary device called *chiasmus*. Appropriately, Paul places the irreducible centerpiece of his instruction at the center of the passage (v. 15b, "wise for salvation through faith in Christ Jesus"), and then encircles this pivotal claim in pairs of the parallel elements of Timothy's religious formation (vv. 14, 17) and Scripture's role in his formation (vv. 15a, 16).[4] Paul appeals to Timothy's personal experience of being made wise by God's salvation, then, as both the aim of his Christian formation and the evidence of Scripture's efficaciousness.

The verbal idea for wisdom rarely occurs (cf. 2 Pet. 1:16) but is consistent with the premise of Israel's Wisdom tradition, which is that God's word is the source of a wise or skillful approach to life — what Paul earlier calls "way of life" (3:10). When it is read correctly (2:15), Scripture's effect is not to impart the kind of knowledge that makes one a true believer; rather, Scripture helps to forge the believer's religious skill set — that is, to become wise in the ways of God that guide

3. Cf. Brevard S. Childs, *The Church's Guide for Reading Paul: The Canonical Shaping of the Pauline Corpus* (Grand Rapids: Eerdmans, 2008), pp. 69-75.

4. Raymond Collins, *1 and 2 Timothy and Titus: A Commentary* (NTL) (Louisville: Westminster John Knox, 2002), p. 262, though he incorrectly posits this claim as part of a polemic against the opponents rather than as an apologia for the Pauline tradition.

one's spiritual formation. The word "enable" implies that acquiring these new skills targets salvation *(eis sōtērian)*. A biblically based wisdom that saves the believer from sin and death is similar to the point scored by the Epistle of James (see James 1:18-21).

The phrase "through faith in Christ Jesus" is quintessentially Pauline (see 1 Tim. 1:14; cf. Gal. 2:16; 3:26; Rom. 3:22). If reading Scripture enables a wisdom that saves, such a salvation is impossible apart from Christ Jesus, a core belief summarized by the various sayings spread across the Pastorals (e.g., 1 Tim. 1:15; 2 Tim. 2:11-13). Affirmation of these core beliefs about Christ Jesus is a prerequisite for a Christian reading of a Scripture way of salvation and the reader's experience of victory over sin and death.[5]

No reason is given why the term for Scripture changes to *pasa graphē* ("every scripture") in 3:16; the meaning of the term itself is ambiguous and remains contested to this day. The terms "holy writings" and "every scripture" do not appear to be used interchangeably. While both refer to Timothy's Bible, the Septuagint, the change from a plural reference ("the holy writings") to a singular one ("every scripture") seems significant to us. "Every scripture" extends the general claim made about "the holy writings" to its every part. If learning "the holy writings" cultivates a wisdom that saves, then the various performances of its "every scripture" are inspired by God to produce this salvation. This is a classic form of deductive logic! Moreover, the noun "scripture" implies simultaneity, so that, even though it is expressed by a different genre or in a different theological idiom, "every scripture" bears common witness to the truth about God, the only God.

This text's two famous adjectives, "God-inspired" *(theopneustos)* and "useful," are the existential marks that commend the performance of "every scripture" as divinely inspired: that is, indispensable for wisdom-making when it is properly used within the community of faithful hearers and readers. We will not go into the interpretation of *theopneustos* — sometimes contentious within Protestant Christianity — or the awkward syntax of Paul's sentence structure.[6] We admit that the "plain meaning" is not very plain! Hellenic religions sometimes de-

---

5. See Robert W. Jenson, "The Religious Power of Scripture," *SJT* 52 (1999): 89-105.

6. A still useful summary of the recent history of the battle for an inspired Bible within evangelical Protestantism is K. R. Trembath, *Evangelical Theories of Biblical Inspiration: A Review and Proposal* (New York: Oxford University Press, 1987).

scribed the speeches of their leaders as "inspired," but usually in reference to their mantic experiences or the reception of the speeches by others who were inspired by their powerful rhetoric. In fact, the Jewish writing 4 Ezra, written about the same time as Paul wrote 2 Timothy, narrates the inspiration of the prophet Ezra this way: "And on the next day a voice called me, saying, 'Ezra, open your mouth and drink what I give you to bring.' So I opened my mouth, and a full cup was offered to me; it was full of something like water, but its color was like fire. I took it and drank; and when I had drunk it, my heart poured forth understanding and my wisdom increased, for my spirit retained its memory and my mouth was opened and no longer closed" (4 Ezra 14:37-38).

But we suspect that Paul himself created the word *theopneustos* by bringing together *theos* ("God") and *pneuō* ("breathed") to echo two familiar Bible stories of God-breathing in order to emphasize his claim of Scripture's power to form a congregation's salvation-generating wisdom. The first is LXX Genesis 2:7: God *(ho theos)* breathed the "breath of life" *(pnoē zōēs)* into the human, who "became alive." The second biblical text is Ezekiel's stunning vision of exiled Israel's "dry bones" rattling around in the desert without life (Ezek. 37:1-14). This text, read as a Passover *haftarah,* reminded Israel of God's promise to restore Israel. Ezekiel reports that the Lord God once again breathes life into Israel's lifeless body, this time via God's spirit. In Paul's Septuagint ("the holy writings"), the prophet recognizes that there is no *pneuma* ("breath") in Israel's corpse (37:8b), which sets the stage for the Lord's commissioning of *to pneuma* ("the spirit") — referring to the Lord's spirit — to command "the fourfold spirit *(tessares pneumatos)* to breathe into these corpses and they will live" (37:9b).

Paul draws on both antecedent texts to retrieve their use of the same theological trope, a breathing God, in order to connect Scripture with God's imparting of new life, or life in covenant with God. The implied voice of *theopneustos* is passive: it is God alone who breathes life into a people, although in this case through scriptural medium, rather than the "ground" of the creation narrative in Genesis or the "fourfold spirit" of Ezekiel's vision: "every scripture" is the creaturely agent that is the auxiliary of God's Spirit (Ezek. 37:9) to enliven God's people for wisdom-making and covenant-keeping.

J. R. Levison considers the importance of these same two Old Testament texts in forging Paul's understanding of the biblical promise of a new creation in arguing that Paul's reading of Genesis 2:7 and Ezekiel

36-37 is transformed by his belief in the resurrection (cf. 2 Tim. 2:8). Rather than locating the "spirit of life" in the first Adam, as do other Jewish interpreters (including Philo), Paul now locates the divine spirit in the risen Christ, the second Adam, in whom the holy Spirit vivifies a new life in all who believe. In Levison's reading, Christ's resurrection and the individual believer's baptism into his spiritual body personalize Ezekiel's prophecy that "bones and sinews and flesh can rekindle, and that the spirit can come from the four corners of the earth to fill the moribund nation, to re-create Israel into a new people who will till the land until it becomes a garden of Eden."[7] The morality of the first Adam of Genesis 2:7, in whom the divine breath is stilled by sin, thus provides the prophetic foil for the second Adam's life-giving spirit, who reorders the relationship between mortality and immortality.

In our reading, Paul's conception of Scripture is reworked within this same matrix of meaning, not only in his coinage of *theopneustos* when we would probably expect another word for inspiration *(enthousia)*, but also in his use of a fully formed (or mature) "man of God" as the endgame of using Scripture recalls the transforming effect the risen Adam's life-giving spirit has on the faithful mortal in whom it breathes new life. Indeed, it is Scripture that this life-giving spirit uses to lead this new creature "through a valley of very many, very dry bones back up the garden path to Eden."[8] Perhaps Paul's concept of individual (and not just national) restoration targets Timothy, in whom the spiritual gift needs rekindling (see 2 Tim. 1:6-7).

The catalog of Scripture's uses, which includes both priestly (teaching, training) and prophetic (showing mistakes, correcting) roles, is also patterned on what rabbis understood as the various roles of Torah.[9] Not only is Torah the "curriculum" used by rabbis-like-Moses when teaching the congregation the truths about God; Torah is also used by prophets-like-Moses, including Jeremiah and Isaiah, when calling the congregation to repentance.[10] Paul's point in exhorting Timo-

---

7. John R. Levison, *Filled with the Spirit* (Grand Rapids: Eerdmans, 2009), p. 315.

8. Levison, *Filled with the Spirit,* p. 316.

9. For this background, see T. Scott Caulley, "The Idea of Inspiration in 2 Peter 1:16-21" (D.Th. dissertation, University of Tübingen, 1983).

10. Luke Timothy Johnson argues that this is thematic of the book of Acts, which narrates the mission of the apostles according to the Moses prophetic typology set out by Stephen's sermon in Acts 7. Johnson, *Acts of the Apostles* (Sacra Pagina) (Collegeville, MN: Liturgical Press, 1992), pp. 12-14.

thy, then, is to emphasize both roles with Scripture in hand: he is to reprove and correct false teachers as a prophet, while teaching and training the congregation to live holy lives before God and each other. Such are the aspirations and "good work" of "the man of God" (3:17a), who is brought to maturity by Scripture.

The repetition of "mature, made mature" (3:17) draws on rarely used words from a glossary of spiritual formation that envisions a process during which things are added to make a person or group complete. In other words, Scripture's different uses supply goods that add to whatever else has been received from the tradition — in this case, from observing Paul's life and listening to him teach (3:10-13). William Abraham reminds us that Scripture is a piece of — and of a piece with — a broader, more expansive canonical heritage that includes creeds, sacramental practices, liturgical conduct, icons, ecclesiastical disciplines, exemplars, and teachers.[11] Whether one agrees with all the historical and philosophical detail in his sophisticated analysis, one must surely agree with his rejection of sola Scriptura as the self-authenticating measure of Christian theology, detached from the other artifacts of the church's apostolic tradition in measuring the orthodoxy of our Christian commitments. The functional importance of Scripture is as a means of grace, used as an auxiliary of God's Spirit to breathe new life into those who use it.

The scope of the final clause, which indicates the purpose ("so that") of Scripture's use, is debated: that is, does it refer only to the maturity of a single "man of God" or to that of the entire congregation? The catch phrase "man of God" (see 1 Tim. 6:11) generally identifies one who belongs to God — no matter whether male or female. However, in this letter of succession it refers to the ideal congregational leader, who safeguards and transmits the Pauline apostolate for future believers. That is, the purpose of the community's "holy writings" is to bring to maturity those who truly are of and for the apostolic tradition.

The phrase "every good work" is repeatedly used in the Pastoral Epistles (1 Tim. 2:10; 2 Tim. 2:21; 3:17; Titus 1:16; 3:1; and similarly in 1 Tim. 3:1; 5:10, 25; 6:18; Titus 2:7, 14; 3:8), and, according to Marshall, is a theologically rather than morally determined concept of Christian existence. Yes and no. That is, it is the manner of a public life produced by

---

11. William J. Abraham, *Canon and Criterion in Christian Theology* (Oxford: Clarendon, 1998), pp. 27-56.

God's saving grace and characterized in the Pastorals by the primary practical virtues of the day.[12] We would say that grace transforms the believer to live in harmony with the *oikonomia theou* — God's way of ordering human existence that aims toward loving relationships (see 1 Tim. 1:4-5). This moral payoff is the target of the redeemed community's use of its every Scripture.

Paul's use of the familiar theological formula "in the presence of God" (4:1) typically introduces a practical implication of prior instruction (cf. 1 Tim. 2:3; 5:4, 21; 6:13; 2 Tim. 2:14). Its juridical significance — similar to "as God is our witness" (see 1 Tim. 5:21) — puts Timothy on notice that the previous claims about Scripture should inspire him to action.[13] The use of the formula here is expanded to make the call to action more pointed and urgent (as in 1 Tim. 2:3 [4-6]): the divine witness is joined by Christ Jesus, "who is coming to judge the living and the dead" (cf. 1 Tim. 5:21). The source and meaning of this messianic formula, which is elaborated by an epiphany saying ("by his appearing and by his kingdom" [4:1b]), are both contested even as the syntax is awkward. The plain sense of the exhortation itself is nonetheless clear: Timothy's present choices are motivated by expectation of a future judgment.

This belief probably reaches back to draw on 2 Timothy 2:8 for added implications for the future appearing of the living Jesus. The purpose of his return to complete his messianic mission is to make judgments about the past and present performances of everyone, including those members of the community who have denied the faith (2:12-13). While Paul nowhere declares the criterion used to render his end-time verdict, in a succession letter it probably assumes a work that presents the apostolate "for that day" (1:12). If so, Timothy's future will

---

12. Cf. I. Howard Marshall, *The Pastoral Epistles* (ICC) (Edinburgh: T. & T. Clark, 1999), pp. 227-29.

13. Scholars have long recognized the difficulty of following the argument line here, whether 4:1-5 follows from the prior claims about Scripture (3:14-17), or from the earlier warning about false teachers (3:13) that is interrupted by the author's excursus on Scripture, or 4:1-5 begins a concluding exhortation to the entire letter. Our sense of the more limited role of 4:1-5 within the letter follows from an assessment of how the formula "in the presence of God" is used elsewhere in 1-2 Timothy and also the repetition of the *su de* conjunction that holds together 3:10–4:5 (see above). In our view, then, the command issued by Paul in 1 Tim. 4:2 is based on Timothy's appropriation of the holy writings in a way that targets the community's salvation.

be measured by whether or not he has remained faithful to "the pattern of healthy teaching" that God entrusted to Paul (1:12-13; cf. 1 Tim. 4:14-16). The apocalyptic idiom of the "reappearing" of the risen Jesus is important to the Pastoral Epistles, where it is linked with the final victory of God's reign over death and evil — Paul's core belief about the future of God's salvation. But Paul's use of "appearing" in 1:10 of Jesus' arrival as Messiah to abolish death and inaugurate life suggests that the Lord's *parousia* is the endgame of a process already underway. In this way, the Messiah's judgment of Timothy's faithfulness to the present tasks of succession that were given him is made more urgent.

The expectation of an imminent judgment, which surely includes Timothy's own (see 1 Tim. 4:16), implicates everybody by using "the living and the dead." While the universal scope of Christ's coming judgment mirrors the universal scope of God's desire to save everyone, its mention here underscores the prior conception of a "man of God" who is brought to maturity by Scripture (2 Tim. 3:17). Only then can the pastoral leader expect to safeguard the congregation from false teachers (cf. 3:1-9; 4:3-4) for the future of God's salvation (cf. 1 Tim 4:16; 2 Tim 4:6-8).

The principal command given Timothy to "proclaim the word *[logos]*" (2 Tim. 4:2a) reiterates Paul's previous instruction elsewhere (cf. 1:13; 2:15; 1 Tim. 4:14-16); and the four commands he adds — "stand ready . . . refute . . . rebuke . . . encourage" (4:2b) — elaborate the purpose of his proclamation. The "word" Timothy is charged to proclaim, which anticipates this robust result, is nothing other than the "pattern" of Paul's teaching (2 Tim. 1:13; 2:8b-9). And the normal sense of the verb "proclaim" is a public speech that clarifies truth. That is, the immediate purpose of Timothy's proclamation of Paul is to refute the falsehood of his opponents (4:3-4) and so to clarify any confusion about the gospel occasioned by their influence (4:8). Moreover, in this setting of exhortation, the tasks of "refuting and rebuking" bad theology and replacing it with good theology (catechesis) are roles assigned to the community's Scripture (3:16b). This connection does not suppose that the *logos* is an exclusively biblical one; rather, it is to affirm that a Pauline concept of Scripture, whose authorized role is to clarify the truth about God, is a sanctified auxiliary for use in conducting this pastoral work.

The resumption of Paul's apocalyptic polemic against false teachers in 4:3-4 (see 3:1-9) adds little to the apostle's canonical correspondence with Timothy, except to concentrate the reader's attention on the problem of a congregation's tendency to favor unreliable conspiracy theories over the healthy teaching of the apostolic tradition. We have translated *mythoi* as "conspiracies" (4:4) to help create a more particular impression of the worry expressed by this text. That is, the situation described is not one created by the teachers themselves but by members of the congregation who do "not tolerate healthy [i.e., Pauline] teaching . . . and accumulate teachers who say what they want to hear" (4:3).

Brevard Childs, following Gerhard Lohfink, contends that the persistent repetition of Paul's warning that his opponents are intolerant of "healthy teaching" (4:3; cf. 1 Tim. 1:10; 4:6; 6:3; Titus 1:9; 2:1) is "the most important normative concept in the Pastoral Epistles."[14] Timothy must be prepared to proclaim an appropriate word in the face of opposition, in imitation of Paul, the apostle to whom God's "glorious gospel" has been entrusted that he might teach truth to the nations (1 Tim. 1:11; 2:7; cf. Titus 1:3). This imitation extends, beyond the doctrinal content of the gospel, to pedagogy as well: a "patient instruction" that includes the rhetoric of refutation and rebuke as necessary (4:2). The reader should assume that this becomes necessary because of the ease with which Christian congregations "turn from hearing the truth toward conspiracies" (4:4).

The picture Paul draws is of a Christian community that has heard this apostolic word proclaimed (4:2), but in response some members have rejected its truth claims (4:4). Presumably, they do not wish to pay its social expense, which is considerable. Paul repeatedly notes in personal reminiscences his imprisonment (1:8; 2:9), suffering (1:8, 12; 2:9; 3:11; 4:14), and rejection (1:15; 4:10, 16); and he boldly predicts that "anyone who desires to live a godly life with Christ Jesus will be persecuted" (3:12). One reasonably doubts that the persuasive power of his opponents in initiating this spiritual disaffection has to do with the superior content of what they claim; or, at least, one cannot imagine that Paul would admit this of an intellectual rival, given the divine source of his gospel! In fact, Paul's word choice of *mythoi* ("conspiracies)" communicates the kind of unreliable evidence that finds a home in self-centered people who are not really interested in considering the gospel truth; *mythoi* are alternative theories of existence for which there is no evidence. The effect is to cultivate an unhealthy outlook that

14. Childs, *Reading Paul*, p. 163.

leaves people utterly unprepared for the future appearing and judgment of Christ Jesus.

The third and final *su de* ("you, however") of this unit of instruction (4:5; cf. 3:10, 14) introduces yet another contrasting image of Timothy as the ideal successor of the Pauline apostolate. The more general exhortation to "remain sober-minded" probably has the preceding "teachers" (4:3) in mind. The virtue of sober-mindedness characterizes the one who does not rock the boat — in this case, maintains Paul's example. If the criterion of succession is whether Paul is imitated, then even as Paul "suffered bad news" (2:9; cf. 3:10-12), so must Timothy; and even as Paul is the preacher of good news (cf. Acts 21:8; cf. 1:8, 11-12), so is this Timothy's "service."

This final exhortation is linked with an emphatic "as for me" (4:6) to Paul's prediction of his imminent death (4:6) and to a confident rehearsal of his life of faithfulness (4:7), which assures a "champion's wreath" when the Lord renders his end-time judgment (4:8; cf. 4:1). This prediction anticipates what every letter of succession must: a formal announcement of the leader's impending "death" (literally, "departure") when a succession, if there is to be one, must take place if the leader's noble work is to continue.

Much has been made of Paul's use of the verb phrase "had my fill," which comes from Scripture's priestly glossary and literally refers to a libation poured over a sacrifice offered to God (see Exod. 30:9; Num. 28:7; Hosea 9:4; 4 Macc. 3:16). An imprisoned Paul's dramatic use of this word, *spendō*, in Philippians 2:17 speaks of his death in sacrificial terms and has led some interpreters to find the prediction of a martyr's death.[15] But this is hardly the plain sense of the text. A better reading is that Paul simply recognizes the end of his life has now arrived, even though he remains busy making plans for the immediate future (see 4:9-13).

It is perhaps significant that Paul predicts his death as he describes his call to his apostolic ministry (Titus 1:3): it is a *kairos* event, a moment in time that sometimes functions as an eschatological catchword for the "God-only-knows" scheduling of important events in the history of salvation. Such events prompt ultimate personal decisions in turn (cf. 1 Thess. 5:1; Acts 1:7). Perhaps Paul's keen sense that his apostolate is a *kairos* moment of salvation's history (Titus 1:3) is what leads

---

15. See George W. Knight, *The Pastoral Epistles: A Commentary on the Greek Text* (NIGTC) (Grand Rapids: Eerdmans, 1992), p. 458.

him to ponder his calling and his death — the holy death of an apostle — as a similar sort of crucial event because it occasions important decisions for Timothy and his other successors.

Some understand that the reward mentioned is granted in this life for faithful work done.[16] But surely Collins is correct to observe that the reference to "on that day" has the Lord's Second Coming in mind and echoes the vision of Zephaniah 1:14 (Septuagint) of "that great day of the Lord." "On that day," if it is "that great day of the Lord," a series of fearsome final events will unfold to bring judgment against the enemies of God's people. This intertext identifies the enemies with subversives mentioned here and earlier (3:1-9) along with those mentioned in the letter's benedictory (4:10, 14-16) who have harmed Paul.[17] Timothy must not be included among them but rather must stand with Paul and his apostolate during this fragile time of transition.

Paul does not anticipate a negative verdict for himself, but a "champion's wreath for rectitude that the Lord will give me on that day" (4:8a). The reason for his optimism is supplied by the memorable triad of metaphors: "I have fought the fight, finished the race, kept the faith" (4:7).[18] This combination of a soldier's completed fight, an athlete's finished race, and a believer's confirmed faith recalls the similar triad of exemplary sufferers in 2:3b-7: the good soldier, the competing athlete, and the hard-working farmer. These are exemplars of laborers whose work is brought to purposeful completion. The implication of the verb here is of action begun in the past that has been brought to completion. And the reader of each trope, whether ancient or contemporary, would naturally assume that the labor envisioned would have followed a battle plan, a race course, a confession of faith that guides the action to its particular end.[19]

---

16. Cf. Jay Twomey, *The Pastoral Epistles Through the Centuries* (Chichester, UK: Wiley-Blackwell, 2009), pp. 182-84.

17. Philip Towner, *The Letters to Timothy and Titus* (NICNT) (Grand Rapids: Eerdmans, 2006), p. 616, also includes Rome and its culpability for Paul's imprisonment (and perhaps Jesus' execution).

18. Towner, along with others, recommends that all three are athletic metaphors that climax in the dramatic image of a champion's victory in 4:8a (Towner, *The Letters to Timothy and Titus*, pp. 612-14). We find this metaphor forced for no good reason.

19. The parallelism between 4:7 and Acts 20:24 is significant, not only because it challenges an axiom of Acts criticism that the narrator does not know the Pauline letters but more importantly for us because it links the speech of succession in Acts 20 with the climax of this letter of succession when Paul predicts his imminent death.

Paul's labor is not necessarily motivated by the prospect of a "champion's wreath," but that is the reasonable expectation based on his Christology: Christ's faithfulness to God's redemptive will is the basis of his resurrection, the vindication of his messiahship, and his exaltation as Lord (cf. Phil. 2:5-11). The additional metaphor noting that the champion's reward is "the wreath for rectitude" indicates that "rectitude" does not explain the wreath's composition but the makeup of true champions: they are righteous. Paul triumphs in the end because he has lived a faithful life, enduring his hardships with sobriety and responding to his many critics with patient and competent instruction. The implication is certain: Timothy must now, as Paul's exemplary successor, do the same (cf. 2:1-2).

Our choice of "rectitude" to signal the eschatological reward is significant in any Pauline text, not only because — as in this case — it describes the apostle's résumé, but also because it establishes the pattern of his apostolate, which includes "all those who have loved his appearance" (4:8c). Readers may discern here an echo of Paul's keynote statement in introducing his magisterial Epistle to the Romans (Rom. 1:17), especially if the final member of the preceding triad — "kept the faith" — is understood as the principal condition for his eschatological reception of a "wreath of rectitude." In this keynote to Romans, Paul quotes Habakkuk 2:4 — "the righteous shall live by faith[fullness]" — to support the central claim of his proclaimed gospel (cf. Rom. 1:15): that God has put to rights what is wrong "to everyone who believes" (Rom. 1:16-17).

Richard Hays argues that Paul's quotation from Habakkuk in this pivotal Romans text is like an epigraph for the entire epistle, which reads like a Christian response to a distinctively Jewish expression of theodicy: whether God has been faithful to promises made to Israel according to the Scripture. Paul's argument in support of God's rectitude is climaxed in Romans 9-11, where he uses Scripture in support of his claim that God has always acted, and will continue to act, faithfully in fulfilling promises made to Israel. In introducing this argument, Hays contends that Paul edits different textual traditions of Habakkuk 2:4 to create a new ambiguity about whose faithfulness actually delivers the promised goods — whether a people's (Hebrew Bible) or God's (the Septuagint [LXX], the Greek translation of the Hebrew Bible). Whereas the Hebrew version of Habakkuk 2:4 exhorts Israel to remain faithful to God in prospect of a future salvation, the Septuagint version speaks of "my" (God's) faithfulness to Israel as the basis of its hope. Paul edits out the referent in his quotation of Habakkuk's prophecy to suspend the identity of the faithful one. It is the letter's taxonomy to make clear that it is God who has acted faithfully in response to the faithfulness of the Messiah to right what is wrong with God's creation, thereby forming a twofold referent of the prophetic epigraph.[20] As he does elsewhere in the Pastorals (see 1 Tim. 1:12-16), Paul personalizes his gospel's core conviction to supply evidence of its veracity; indeed, his faithfulness to the Lord — he has "kept the faith" — will be rewarded by the Lord's faithfulness to him on that day when he appears to judge the living and the dead.

The meaning of the final phrase of this passage, which we have translated quite literally ("all those who have loved his appearance" [4:8c]), remains difficult for Protestants whose *sola* fideism inclines them — against Paul! — to detach their future "wreath of rectitude" from their present performance of rectitude. The verb form *agapaō* is actively intensive, indicating that one's love (or longing) for the Lord's reappearing is cumulative and is confirmed concretely by acts of love for him (cf. Phil. 3:20).[21]

Part 2: Engaging 2 Timothy 1:10–4:8 for Congregational Leaders

In my ecclesiastical tradition it is a convention at the ordination to ministry — and at the ceremonies for the installation of a new pastor — for the worship service to include two charges in addition to a sermon. One charge is to the congregation, reminding the church of its covenantal relationship with its pastor and the responsibilities that covenant entails. The other charge is to the minister, whether freshly ordained or an already ordained but now newly installed pastor.

In one sense, the canonical letters of the apostle Paul to the series of congregations that begin with Romans and conclude with 1 and 2 Thessalonians are all, in their way, charges to congregations. Each one has a different Christian congregation in view, each with its own con-

---

20. Richard B. Hays, *Echoes of Scripture in the Letters of Paul* (New Haven, CT: Yale University Press, 1989), pp.36-41.

21. Marshall, *The Pastoral Epistles*, pp. 809-10.

text, issues, and challenges. In various ways, Paul instructs and charges these congregations to be faithful incarnations of the gospel of Jesus Christ. But the Pastoral Epistles, 1 and 2 Timothy and Titus, are different. They are instructions and charges to Paul's associates: Timothy in Ephesus and Titus in Crete. They are, in a sense, charges to the pastor, full of instruction about the proper role and functioning of a pastoral leader in the household of God, the church. Now, as we approach the end of 2 Timothy, this final text in our study is quintessentially a charge — indeed, the final charge — of a dying Paul to his student and successor, Timothy.

As the preceding exegetical study indicates, there is in this text a repeated and unifying grammatical device that structures Paul's final charge to Timothy: *su de,* a rhetorical formula that we translate as "you, however." Three times (3:10; 3:14; 4:5) Paul acknowledges false paths that fail in healthy teaching; and then with *su de,* "you, however," he firmly places Timothy on the proper path, charging him to be faithful to his calling and to his role as Paul's successor. The literary structure of a repeated *su de* makes clear the way in which faithfulness as a minister of the gospel and leader of a congregation entails making difficult choices over against common and more popular alternative paths. Moreover, faithfulness requires intentionality in choosing a way that is neither easy nor free of risk. Jesus' words in the Sermon on the Mount capture this same sense of "you, however": "Enter through the narrow gate; for the gate is wide and the road is easy that leads to destruction, and there are many who take it. For the gate is narrow and the road is hard that leads to life, and there are few who find it" (Matt. 7:13-14). Paul's final charge to Timothy guides him beyond the wide gate and easy road to the narrow gate and hard road that leads to life.

Guided by Paul's use of the *su de* formula, I will focus my comments on the three core elements of Paul's final charge: the importance of attending to the role model that Paul provides; the centrality of Scripture as the core text for the work of the pastor and teacher; and urgency in proclaiming the gospel. For the contemporary practice of ordained ministry and pastoral leadership, each of the three is axiomatic, though none in our contemporary setting can be taken for granted. In other words, all three are as neglected or misunderstood as they are important, and Paul's final charge to his successor Timothy stands as an urgent charge to pastoral leaders today.

The Role Model and Ministry Mentor

Paul begins the first of the three elements of his charge with the words, "You, however, have closely observed me . . ." (3:10). Within this topic of "the role model and mentor" lie two elements and possibilities: the particular and the general. By "the particular" I mean the particular role model that Paul provides to Timothy. By "the general" I mean the larger topic of role models and mentors for ordained ministers and pastoral leaders. Both of these — the particular and the general — merit attention, and they are in a sense bound together as two parts of one whole.

First, Paul is not reluctant to offer himself as an example to be followed — and even imitated. If contemporary sensibilities sometimes look askance at imitation, seeing it as a form of inauthenticity — as they urge people to find and be their own unique selves — Paul seems untroubled by any such reservations. Though the recurrent exhortation to "be yourself" is the conventional wisdom of the late modern West and reflects our cultural predisposition, I suspect that Paul's emphasis on imitation may also have to do with a pattern of practice and instruction more common in his world than in our own, though not wholly unheard of today: the pattern of the master and apprentice. As a way of learning what it meant to practice a profession, whether medicine, law, or ministry, or a craft, whether carpentry, farming, or potmaking, the master/apprentice pattern has probably been dominant during most of human history, only giving way in relatively recent times to a newer model, that of professional schooling and an attendant credentialing process.

As we have noted in the exegesis above, the word we have translated as "observe" holds larger implications: it suggests that the relationship of Paul and Timothy is a form of catechesis "into a manner of life." That manner of life is elaborated in a list of nine virtues that range from moral qualities (faith, loyalty, love, and patience) to vocational tasks (teaching and purpose) to experiences of suffering and physical abuse. While the nine do not appear to be systematic or comprehensive, they illustrate a particular way of life. This way of life is characterized by tasks and skills but also by qualities of character and being. Ministry is like that. It is not either job skills or personal qualities. It is both. It is not either what you do or who you are; it is both. It includes your doing and your being, bound inextricably in your way of life.

It is perhaps unexpected — certainly striking — that this list of nine virtues ends with "physical abuse" and suffering." As outcomes of vocational practices and qualities of character, one might expect something in a more positive vein, say, peace or honor in the eyes of others. Though, along with Jesus (Matt. 7:13-14), Paul does anticipate a final fulfillment, the short-term consequence of this way of life has a cost not only because it is characterized by integrity but because of the content of the proclamation of Jesus Christ. Those who imagine that ordination is a ticket to status, power, prominence, and acclaim may, in light of Paul's example, wish to think again. As one of my colleagues remarked to me when I was lamenting the suffering and duress of ministry, "What part of the cross don't you get?"

Therefore, Paul's particular example as role model conveys at least the following elements. Ministers are neither self-creations nor solo operators. We follow others. We are apprentices to a master, students of a teacher. Furthermore, this is not a job but a way of life. And finally, this way of life is not cost- or risk-free. Faithful practice of it may very well — will most likely — entail suffering and even persecution.

Turning, then, to some additional and more general thoughts about the importance of role models and mentors in ministry, I observe that such relationships are making a comeback in our own time. Under the rubric of "spiritual formation," mentoring relationships are both being more routinely structured into schools and courses that prepare clergy, and they are being sought out, in official and unofficial ways, by students preparing for ministry and by clergy who are new to the practice of ministry.

The origins of the term "mentor" lie in Greek mythology. Barbara Blodgett explains: "Mentor was the close friend of Odysseus to whom Odysseus entrusted his son Telemachus when he departed to fight the Trojan War. Mentor guided Telemachus and, as he grew, helped him become a man worthy of being his father's son." In a certain sense, Paul was to Timothy what Mentor was to Telemachus (with Odysseus being an analogue to Christ). "Over time," Blodgett concludes, "the term [mentor] has developed many meanings, but the basic idea is that a mentor is a wise, trusted and experienced person who takes an interest in the life and career of a novice and commits to helping him or her grow into a role."[22]

---

22. Barbara Blodgett, *Becoming the Pastor You Hope to Be* (Herndon, VA: Alban, 2011), p. 42.

If my observation is accurate, the role of mentor or role model — sometimes styled as "coach" or "spiritual director" — is making a come-back in the preparation and practice of ministry. What accounts for that? As the preparation of clergy joined other professions in the schooling/credentialing model, the operating assumption was that, in professional schooling, future clergy acquired theoretical knowledge that they then applied in the practice of ministry. However, seldom has it proven so simple. More often, both academics and clergy complain of a gap between theory and practice. This does not mean that theoretical and academic knowledge is unimportant or without value. I, for one, count it extremely valuable and absolutely necessary. But in the theory-to-practice model, there is a missing link: that link is the unique knowledge that professionals acquire as they practice ministry. Philosopher Michael Polanyi speaks of the knowledge of the professional as "tacit knowledge." Engineer and educator Donald Schon suggests the same with his work on the "reflective practitioner."[23] There are forms of knowledge acquired only in practice and conveyed best by those who have the capacity to be "reflective practitioners." Such reflective practitioners are able to "play the game" and "see the game whole" — often simultaneously — a combination that Magic Johnson, for example, managed as a player/coach in basketball. For others, the action/reflection may be more sequential, but the capacity to do both is what characterizes the skilled mentor. Such people are the missing link, bridging the gap between theory and practice with knowledge gained in the midst of practice. This, I believe, accounts for the new — or at least renewed — emphasis on mentors, role models, and coaches.

Here is an observation from my own practice as a consultant, coach, and teacher working primarily with clergy and other church leaders. For a number of years the norm for the continuing education of clergy was for ministers/pastoral leaders to return to the academic setting (seminary or university) for updates on the newest theory and research with the apparent assumption that their job was to take the theory back and put it into practice in the church. While not without some value, this pattern neglected what clergy members were themselves learning in the practice of ministry and provided little or no opportunity to reflect on and benefit from that learning. Rather, this

23. Donald Schon, *The Reflective Practitioner: How Professionals Think in Action* (New York: Basic Books, 1983).

model of continuing education was like hitting the button on one's computer for a new "download": clergy return to seminary or university for new "downloads." Not only does such a model fail to acknowledge and respect the knowledge gained in practice, but it rests on a false assumption, the assumption that ministry is simply a matter of applying theoretical knowledge to practice. It ain't that simple!

Much of my own work today is with groups of clergy who make up "communities of practice." In such groups, clergy members reflect on the practice of ministry with colleagues and mentors in order to make sense of their experience, to learn from it, and to illuminate what might be considered "best practices." Such alternative forms of continuing education pay attention to the unique knowledge of professionals, to the role of mentors, and to developing the capacity to reflect on action — and actually to reflect in the midst of action. Such use of mentors, role models, and peer groups has been shown to be especially effective in overcoming the sense of isolation and loneliness reported by many clergy, as well as encouraging excellence in the practice of ministry through peer learning and the guidance of mentors. All of this is to say that when Paul counseled Timothy to "closely observe" his practice and instruction, he may have been on to something.

The Role and Centrality of Scripture

If one source of guidance and instruction for the minister and pastoral leader is the role model or mentor, a second is Scripture. The second *su de* of Paul's final charge to Timothy points him to "the holy writings, which enable you to be wise for salvation," affirming that "every scripture is God-inspired and useful for teaching . . ." (3:15-16). If, as we have argued, Paul's instruction to Timothy is catechesis into a way and manner of life, then the principal course textbook is Scripture.

But what is "Scripture," and how are we, as believers and church leaders, to take it? Here in 2 Timothy the technical referent of "Scripture" is the Septuagint, Israel's Scripture in Greek translation. But after acknowledging that this is the case, it seems legitimate for our purposes to speak of Scripture as the church does, as the canonical texts of the Old and New Testaments. What, then, are they? There are no simple or easy answers to such a question. Still, we must make a response. Ordained ministers and pastoral leaders must have some operative "doctrine of Scripture," some notion of the Bible's role and function. This is necessary, in good part, because such questions are contested in both church and society at large. Answers to the question of what is the role and function of Scripture range from "It is the literal and inerrant word of God" to "It's just another book" — and pretty much everything in between.

Entire books — an enormous number of them — have been written on the subject of the role, nature, and function of Scripture. Nothing written here will begin to be fully adequate to the questions. Still, one helpful response is to describe the Bible as "the church's book."[24] This is not intended to suggest exclusive rights or control of the Bible on the part of the church or churches. It is intended to affirm two things. One is that Scripture, the canon as we know it, is the product of the church. Actual communities of faith have heard, read, used, and tested many texts over a period of centuries and settled on these sixty-six books (or seventy-three in the case of Roman Catholicism) as, in some sense, the church's own unique "library." So Scripture is the church's book in the sense that the church, with the guidance of the Holy Spirit, determined Scripture's shape and content. To speak of the Bible as "the church's book," however, is to posit a second affirmation: that in some sense the church itself belongs to and is accountable to Scripture. This relationship is analogous to the way the nation of the United States belongs to and is accountable to its own Constitution as the expression of its values and normative practices. Thus does Scripture define the nature of the church, its identity and mission, its convictions and practices.[25]

While it is necessary for pastoral leaders to hold informed convictions about the role, nature, and function of Scripture, these matters, important as they are, are only preliminary points to a discussion of what Paul urges on Timothy here in this final charge and to the implications of those remarks for contemporary pastoral leaders. By urging Timothy to take with deep seriousness the place of Scripture and the power of Scripture to form and reform, Paul challenges both the disuse

24. Martin Copenhaver, *To Begin at the Beginning* (Cleveland: Pilgrim Press, 1994), p. 103.

25. For further reading, see Copenhaver, *To Begin at the Beginning*, esp. chapter 6; Stephen Fowl, *Theological Interpretation of Scripture* (Eugene, OR: Wipf and Stock, 2009); and Anthony Robinson, *What's Theology Got to Do with It?* (Herndon, VA: Alban, 2006), esp. chapter 3.

and misuse of Scripture in the church today. Sometimes the problem is disuse: Scripture takes an almost ornamental role. We read it in worship, though we may not be sure quite why. Sermons refer to its texts without deeply engaging them; for many, the Bible seems more of a resource than a source. If one must generalize, these particular forms of disuse tend to characterize the more theologically liberal churches. But the theological conservative churches are not without culpability, though theirs tends more to the misuse category: texts are used as "proof-texts" to support positions already arrived at or to bolster culturally acquired practices and prejudices. In this use the texts of Scripture may be given authority and yet not be known, which seems especially dangerous.

Noting the critical importance of Scripture to virtually every movement of reform and renewal in church history, Walter Brueggemann says, "Serious Scripture study calls one to repentance and invites one to a changed perceptual world."[26] A somewhat different way to put this same crucial point was made by New Testament scholar J. Louis Martyn. Imagine, I recall Martyn musing, a team of archaeologists on a dig, patiently working to unearth what promised to be a very fine skeleton. They used all sorts of tools and devices — scoops and shovels, brushes and measuring instruments. Finally, after much painstaking work, the skeleton was laid bare, fully exposed. Then, suddenly, as the scientists pored over their find, the skeleton sat up, grabbed a shovel, and whumped the scientists upside the head. The Bible is like that, says Martyn. Scripture is alive. It is not a dead or inert object to be examined or housed in a museum. It is a living subject that summons us to listen to it and to dialogue with it.

Scripture, working in tandem with the Holy Spirit, is the message of truth about the living God and an instrument of God's presence and power. Paul emphasizes this living and active quality of Scripture to his successor Timothy, noting that Scripture has the capacity of making people "wise for salvation." Moreover, for Paul, Jesus Christ is the decisive revelation through which Scripture, in concert with the Holy Spirit, does something: it saves, it teaches, it corrects.

My own sense is that in much of the contemporary church our confidence in the power of Scripture to mediate saving truths — our

---

26. Walter Brueggemann, *The Bible Makes Sense* (Winona, MN: St. Mary's Press, 1977), p. 137.

confidence in the power of the Word of God — is greatly diminished. A result of this diminished confidence in the power of God's Word is, among other things, that sermons are not usually events of the living Word. The words of Jesus to the religious leaders of his day seem apt for our time as well: "Jesus answered them, 'You are wrong, because you know neither the scriptures nor the power of God'" (Matt. 22:29, NRSV). Thomas G. Long made a similar point recently: "As one of my keenest students complained, the sermons she has heard were often 'like listening to something on National Public Radio: well researched, very well written prose, clever and witty in places, well voiced, but oral religious essays nevertheless.'"[27]

Something is missing, and what is missing has to do with a loss of confidence in the power of God's word in Scripture to mediate God's presence and transforming power. Another way of putting this comes from Fleming Rutledge: "We have forgotten how to be theo-logical. We have not even noticed that our sermons are anthropo-logical. We have made ourselves the subject of all the verbs."[28] As one illustration of this tendency, I recall the fairly recent evangelistic campaign known and promoted as "I Found It!" Were we more theological and less anthro-pological, it might have been "It Found Me!" The primary referent, the central character, the main actor, the primary dramatis persona of Scripture is not the human being — it is God. To read Scripture theo-logically is to read it as God's story.[29] Moreover, to interpret Scripture faithfully is to theologize before we moralize, which means speaking of who God is, what God has done and is doing, and what God will do be-fore and as the context for all speaking of who we are and what we are to do. Apart from this, instead of offering good news, we offer, at best, good advice. Contrary to the well-known and proverbial "no news is good news," as Long notes about preaching, "no news is bad news."[30] In placing Scripture at the center of his final charge to Timothy, Paul urges its centrality to the church and to ministry.

27. Thomas G. Long, *Preaching: From Memory to Hope* (Louisville: Westminster John Knox, 2009), p. 34.

28. Fleming Rutledge, unpublished lecture, "And God Said," presented at Wycliffe College, University of Toronto, 2008.

29. James A. Sanders, *God Has a Story Too* (Philadelphia: Fortress, 1979).

30. Long, *Preaching: From Memory to Hope*, p. 27.

Urgency in Proclaiming the Gospel

It is difficult to imagine a more direct and insistent call to urgency in proclaiming the gospel than one finds near the end of 2 Timothy. "In the presence of God and Christ Jesus, who is coming to judge the living and the dead, by his appearing and by his kingdom, I firmly command: Proclaim the word! Stand ready at all times! Refute! Rebuke! Always encourage with patient instruction! For a time will come when people will not tolerate healthy teaching."

This is a stirring exhortation, one that reprises a recurrent theme of 1 and 2 Timothy, especially 2 Timothy. We also heard it in 2 Timothy 1:7: "For God did not give us a cowardly spirit but a Spirit of power, love and discernment." There is a steady exhortation to courage in the preaching of the gospel and to urgency throughout these letters. And yet I agree with Fleming Rutledge in her analysis of much contemporary preaching. She says bluntly: "I do not hear enough sermons that convey passionate conviction about the gospel. Many sermons come across as collections of religious thoughts offered in a hesitant, tentative way."[31]

These are complex matters bound up with our deep contemporary ambivalence about power, authority, and conviction. Too often, as we have noted above, power is suspect; authority is construed as inevitably authoritarian; and conviction is relegated to ideological purists and "true believers" (Eric Hoffer's term) who are considered automatically suspect in many quarters. More suited to the spirit of the age are qualities of hesitancy, doubt, tentativeness, and tolerance. There is, of course, much to be said for tolerance and for humility. But like all virtues, these can, when taken too far or too single-mindedly, flip over and become vices. They can become an inability or unwillingness of parents to confidently rear and guide their children by communicating values and conveying wisdom that give the latter a secure foundation. They can become the mantra of educators who tell students, "It's up to you to figure out what's true for you" (thus positing a kind of truth claim in its own right), which perhaps leaves students wondering, "If that's true, what's the point of being here and listening to you?" They become words from the pulpit that urge us to be considerate and inclusive but are either unwilling or unable to help people sort out differing

31. Rutledge, "And God Said," p. 5.

and competing truth claims as a way to locate a philosophical and moral center for living. The result, as the pioneer sociologist Emile Durkheim has noted, is anomie, the loss of both a sense of belonging and of meaning. Some would go further and describe the resulting social pathology as nihilism.

Paul Scott Wilson has charged that there has been a loss of "proclamation," a central genre of preaching in our time. In his book *Setting Words on Fire: Putting God at the Center of the Sermon,* Wilson posits a broad distinction between teaching and proclamation:

> Teaching provides the theological, historical, and cultural information that people need about who God is now and in history, but it does not introduce them to God. Information about someone is no substitute for actually meeting the person. . . . People need not just information about God — they need communication from God. They need to hear God speaking. . . . Effective proclaimers say words like, "Change your ways. I love you. I forgive you. I died for you. Death has no more power over you." That is proclamation. Without foundation in teaching, it may sound frivolous, naive, irrelevant, or offensive. [But] proclamation picks up where teaching leaves off and brings it to necessary completion.[32]

A somewhat different way of putting this is to note that the current emphasis on "spirituality" may be a mixed blessing. It expresses a genuine longing for something more. But too often the focus is entirely on "my spirituality," on "my own individual experience," and on those things a person can or should do to enhance, deepen, or stimulate his or her spirituality. For those shaped by Scripture and God's revelation or apocalypse in Jesus Christ, this puts the emphasis in the wrong place. It leads people to imagine an all-loving but inactive God who is the object of our religious or spiritual search and goal of our "faith journey." Instead, the proper emphasis of Christian preaching and proclamation is the God who in Jesus Christ has searched for and found us. The emphasis is on the God who, as Barth put it, has initiated the "journey of the Son of God into the far country" in search of a lost and prodigal humanity. When the focus shifts from the God who has come to and for us, to our own search for God, something crucial

---

32. Paul Scott Wilson, *Setting Words on Fire* (Nashville: Abingdon, 2009), p. 92.

has changed and urgency dissipates. There is no news of God or about God, but only moralistic counsel and advice. Or, as Long sums it up,

> What has happened to the pulpit is more like a habit of speech, being accommodated to the way our culture uses religious language, namely, as holy sounding talk with all the edges filed away, so that it refers not to the wild, undomesticated presence of the living God, but only to us, to our sincere hearts, spiritual intentions, and our desire to do good things in life. In other words, there is plenty of morality and good counsel, but no desert bush bursting into flame.[33]

There are, of course, notable and wondrous exceptions to these generalizations. But that's the point — they are the exceptions. Paul's final *su de* — "you, however, do the work of a preacher of the good news" — is a call for urgency in the proclamation of the gospel that is as timely now as it was then.

DISCUSSION QUESTIONS

1. What relationship is there between "the last days" (2 Tim. 3:1-9; 4:3-4) and the quality of a leader's theological education (3:10-17)?

2. What are the intended results of God's inspiration of Scripture (3:15-17), and how does the leader's use of Scripture inspire Christian ministry (4:1-8)?

3. What particular role or function does a good mentor play in the life of a pastoral leader? Have you had a good mentor? What did he/she do?

4. How would you rate "the sense of urgency" in the preaching you do or the preaching you hear?

33. Long, *Preaching: From Memory to Hope*, p. 34.

For Further Reading on 1 and 2 Timothy and Leadership

Aageson, J. W. *Paul, the Pastoral Epistles, and the Early Church*. Library of Pauline Studies. Grand Rapids: Baker, 2008.

Bassler, J. M. *1 Timothy, 2 Timothy, Titus*. Abingdon New Testament Commentaries. Nashville: Abingdon, 1996.

Collins, R. F. *1 and 2 Timothy and Titus: A Commentary*. New Testament Library. Louisville: Westminster John Knox, 2002.

Fee, G. D. *1 and 2 Timothy, Titus*. New International Biblical Commentary. Grand Rapids: Baker, 1988.

Friedman, E. H. *A Failure of Nerve: Leadership in the Age of the Quick Fix*. New York: Seabury, 2007.

Heifetz, R., and M. Linsky. *Leadership on the Line: Staying Alive through the Dangers of Leading*. Boston: Harvard Business School Press, 2002.

Johnson, L. T. *The First and Second Letters to Timothy*. Anchor Bible 35A. Garden City, N.Y.: Doubleday, 2001.

_____. *Letters to Paul's Delegates: 1 Timothy, 2 Timothy, Titus*. New Testament in Context. Valley Forge, PA: Trinity Press International, 1996.

Knight, G. W. *Commentary on the Pastoral Epistles*. New International Greek Testament Commentary. Grand Rapids: Eerdmans, 1992.

Marshall, I. H. *The Pastoral Epistles*. International Critical Commentary. Edinburgh: T&T Clark, 1999.

Mounce, W. D. *The Pastoral Epistles*. Word Biblical Commentary. Dallas: Word, 2000.

Ngewa, S. M. *1 & 2 Timothy and Titus*. Grand Rapids: Zondervan, 2009.

Robinson, A. B. *Leadership for Vital Congregations*. Cleveland: Pilgrim Press, 2006

Steinke, P. *Congregational Leadership in Anxious Times: Being Calm and Courageous No Matter What*. Herndon, VA: Alban, 2006.

Towner, P. H. *The Letters to Timothy and Titus*. New International Commentary on the New Testament. Grand Rapids: Eerdmans, 2006.

_____. *1-2 Timothy & Titus*. IVP New Testament Commentary. Downers Grove, Ill.: InterVarsity Press, 1994.

Twomey, J. *The Pastoral Epistles through the Centuries*. Black Bible Commentaries. Oxford: Wiley-Blackwell, 2009.

Wall, R. W. *The Pastoral Epistles*. Two Horizons Commentary. Grand Rapids: Eermdans, 20XX.

Young, F. *The Theology of the Pastoral Letters*. New Testament Theology. Cambridge: University Press, 1994.

Index